Wilhelm Grimm, Walter Crane, Jacob Grimm

Household Stories

Wilhelm Grimm, Walter Crane, Jacob Grimm

Household Stories

ISBN/EAN: 9783744649230

Printed in Europe, USA, Canada, Australia, Japan

Cover: Foto ©Thomas Meinert / pixelio.de

More available books at **www.hansebooks.com**

HOUSEHOLD·STORIES
·GRIMM·

THE
·SLEEPING·
BEAUTY·

"·AT·LAST·HE·CAME·TO·THE·
·TOWER·&·OPENED·THE·DOOR·
·OF·THE·LITTLE·ROOM·WHERE·
·ROSAMOND·LAY·"

Frontispiece.

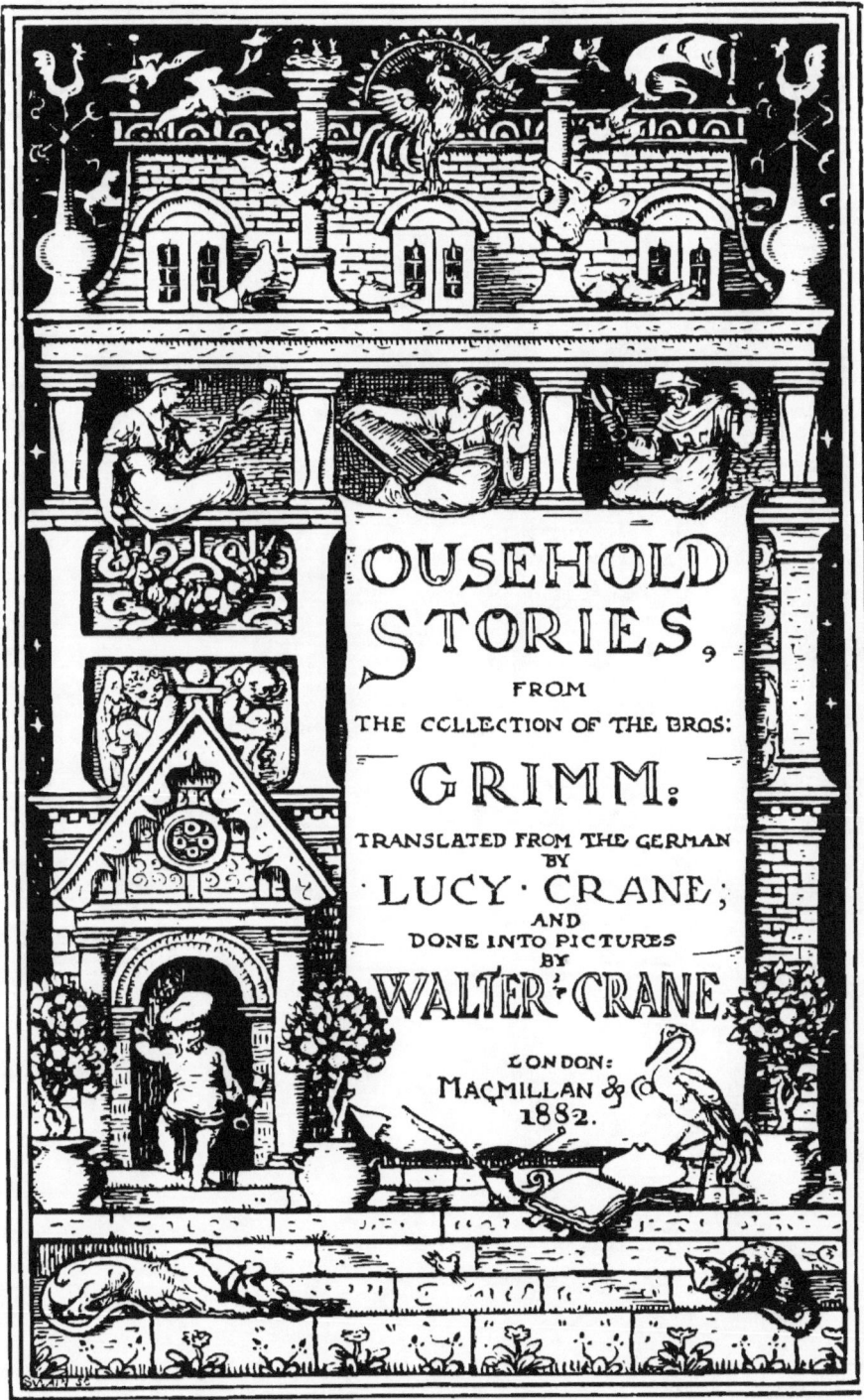

OUSEHOLD STORIES,

FROM

THE COLLECTION OF THE BROS:

GRIMM:

TRANSLATED FROM THE GERMAN
BY
LUCY · CRANE;
AND
DONE INTO PICTURES
BY
WALTER · CRANE.

LONDON:
MACMILLAN & C⁰
1882.

LIST OF ILLUSTRATIONS

HALF-TITLE.

THE SLEEPING BEAUTY. . . . *Frontispiece*

TITLE-PAGE. PAGE

THE RABBIT'S BRIDE, Headpiece . . . 1

     Tailpiece . . 2

SIX SOLDIERS OF FORTUNE, Headpiece . . 3

       Tailpiece . . 8

CLEVER GRETHEL, Headpiece . . . 9

     Tailpiece . . 11

THE DEATH OF THE HEN, Headpiece . . 12

     Tailpiece . 13

HANS IN LUCK, Headpiece . . . 14

     Tailpiece . . 19

THE GOOSE GIRL . . . . *To face page* 20

     Headpiece . . 20

     Tailpiece . . 25

THE RAVEN, Headpiece . . . 26

     Tailpiece . . . 31

THE FROG PRINCE, Headpiece . . . 32

     Tailpiece . . . 36

CAT AND MOUSE IN PARTNERSHIP, Headpiece . . 37

       Tailpiece . 39

THE WOLF AND THE SEVEN GOSLINGS, Headpiece 40

       Tailpiece . . 42

FAITHFUL JOHN . . *To face page* 43

     Headpiece . . 43

     Tailpiece . . 51

		PAGE
THE WONDERFUL MUSICIAN, Headpiece . . .		52
Tailpiece		55
THE TWELVE BROTHERS, Headpiece		56
Tailpiece		61
THE VAGABONDS, Headpiece		62
Tailpiece		64
THE BROTHER AND SISTER, Headpiece		65
Tailpiece		71
RAPUNZEL	*To face page*	72
Headpiece		72
Tailpiece		75
THE THREE LITTLE MEN IN THE WOOD, Headpiece . .		76
Tailpiece . .		81
THE THREE SPINSTERS, Headpiece		82
Tailpiece . . .		84
HANSEL AND GRETHEL, Headpiece . . .		85
Tailpiece		92
THE WHITE SNAKE	*To face page*	93
Headpiece		93
Tailpiece		97
THE STRAW, THE COAL, AND THE BEAN, Headpiece . .		98
Tailpiece . .		99
THE FISHERMAN AND HIS WIFE, Headpiece . . .		100
Tailpiece . .		108
THE GALLANT TAILOR, Headpiece . . .		109
Tailpiece		117
ASCHENPUTTEL, Headpicce		118
Tailpiece		125
THE MOUSE, THE BIRD, AND THE SAUSAGE, Headpiece .		126
Tailpiece . .		127
MOTHER HULDA	*To face page*	128
Headpiece		128
Tailpiece		131
LITTLE RED-CAP, Headpiece		132
Tailpiece		135
THE BREMEN TOWN MUSICIANS, Headpiece . .		136
Tailpiece . . .		139

PAGE

PRUDENT HANS, Headpiece 140
    Tailpiece 144
CLEVER ELSE, Headpiece 145
    Tailpiece 148
THE TABLE, THE ASS, AND THE STICK, Headpiece . . 149
    Tailpiece . . 159
TOM THUMB, Headpiece 160
    Tailpiece 166
HOW MRS. FOX MARRIED AGAIN, Headpiece . . . 167
    Initial . . . 169
    Tailpiece . . . 170
THE ELVES, Headpiece 171
    Initial 173
    Initial 174
    Tailpiece 174
THE ROBBER BRIDEGROOM . . . To face page 175
    Headpiece 175
    Tailpiece 178
MR. KORBES, Headpiece 179
    Tailpiece 180
TOM THUMB'S TRAVELS, Headpiece . . . 181
    Tailpiece . . . 185
THE ALMOND TREE . . To face page 186
    Headpiece 186
    Tailpiece 194
OLD SULTAN, Headpiece 195
    Tailpiece 197
THE SIX SWANS . . . To face page 198
    Headpiece . . . 198
    Tailpiece 203
THE SLEEPING BEAUTY, Headpiece . . 204
    Tailpiece 207
KING THRUSHBEARD, Headpiece . . . 208
    Tailpiece 212
SNOW-WHITE . . . . To face page 213
    Headpiece . . . 213
    Tailpiece . . . 221

PAGE

THE KNAPSACK, THE HAT, AND THE HORN, Headpiece   222

Tailpiece .   .   227

RUMPELSTILTSKIN, Headpiece   228

Tailpiece   231

ROLAND, Headpiece   232

Tailpiece   235

THE GOLDEN BIRD,   .   .   .   *To face page* 236

Headpiece   236

Tailpiece   243

THE DOG AND THE SPARROW, Headpiece   .   .   .   244

Tailpiece   .   .   247

FRED AND KATE, Headpiece   .   .   .   248

Tailpiece   255

THE LITTLE FARMER, Headpiece   .   .   256

Tailpiece   .   .   261

THE QUEEN BEE, Headpiece   .   .   262

Tailpiece   .   .   .   264

THE GOLDEN GOOSE, Headpiece   .   .   .   265

Tailpiece   269

·THE·RABBIT'S·BRIDE·

HERE was once a woman who lived with her daughter in a beautiful cabbage-garden; and there came a rabbit and ate up all the cabbages. At last said the woman to her daughter,

"Go into the garden, and drive out the rabbit."

"Shoo! shoo!" said the maiden; "don't eat up all our cabbages, little rabbit!"

"Come, maiden," said the rabbit, "sit on my tail and go with me to my rabbit-hutch." But the maiden would not.

Another day, back came the rabbit, and ate away at the cabbages, until the woman said to her daughter,

"Go into the garden, and drive away the rabbit."

"Shoo! shoo!" said the maiden; "don't eat up all our cabbages, little rabbit!"

"Come, maiden," said the rabbit, "sit on my tail and go with me to my rabbit-hutch." But the maiden would not.

Again, a third time back came the rabbit, and ate away at the cabbages, until the woman said to her daughter,

"Go into the garden, and drive away the rabbit."

"Shoo! shoo!" said the maiden; "don't eat up all our cabbages, little rabbit!"

"Come, maiden," said the rabbit, "sit on my tail and go with me to my rabbit-hutch."

And then the girl seated herself on the rabbit's tail, and the rabbit took her to his hutch.

B

"Now," said he, "set to work and cook some bran and cabbage; I am going to bid the wedding guests." And soon they were all collected. Would you like to know who they were? Well, I can only tell you what was told to me; all the hares came, and the crow who was to be the parson to marry them, and the fox for the clerk, and the altar was under the rainbow. But the maiden was sad, because she was so lonely.

"Get up! get up!" said the rabbit, "the wedding folk are all merry."

But the bride wept and said nothing, and the rabbit went away, but very soon came back again.

"Get up! get up!" said he, "the wedding folk are waiting." But the bride said nothing, and the rabbit went away. Then she made a figure of straw, and dressed it in her own clothes, and gave it a red mouth, and set it to watch the kettle of bran, and then she went home to her mother. Back again came the rabbit, saying, "Get up! get up!" and he went up and hit the straw figure on the head, so that it tumbled down.

And the rabbit thought that he had killed his bride, and he went away and was very sad.

THERE was once a man who was a Jack-of-all-trades; he had served in the war, and had been brave and bold, but at the end of it he was sent about his business, with three farthings and his discharge.

"I am not going to stand this," said he; "wait till I find the right man to help me, and the king shall give me all the treasures of his kingdom before he has done with me."

Then, full of wrath, he went into the forest, and he saw one standing there by six trees which he had rooted up as if they had been stalks of corn. And he said to him,

"Will you be my man, and come along with me?"

"All right," answered he; "I must just take this bit of wood home to my father and mother." And taking one of the trees, he bound it round the other five, and putting the faggot on his shoulder, he carried it off; then soon coming back, he went along with his leader, who said,

"Two such as we can stand against the whole world."

And when they had gone on a little while, they came to a huntsman who was kneeling on one knee and taking careful aim with his rifle.

"Huntsman," said the leader, "what are you aiming at?"

"Two miles from here," answered he, "there sits a fly on the bough of an oak-tree, I mean to put a bullet into its left eye."

"Oh, come along with me," said the leader; "three of us together can stand against the world."

The huntsman was quite willing to go with him, and so they went on till they came to seven windmills, whose sails were going round briskly, and yet there was no wind blowing from any quarter, and not a leaf stirred.

"Well," said the leader, "I cannot think what ails the windmills, turning without wind;" and he went on with his followers about two miles farther, and then they came to a man sitting up in a tree, holding one nostril and blowing with the other.

"Now then," said the leader, "what are you doing up there?"

"Two miles from here," answered he, "there are seven windmills; I am blowing, and they are going round."

"Oh, go with me," cried the leader, "four of us together can stand against the world."

So the blower got down and went with them, and after a time they came to a man standing on one leg, and the other had been taken off and was lying near him.

"You seem to have got a handy way of resting yourself," said the leader to the man.

"I am a runner," answered he, "and in order to keep myself from going too fast I have taken off a leg, for when I run with both, I go faster than a bird can fly."

"Oh, go with me," cried the leader, "five of us together may well stand against the world."

So he went with them all together, and it was not long before they met a man with a little hat on, and he wore it just over one ear.

"Manners! manners!" said the leader; "with your hat like that, you look like a jack-fool."

"I dare not put it straight," answered the other; "if I did, there would be such a terrible frost that the very birds would be frozen and fall dead from the sky to the ground."

"Oh, come with me," said the leader; "we six together may well stand against the whole world."

So the six went on until they came to a town where the king had caused it to be made known that whoever would run a race with his daughter and win it might become her husband, but that whoever lost must lose his head into the bargain. And the leader came forward and said one of his men should run for him.

"Then," said the king, "his life too must be put in pledge, and if he fails, his head and yours too must fall."

When this was quite settled and agreed upon, the leader called the runner, and strapped his second leg on to him.

"Now, look out," said he, "and take care that we win."

It had been agreed that the one who should bring water first from a far distant brook should be accounted winner. Now the king's daughter and the runner each took a pitcher, and they started both at the same time; but in one moment, when the king's daughter had gone but a very little way, the runner was out of sight, for his running was as if the wind rushed by. In a short time he reached the brook, filled his pitcher full of water, and turned back again. About half-way home, however, he was overcome with weariness, and setting down his pitcher, he lay down on the ground to sleep. But in order to awaken soon again by not lying too soft he had taken a horse's skull which lay near and placed it under his head for a pillow. In the meanwhile the king's daughter, who really was a good runner, good enough to beat an ordinary man, had reached the brook, and filled her pitcher, and was hastening with it back again, when she saw the runner lying asleep.

"The day is mine," said she with much joy, and she emptied his pitcher and hastened on. And now all had been lost but for the huntsman who was standing on the castle wall, and with his keen eyes saw all that happened.

"We must not be outdone by the king's daughter," said he, and he loaded his rifle and took so good an aim that he shot the horse's skull from under the runner's head without doing him any harm. And the runner awoke and jumped up, and saw his pitcher standing empty and the king's daughter far on her way home. But, not losing courage, he ran swiftly to the brook, filled it again with water, and for all that, he got home ten minutes before the king's daughter.

"Look you," said he; "this is the first time I have really stretched my legs; before it was not worth the name of running."

The king was vexed, and his daughter yet more so, that she should be beaten by a discharged common soldier; and they took counsel together how they might rid themselves of him and of his companions at the same time.

"I have a plan," said the king; "do not fear but that we shall be quit of them for ever." Then he went out to the men and bade them to feast and be merry and eat and drink; and he led them into a room, which had a floor of iron, and the doors were iron, the windows had iron frames and bolts; in the room was a table set out with costly food.

"Now, go in there and make yourselves comfortable," said the king.

And when they had gone in, he had the door locked and bolted. Then he called the cook, and told him to make a big fire underneath the room, so that the iron floor of it should be red hot. And the cook did so, and the six men began to feel the room growing very warm, by reason, as they thought at first, of the good dinner; but as the heat grew greater and greater, and they found the doors and windows fastened, they began to think it was an evil plan of the king's to suffocate them.

"He shall not succeed, however," said the man with the little hat; "I will bring on a frost that shall make the fire feel ashamed of itself, and creep out of the way."

So he set his hat straight on his head, and immediately there came such a frost that all the heat passed away and the food froze in the dishes. After an hour or two had passed, and the king thought they must have all perished in the heat, he caused the door to be opened, and went himself to see how they fared. And when the door flew back, there they were all six quite safe and sound, and they said they were quite ready to come out, so that they might warm themselves, for the great cold of that room had caused the food to freeze in the dishes. Full of wrath, the king went to the cook and scolded him, and asked why he had not done as he was ordered.

"It is hot enough there: you may see for yourself," answered the cook. And the king looked and saw an immense fire burning underneath the room of iron, and he began to think that the six men were not to be got rid of in that way. And he thought of a new plan by which it might be managed, so he sent for the leader and said to him,

"If you will give up your right to my daughter, and take gold instead, you may have as much as you like."

"Certainly, my lord king," answered the man; "let me have as much gold as my servant can carry, and I give up all claim to your daughter." And the king agreed that he should come again in a fortnight to fetch the gold. The man then called together all the tailors in the kingdom, and set them to work to make a sack, and it took them a fortnight. And when it was ready, the strong man who had been found rooting up trees took it on his shoulder, and went to the king.

"Who is this immense fellow carrying on his shoulder a bundle of stuff as big as a house?" cried the king, terrified to think how much gold he would carry off. And a ton of gold was dragged in by sixteen strong men, but he put it all into the sack with one hand, saying,

"Why don't you bring some more? this hardly covers the bottom!" So the king bade them fetch by degrees the whole of his treasure, and even then the sack was not half full.

"Bring more!" cried the man; "these few scraps go no way at all!" Then at last seven thousand waggons laden with gold collected through the whole kingdom were driven up; and he threw them in his sack, oxen and all.

"I will not look too closely," said he, "but take what I can get, so long as the sack is full." And when all was put in there was still plenty of room.

"I must make an end of this," he said; "if it is not full, it is so much the easier to tie up." And he hoisted it on his back, and went off with his comrades.

When the king saw all the wealth of his realm carried off by a single man he was full of wrath, and he bade his cavalry mount, and follow after the six men, and take the sack away from the strong man.

Two regiments were soon up to them, and called them to consider themselves prisoners, and to deliver up the sack, or be cut in pieces.

"Prisoners, say you?" said the man who could blow, "suppose you first have a little dance together in the air," and holding one nostril, and blowing through the other, he sent the regiments flying head over heels, over the hills and far away. But a sergeant who had nine wounds and was a brave fellow, begged not to be put to so much shame. And the blower let him down easily, so that he came to no harm, and he bade him go to the king and tell him that whatever regiments he liked to send more should be blown away just the same.   And the king, when he got the message, said,

"Let the fellows be; they have some right on their side."
So the six comrades carried home their treasure, divided it among them, and lived contented till they died.

✿ · CLEVER · GRETHEL · ✿

HERE was once a cook called Grethel, who wore shoes with red heels, and when she went out in them she gave herself great airs, and thought herself very fine indeed. When she came home again, she would take a drink of wine to refresh herself, and as that gave her an appetite, she would take some of the best of whatever she was cooking, until she had had enough ;—"for," said she, "a cook must know how things taste."

Now it happened that one day her master said to her,—

"Grethel, I expect a guest this evening; you must make ready a pair of fowls."

"Certainly, sir, I will," answered Grethel. So she killed the fowls, cleaned them, and plucked them, and put them on the spit, and then, as evening drew near, placed them before the fire to roast. And they began to be brown, and were nearly done, but the guest had not come.

"If he does not make haste," cried Grethel to her master, "I must take them away from the fire; it's a pity and a shame not to eat them now, just when they are done to a turn." And the master said he would run himself and fetch the guest. As soon as he had turned his back, Grethel took the fowls from before the fire.

"Standing so long before the fire," said she, "makes one hot and thirsty,—and who knows when they will come! in the meanwhile I will go to the cellar and have a drink." So down she ran, took up a mug, and saying, "Here's to me!" took a good draught. "One good drink deserves another," she said "and it should not be cut short;" so she took another hearty draught. Then she went and put the fowls down to the fire again, and, basting them with butter, she turned the spit briskly round. And now they began to smell so good that Grethel saying, "I must find out whether they really are all right," licked her fingers, and then cried, "Well, I never! the fowls are good; it's a sin and a shame that no one is here to eat them!"

So she ran to the window to see if her master and his guest were coming, but as she could see nobody she went back to her fowls. "Why, one of the wings is burning!" she cried presently, "I had better eat it and get it out of the way." So she cut it off and ate it up, and it tasted good, and then she thought,

"I had better cut off the other too, in case the master should miss anything." And when both wings had been disposed of she went and looked for the master, but still he did not come.

"Who knows," said she, "whether they are coming or not? they may have put up at an inn." And after a pause she said again, "Come, I may as well make myself happy, and first I will make sure of a good drink and then of a good meal, and when all is done I shall be easy; the gifts of the gods are not to be despised." So first she ran down into the cellar and had a famous drink, and ate up one of the fowls with great relish. And when that was done, and still the master did not come, Grethel eyed the other fowl, saying, "What one is the other must be, the two belong to each other, it is only fair that they should be both treated alike; perhaps, when I have had another drink, I shall be able to manage it." So she took another hearty drink, and then the second fowl went the way of the first.

Just as she was in the middle of it the master came back. "Make haste, Grethel," cried he, "the guest is coming directly!" "Very well, master," she answered, "it will soon be ready." The master went to see that the table was properly laid, and, taking the great carving knife with which he meant to carve the fowls, he sharpened it upon the step. Presently came the guest, knocking very genteelly and softly at the front door. Grethel ran and looked to see who it was, and when she caught sight of the guest she put her finger on her lip saying, "Hush! make the best haste you can out of this, for if my master catches you, it will be bad for you; he asked you to come to supper, but he really means to cut off your ears! Just listen how he is sharpening his knife!"

The guest, hearing the noise of the sharpening, made off as fast as he could go. And Grethel ran screaming to her master. "A pretty guest you have asked to the house!" cried she.

"How so, Grethel? what do you mean?" asked he.

"What indeed!" said she; "why, he has gone and run away with my pair of fowls that I had just dished up."

"That's pretty sort of conduct!" said the master, feeling very sorry about the fowls; "he might at least have left me one, that I might have had something to eat." And he called out to him to stop, but the guest made as if he did not hear him; then he ran after him, the knife still in his hand, crying out, "Only one! only one!" meaning that the guest should let him have one of the fowls and not take both, but the guest thought he meant to have only one of his ears, and he ran so much the faster that he might get home with both of them safe.

The DEATH of the HEN:

NCE on a time the cock and the hen went to the nut mountain, and they agreed beforehand that whichever of them should find a nut was to divide it with the other. Now the hen found a great big nut, but said nothing about it, and was going to eat it all alone, but the kernel was such a fat one that she could not swallow it down, and it stuck in her throat, so that she was afraid she should choke.

"Cock!" cried she, "run as fast as you can and fetch me some water, or I shall choke!"

So the cock ran as fast as he could to the brook, and said, "Brook, give me some water, the hen is up yonder choking with a big nut stuck in her throat." But the brook answered, "First run to the bride and ask her for some red silk."

So the cock ran to the bride and said,

"Bride, give me some red silk; the brook wants me to give him some red silk; I want him to give me some water, for the hen lies yonder choking with a big nut stuck in her throat."

But the bride answered,

"First go and fetch me my garland that hangs on a willow." And the cock ran to the willow and pulled the garland from the bough and brought it to the bride, and the bride gave him red silk, and he brought it to the brook, and the brook gave him water. So then the cock brought the water to the hen, but alas, it was too late; the hen had choked in the meanwhile,

and lay there dead.   And the cock was so grieved that he
cried aloud, and all the beasts came and lamented for the hen ;
and six mice built a little waggon, on which to carry the poor
hen to her grave, and when it was ready they harnessed themselves to it, and the cock drove.   On the way they met the
fox.

"Halloa, cock," cried he, "where are you off to ?"

"To bury my hen," answered the cock.

"Can I come too ?" said the fox.

"Yes, if you follow behind," said the cock.

So the fox followed behind and he was soon joined by the
wolf, the bear, the stag, the lion, and all the beasts in the wood.
And the procession went on till they came to a brook.

"How shall we get over ?" said the cock.   Now in the
brook there was a straw, and he said,

"I will lay myself across, so that you may pass over
on me."   But when the six mice had got upon this bridge, the
straw slipped and fell into the water and they all tumbled in
and were drowned.   So they were as badly off as ever, when
a coal came up and said he would lay himself across and they
might pass over him ; but no sooner had he touched the water
than he hissed, went out, and was dead.   A stone seeing this
was touched with pity, and, wishing to help the cock, he laid
himself across the stream.   And the cock drew the waggon with
the dead hen in it safely to the other side, and then began to
draw the others who followed behind across too, but it was
too much for him, the waggon turned over, and all tumbled
into the water one on the top of another, and were drowned.

So the cock was left all alone with the dead hen, and he
digged a grave and laid her in it, and he raised a mound
above her, and sat himself down and lamented so sore that at
last he died.   And so they were all dead together.

·HANS IN LUCK·

HANS had served his master seven years, and at the end of the seventh year he said,

"Master, my time is up; I want to go home and see my mother, so give me my wages."

"You have served me truly and faithfully," said the master; "as the service is, so must the wages be," and he gave him a lump of gold as big as his head. Hans pulled his handkerchief out of his pocket and tied up the lump of gold in it, hoisted it on his shoulder, and set off on his way home. And as he was trudging along, there came in sight a man riding on a spirited horse, and looking very gay and lively. "Oh!" cried Hans aloud, "how splendid riding must be! sitting as much at one's ease as in an arm-chair, stumbling over no stones, saving one's shoes, and getting on one hardly knows how!"

The horseman heard Hans say this, and called out to him,

"Well Hans, what are you doing on foot?"

"I can't help myself," said Hans, "I have this great lump to carry; to be sure, it is gold, but then I can't hold my head straight for it, and it hurts my shoulder."

"I'll tell you what," said the horseman, "we will change; I will give you my horse, and you shall give me your lump of gold."

"With all my heart," said Hans; "but I warn you, you will find it heavy." And the horseman got down, took the gold, and, helping Hans up, he gave the reins into his hand.

"When you want to go fast," said he, "you must click your tongue and cry 'Gee-up!'"

And Hans, as he sat upon his horse, was glad at heart, and rode off with merry cheer. After a while he thought he should like to go quicker, so he began to click with his tongue and to cry "Gee-up!" And the horse began to trot, and Hans was thrown before he knew what was going to happen, and there he lay in the ditch by the side of the road. The horse would have got away but that he was caught by a peasant who was passing that way and driving a cow before him. And Hans pulled himself together and got upon his feet, feeling very vexed. "Poor work, riding," said he, "especially on a jade like this, who starts off and throws you before you know where you are, going near to break your neck; never shall I try that game again; now, your cow is something worth having, one can jog on comfortably after her and have her milk, butter, and cheese every day, into the bargain. What would I not give to have such a cow!"

"Well now," said the peasant, "since it will be doing you such a favour, I don't mind exchanging my cow for your horse."

Hans agreed most joyfully, and the peasant, swinging himself into the saddle, was soon out of sight.

And Hans went along driving his cow quietly before him, and thinking all the while of the fine bargain he had made.

"With only a piece of bread I shall have everything I can possibly want, for I shall always be able to have butter and cheese to it, and if I am thirsty I have nothing to do but to milk my cow; and what more is there for heart to wish!"

And when he came to an inn he made a halt, and in the joy of his heart ate up all the food he had brought with him, dinner and supper and all, and bought half a glass of beer with his last two farthings. Then on he went again driving his cow, until he should come to the village where his mother lived. It was now near the middle of the day, and the sun grew hotter and hotter, and Hans found himself on a heath which it would be an hour's journey to cross. And he began to feel very hot, and so thirsty that his tongue clove to the roof of his mouth.

"Never mind," said Hans; "I can find a remedy. I will milk my cow at once." And tying her to a dry tree, and taking off his leather cap to serve for a pail, he began to milk, but not a drop came. And as he set to work rather awkwardly, the impatient beast gave him such a kick on the head with his hind foot that he fell to the ground, and for some time could not think where he was; when luckily there came by a butcher who was wheeling along a young pig in a wheelbarrow.

"Here's a fine piece of work!" cried he, helping poor Hans on his legs again. Then Hans related to him all that had happened; and the butcher handed him his pocket-flask, saying,

"Here, take a drink, and be a man again; of course the cow would give no milk; she is old and only fit to draw burdens, or to be slaughtered."

"Well, to be sure," said Hans, scratching his head. "Who would have thought it? of course it is a very handy way of getting meat when a man has a beast of his own to kill; but for my part I do not care much about cow beef, it is rather tasteless. Now, if I had but a young pig, that is much better meat, and then the sausages!"

"Look here, Hans," said the butcher, "just for love of you I will exchange, and will give you my pig instead of your cow."

"Heaven reward such kindness!" cried Hans, and handing over the cow, received in exchange the pig, who was turned out of his wheelbarrow and was to be led by a string.

So on went Hans, thinking how everything turned out according to his wishes, and how, if trouble overtook him, all was sure to be set right directly. After a while he fell in with a peasant, who was carrying a fine white goose under his arm. They bid each other good-day, and Hans began to tell about his luck, and how he had made so many good exchanges. And the peasant told how he was taking the goose to a christening feast.

"Just feel how heavy it is," said he, taking it up by the wings; "it has been fattening for the last eight weeks; and when it is roasted, won't the fat run down!"

"Yes, indeed," said Hans, weighing it in his hand, "very fine to be sure; but my pig is not to be despised."

Upon which the peasant glanced cautiously on all sides, and shook his head.

"I am afraid," said he, "that there is something not

quite right about your pig. In the village I have just left one had actually been stolen from the bailiff's yard. I fear, I fear you have it in your hand; they have sent after the thief, and it would be a bad look-out for you if it was found upon you; the least that could happen would be to be thrown into a dark hole."

Poor Hans grew pale with fright. "For heaven's sake," said he, "help me out of this scrape, I am a stranger in these parts; take my pig and give me your goose."

"It will be running some risk," answered the man, "but I will do it sooner than that you should come to grief." And so, taking the cord in his hand, he drove the pig quickly along a by-path, and lucky Hans went on his way home with the goose under his arm. "The more I think of it," said he to himself, "the better the bargain seems; first I get the roast goose; then the fat; that will last a whole year for bread and dripping; and lastly the beautiful white feathers which I can stuff my pillow with; how comfortably I shall sleep upon it, and how pleased my mother will be!"

And when he reached the last village, he saw a knife-grinder with his barrow; and his wheel went whirring round, and he sang,

> " My scissors I grind, and my wheel I turn;
> And all good fellows my trade should learn,
> For all that I meet with just serves my turn."

And Hans stood and looked at him; and at last he spoke to him and said,

"You seem very well off, and merry with your grinding."

" Yes," answered the knife-grinder, " my handiwork pays very well. I call a man a good grinder who, every time he puts his hand in his pocket finds money there. But where did you buy that fine goose?"

" I did not buy it, but I exchanged it for my pig," said Hans.

" And the pig?"

" That I exchanged for a cow."

" And the cow?"

" That I exchanged for a horse."

" And the horse?"

" I gave for the horse a lump of gold as big as my head."

C

" And the gold ?"

" Oh, that was my wage for seven years' service."

" You seem to have fended for yourself very well," said the knife-grinder. " Now, if you could but manage to have money in your pocket every time you put your hand in, your fortune is made."

" How shall I manage that ?" said Hans.

" You must be a knife-grinder like me," said the man. " All you want is a grindstone, the rest comes of itself : I have one here ; to be sure it is a little damaged, but I don't mind letting you have it in exchange for your goose ; what say you ?"

" How can you ask ?" answered Hans. " I shall be the luckiest fellow in the world, for if I find money whenever I put my hand in my pocket, there is nothing more left to want."

And so he handed over the goose to the pedlar and received the grindstone in exchange.

" Now," said the knife-grinder, taking up a heavy common stone that lay near him, " here is another proper sort of stone that will stand a good deal of wear and that you can hammer out your old nails upon. Take it with you, and carry it carefully."

Hans lifted up the stone and carried it off with a contented mind. " I must have been born under a lucky star !" cried he, while his eyes sparkled for joy. " I have only to wish for a thing and it is mine."

After a while he began to feel rather tired, as indeed he had been on his legs since daybreak ; he also began to feel rather hungry, as in the fulness of his joy at getting the cow, he had eaten up all he had. At last he could scarcely go on at all, and had to make a halt every moment, for the stones weighed him down most unmercifully, and he could not help wishing that he did not feel obliged to drag them along. And on he went at a snail's pace until he came to a well ; then he thought he would rest and take a drink of the fresh water. And he placed the stones carefully by his side at the edge of the well ; then he sat down, and as he stooped to drink, he happened to give the stones a little push, and they both fell into the water with a splash. And then Hans, having watched them disappear, jumped for joy, and thanked his stars that he had been so lucky as to get rid of the stones that had weighed upon him so long without any effort of his own.

"I really think," cried he, "I am the luckiest man under the sun." So on he went, void of care, until he reached his mother's house.

THE GOOSE GIRL.

HERE lived once an old Queen, whose husband had been dead many years. She had a beautiful daughter who was promised in marriage to a King's son living a great way off. When the time appointed for the wedding drew near, and the old Queen had to send her daughter into the foreign land, she got together many costly things, furniture and cups and jewels and adornments, both of gold and silver, everything proper for the dowry of a royal Princess, for she loved her daughter dearly. She gave her also a waiting gentlewoman to attend her and to give her into the bridegroom's hands; and they were each to have a horse for the journey, and the Princess's horse was named Falada, and he could speak. When the time for parting came, the old Queen took her daughter to her chamber, and with a little knife she cut her own finger so that it bled; and she held beneath it a white napkin, and on it fell three drops of blood; and she gave it to her daughter, bidding her take care of it, for it would be needful to her on the way. Then they took leave of each other; and the Princess put the napkin in her bosom, got on her horse, and set out to go to the bridegroom. After she had ridden an hour, she began to feel very thirsty, and she said to the waiting-woman,

"Get down, and fill my cup that you are carrying with water from the brook; I have great desire to drink."

"Get down yourself," said the waiting-woman, "and if you are thirsty stoop down and drink; I will not be your slave."

GOOSE GIRL

O WIND, BLOW CONRADS HAT AWAY,
AND MAKE HIM FOLLOW AS IT FLIES,
WHILE I WITH MY GOLD HAIR WILL PLAY
AND BIND IT UP IN SEEMLY WISE!

And as her thirst was so great, the Princess had to get down and to stoop and drink of the water of the brook, and could not have her gold cup to serve her. " Oh dear !" said the poor Princess. And the three drops of blood heard her, and said,

" If your mother knew of this, it would break her heart."

But the Princess answered nothing, and quietly mounted her horse again. So they rode on some miles farther; the day was warm, the sun shone hot, and the Princess grew thirsty once more. And when they came to a water-course she called again to the waiting-woman and said,

" Get down, and give me to drink out of my golden cup." For she had forgotten all that had gone before. But the waiting-woman spoke still more scornfully and said,

" If you want a drink, you may get it yourself; I am not going to be your slave."

So, as her thirst was so great, the Princess had to get off her horse and to stoop towards the running water to drink, and as she stooped, she wept and said, " Oh dear !" And the three drops of blood heard her and answered,

" If your mother knew of this, it would break her heart !"

And as she drank and stooped over, the napkin on which were the three drops of blood fell out of her bosom and floated down the stream, and in her distress she never noticed it; not so the waiting-woman, who rejoiced because she should have power over the bride, who, now that she had lost the three drops of blood, had become weak, and unable to defend herself. And when she was going to mount her horse again the waiting-woman cried,

" Falada belongs to me, and this jade to you." And the Princess had to give way and let it be as she said. Then the waiting-woman ordered the Princess with many hard words to take off her rich clothing and to put on her plain garments, and then she made her swear to say nothing of the matter when they came to the royal court; threatening to take her life if she refused. And all the while Falada noticed and remembered.

The waiting-woman then mounting Falada, and the Princess the sorry jade, they journeyed on till they reached the royal castle. There was great joy at their coming, and the

King's son hastened to meet them, and lifted the waiting-woman from her horse, thinking she was his bride ; and then he led her up the stairs, while the real Princess had to remain below.   But the old King, who was looking out of the window, saw her standing in the yard, and noticed how delicate and gentle and beautiful she was, and then he went down and asked the seeming bride who it was that she had brought with her and that was now standing in the courtyard.

"Oh!" answered the bride, "I only brought her with me for company; give the maid something to do, that she may not be for ever standing idle."

But the old King had no work to give her ; until he bethought him of a boy he had who took care of the geese, and that she might help him.   And so the real Princess was sent to keep geese with the goose-boy, who was called Conrad.

Soon after the false bride said to the Prince,

"Dearest husband, I pray thee do me a pleasure."

"With all my heart," answered he.

"Then" said she, "send for the knacker, that he may carry off the horse I came here upon, and make away with him ; he was very troublesome to me on the journey."   For she was afraid that the horse might tell how she had behaved to the Princess.   And when the order had been given that Falada should die, it came to the Princess's ears, and she came to the knacker's man secretly, and promised him a piece of gold if he would do her a service.   There was in the town a great dark gate-way through which she had to pass morning and evening with her geese, and she asked the man to take Falada's head and to nail it on the gate, that she might always see it as she passed by.   And the man promised, and he took Falada's head and nailed it fast in the dark gate-way.

Early next morning as she and Conrad drove their geese through the gate, she said as she went by,

"O Falada, dost thou hang there ?"

And the head answered,

"Princess, dost thou so meanly fare?
But if thy mother knew thy pain,
Her heart would surely break in twain."

But she went on through the town, driving her geese to the field. And when they came into the meadows, she sat down and undid her hair, which was all of gold, and when Conrad saw how it glistened, he wanted to pull out a few hairs for himself. And she said,

> "O wind, blow Conrad's hat away,
> Make him run after as it flies,
> While I with my gold hair will play,
> And twist it up in seemly wise."

Then there came a wind strong enough to blow Conrad's hat far away over the fields, and he had to run after it; and by the time he came back she had put up her hair with combs and pins, and he could not get at any to pull it out; and he was sulky and would not speak to her; so they looked after the geese until the evening came, and then they went home.

The next morning, as they passed under the dark gate-way, the Princess said,

> "O Falada, dost thou hang there?"

And Falada answered,

> "Princess, dost thou so meanly fare?
> But if thy mother knew thy pain,
> Her heart would surely break in twain."

And when they reached the fields she sat down and began to comb out her hair; then Conrad came up and wanted to seize upon some of it, and she cried,

> "O wind, blow Conrad's hat away,
> Make him run after as it flies,
> While I with my gold hair will play,
> And do it up in seemly wise."

Then the wind came and blew Conrad's hat very far away, so that he had to run after it, and when he came back again her hair was put up again, so that he could pull none of it out; and they tended the geese until the evening.

And after they had got home, Conrad went to the old King and said, "I will tend the geese no longer with that girl!"

"Why not?" asked the old King.

"Because she vexes me the whole day long," answered
Conrad. Then the old King ordered him to tell how it was.

"Every morning," said Conrad, "as we pass under the
dark gate-way with the geese, there is an old horse's head hanging on the wall, and she says to it,

> "O Falada, dost thou hang there?"

And the head answers,

> "Princess, dost thou so meanly fare?
> But if thy mother knew thy pain,
> Her heart would surely break in twain."

And besides this, Conrad related all that happened in the
fields, and how he was obliged to run after his hat.

The old King told him to go to drive the geese next morning as usual, and he himself went behind the gate and listened
how the maiden spoke to Falada ; and then he followed them
into the fields, and hid himself behind a bush ; and he watched
the goose-boy and the goose-girl tend the geese ; and after a
while he saw the girl make her hair all loose, and how it
gleamed and shone. Soon she said,

> "O wind, blow Conrad's hat away,
> And make him follow as it flies,
> While I with my gold hair will play,
> And bind it up in seemly wise."

Then there came a gust of wind and away went Conrad's
hat, and he after it, while the maiden combed and bound up
her hair ; and the old King saw all that went on. At last he
went unnoticed away, and when the goose-girl came back in
the evening he sent for her, and asked the reason of her doing
all this.

"That I dare not tell you," she answered, "nor can I tell
any man of my woe, for when I was in danger of my life I
swore an oath not to reveal it." And he pressed her sore, and
left her no peace, but he could get nothing out of her. At
last he said,

"If you will not tell it me, tell it to the iron oven," and
went away. Then she crept into the iron oven, and began to
weep and to lament, and at last she opened her heart and
said,

" Here I sit forsaken of all the world, and I am a King's daughter, and a wicked waiting-woman forced me to give up my royal garments and my place at the bridegroom's side, and I am made a goose-girl, and have to do mean service. And if my mother knew, it would break her heart."

Now the old King was standing outside by the oven-door listening, and he heard all she said, and he called to her and told her to come out of the oven. And he caused royal clothing to be put upon her, and it was a marvel to see how beautiful she was. The old King then called his son and proved to him that he had the wrong bride, for she was really only a waiting-woman, and that the true bride was here at hand, she who had been the goose-girl. The Prince was glad at heart when he saw her beauty and gentleness; and a great feast was made ready, and all the court people and good friends were bidden to it. The bridegroom sat in the midst with the Princess on one side and the waiting-woman on the other; and the false bride did not know the true one, because she was dazzled with her glittering braveries. When all the company had eaten and drunk and were merry, the old King gave the waiting-woman a question to answer, as to what such an one deserved, who had deceived her masters in such and such a manner, telling the whole story, and ending by asking,

" Now, what doom does such an one deserve ?"

" No better than this," answered the false bride, " that she be put naked into a cask, studded inside with sharp nails, and be dragged along in it by two white horses from street to street, until she be dead."

"Thou hast spoken thy own doom," said the old King; "as thou hast said, so shall it be done." And when the sentence was fulfilled, the Prince married the true bride, and ever after they ruled over their kingdom in peace and blessedness.

·THE RAVEN·

HERE was once a Queen and she had a little daughter, who was as yet a babe in arms; and once the child was so restless that the mother could get no peace, do what she would; so she lost patience, and seeing a flight of ravens passing over the castle, she opened the window and said to her child,

"Oh, that thou wert a raven and couldst fly away, that I might be at peace."

No sooner had she uttered the words, than the child was indeed changed into a raven, and fluttered from her arms out of the window. And she flew into a dark wood and stayed there a long time, and her parents knew nothing of her. Once a man was passing through the wood, and he heard the raven cry, and he followed the voice; and when he came near it said,

"I was born a King's daughter, and have been bewitched, but thou canst set me free."

"What shall I do?" asked the man.

"Go deeper into the wood," said she, "and thou shalt find a house and an old woman sitting in it: she will offer thee meat and drink, but thou must take none; if thou eatest or drinkest thou fallest into a deep sleep, and canst not set me free at all. In the garden behind the house is a big heap of tan, stand upon that and wait for me. Three days, at about the middle of the day, shall I come to thee in a car drawn by four white horses the first time, by four red ones the second time, and lastly by four black ones; and if thou art not waking but sleeping, thou failest to set me free."

The man promised to do all she said.

" But ah !" cried she, "I know quite well I shall not be set free of thee; something thou wilt surely take from the old woman."

But the man promised yet once more that certainly he would not touch the meat or the drink. But when he came to the house the old woman came up to him.

" My poor man," said she to him, " you are quite tired out, come and be refreshed, and eat and drink."

" No," said the man, " I will eat and drink nothing."

But she left him no peace, saying,

" Even if you eat nothing, take a draught out of this cup once and away."

So he was over-persuaded, and he drank.

In the afternoon, about two o'clock, he went out into the garden to stand upon the tan-heap and wait for the raven. As he stood there he felt all at once so tired, that he could bear it no longer, and laid himself down for a little; but not to sleep. But no sooner was he stretched at length than his eyes closed of themselves, and he fell asleep, and slept so sound, as if nothing in the world could awaken him.

At two o'clock came the raven in the car drawn by four white horses, but she was sad, knowing already that the man would be asleep, and so, when she came into the garden, there he lay sure enough. And she got out of the car and shook him and called to him, but he did not wake. The next day at noon the old woman came and brought him meat and drink, but he would take none. But she left him no peace, and persuaded him until he took a draught out of the cup. About two o'clock he went into the garden to stand upon the tan-heap, and to wait for the raven, but he was overcome with so great a weariness that his limbs would no longer hold him up; and whether he would or no he had to lie down, and he fell into a deep sleep. And when the raven came up with her four red horses, she was sad, knowing already that the man would be asleep. And she went up to him, and there he lay, and nothing would wake him.

The next day the old woman came and asked what was

the matter with him, and if he wanted to die, that he would neither eat nor drink ; but he answered,

"I neither can nor will eat and drink."

But she brought the dishes of food and the cup of wine, and placed them before him, and when the smell came in his nostrils he could not refrain, but took a deep draught. When the hour drew near, he went into the garden and stood on the tan-heap to wait for the king's daughter ; as time went on he grew more and more weary, and at last he laid himself down and slept like a stone. At two o'clock came the raven with four black horses, and the car and all was black ; and she was sad, knowing already that he was sleeping, and would not be able to set her free ; and when she came up to him, there he lay and slept. She shook him and called to him, but she could not wake him. Then she laid a loaf by his side and some meat, and a flask of wine, for now, however much he ate and drank, it could not matter. And she took a ring of gold from her finger, and put it on his finger, and her name was engraven on it. And lastly she laid by him a letter, in which was set down what she had given him, and that all was of no use, and further also it said,

"I see that here thou canst not save me, but if thy mind is to the thing, come to the golden castle of Stromberg : I know well that if thou willst thou canst." And when all this was done, she got again into her car, and went to the golden castle of Stromberg.

When the man waked up and perceived that he had been to sleep, he was sad at heart to think that she had been, and gone, and that he had not set her free. Then, catching sight of what lay beside him, he read the letter that told him all. And he rose up and set off at once to go to the golden castle of Stromberg, though he knew not where it was. And when he had wandered about in the world for a long time, he came to a dark wood, and there spent a fortnight trying to find the way out, and not being able. At the end of this time, it being towards evening, he was so tired that he laid himself down under a clump of bushes and went to sleep. The next day he went on again, and in the evening, when he was going to lie down again to rest, he heard howlings and lamentations, so that he could not sleep. And about the hour when lamps are lighted, he looked up and saw a light glimmer in the forest ; and he got up and followed it, and he found that it came from a house that looked very small indeed, because there stood a giant before it. And the man thought to himself that if he were to try to enter and the giant were to see him, it would go hard but he should lose his life. At last he made up his mind, and walked in. And the giant saw him.

"I am glad thou art come," said he ; "it is now a long time since I have had anything to eat ; I shall make a good supper of thee."

" That may be," said the man, " but I shall not relish it ; besides, if thou desirest to eat, I have somewhat here that may satisfy thee."

" If that is true," answered the giant, "thou mayest make thy mind easy ; it was only for want of something better that I wished to devour thee."

Then they went in and placed themselves at the table, and the man brought out bread, meat, and wine in plenty.

" This pleases me well," said the giant, and he ate to his heart's content. After a while the man asked him if he could tell him where the golden castle of Stromberg was.

" I will look on my land-chart," said the giant, " for on it all towns and villages and houses are marked."

So he fetched the land-chart which was in his room, and sought for the castle, but it was not to be found.

" Never mind," said he, " I have up-stairs in the cupboard much bigger maps than this ; we will have a look at them." And so they did, but in vain.

And now the man wanted to pursue his journey, but the giant begged him to stay a few days longer, until his brother, who had gone to get in a store of provisions, should return. When the brother came, they asked him about the golden castle of Stromberg.

" When I have had time to eat a meal and be satisfied, I will look at the map."

That being done, he went into his room with them, and they looked at his maps, but could find nothing : then he fetched other old maps, and they never left off searching until they found the golden castle of Stromberg, but it was many thousand miles away.

" How shall I ever get there ?" said the man.

" I have a couple of hours to spare," said the giant, " and I will set you on your way, but I shall have to come back and look after the child that we have in the house with us."

Then the giant bore the man until within about a hundred hours' journey from the castle, and saying,

" You can manage the rest of the way by yourself," he departed; and the man went on day and night, until at last he came to the golden castle of Stromberg. It stood on a mountain of glass, and he could see the enchanted Princess driving round it, and then passing inside the gates. He was rejoiced when he saw her, and began at once to climb the mountain to get to her; but it was so slippery, as fast as he went he fell back again. And when he saw this he felt he should never reach her, and he was full of grief, and resolved at least to stay at the foot of the mountain and wait for her. So he built himself a hut, and sat there and waited a whole year; and every day he saw the Princess drive round and pass in, and was never able to reach her.

One day he looked out of his hut and saw three robbers fighting, and he called out, " Mercy on us !" Hearing a voice, they stopped for a moment, but went on again beating one another in a dreadful manner. And he cried out again, " Mercy on us !" They stopped and listened, and looked about them, and then went on again. And he cried out a third time, " Mercy on us !" and then, thinking he would go and see what was the matter, he went out and asked them what they were fighting for. One of them told him he had found a stick which would open any door only by knocking at it; the second said he had found a cloak which, if he put it on, made him invisible; the third said he was possessed of a horse that would ride over everything, even the glass mountain. Now they had fought because they could not agree whether they should enjoy these things in common or separately.

" Suppose we make a bargain," said the man; " it is true I have no money, but I have other things yet more valuable to exchange for these; I must, however, make trial of them beforehand, to see if you have spoken truth concerning them."

So they let him mount the horse, and put the cloak round him, and they gave him the stick into his hand, and as soon as he had all this he was no longer to be seen; but laying about him well, he gave them all a sound thrashing, crying out,

"Now, you good-for-nothing fellows, you have got what you deserve; perhaps you will be satisfied now!"

Then he rode up the glass mountain, and when he reached the castle gates he found them locked; but he beat with his stick upon the door and it opened at once. And he walked in, and up the stairs to the great room where sat the Princess with a golden cup and wine before her: she could not see him so long as the cloak was on him, but drawing near to her he pulled off the ring she had given him, and threw it into the cup with a clang.

"This is my ring," she cried, "and the man who is to set me free must be here too!"

But though she sought through the whole castle she found him not; he had gone outside, seated himself on his horse, and thrown off the cloak. And when she came to look out at the door, she saw him and shrieked out for joy; and he dismounted and took her in his arms, and she kissed him, saying,

"Now hast thou set me free from my enchantment, and to-morrow we will be married."

: THE FROG PRINCE :

IN the old times, when it was still of some use to wish for the thing one wanted, there lived a King whose daughters were all handsome, but the youngest was so beautiful that the sun himself, who has seen so much, wondered each time he shone over her because of her beauty. Near the royal castle there was a great dark wood, and in the wood under an old linden-tree was a well ; and when the day was hot, the King's daughter used to go forth into the wood and sit by the brink of the cool well, and if the time seemed long, she would take out a golden ball, and throw it up and catch it again, and this was her favourite pastime.

Now it happened one day that the golden ball, instead of falling back into the maiden's little hand which had sent it aloft, dropped to the ground near the edge of the well and rolled in. The king's daughter followed it with her eyes as it sank, but the well was deep, so deep that the bottom could not be seen. Then she began to weep, and she wept and wept as if she could never be comforted. And in the midst of her weeping she heard a voice saying to her,

"What ails thee, king's daughter? thy tears would melt a heart of stone."

And when she looked to see where the voice came from, there was nothing but a frog stretching his thick ugly head out of the water.

"Oh, is it you, old waddler?" said she; "I weep because my golden ball has fallen into the well."

"Never mind, do not weep," answered the frog; "I can help you; but what will you give me if I fetch up your ball again?"

"Whatever you like, dear frog," said she; "any of my clothes, my pearls and jewels, or even the golden crown that I wear."

"Thy clothes, thy pearls and jewels, and thy golden crown are not for me," answered the frog; "but if thou wouldst love me, and have me for thy companion and play-fellow, and let me sit by thee at table, and eat from thy plate, and drink from thy cup, and sleep in thy little bed,—if thou wouldst promise all this, then would I dive below the water and fetch thee thy golden ball again."

"Oh yes," she answered; "I will promise it all, whatever you want, if you will only get me my ball again."

But she thought to herself, "What nonsense he talks! as if he could do anything but sit in the water and croak with the other frogs, or could possibly be any one's companion."

But the frog, as soon as he heard her promise, drew his head under the water and sank down out of sight, but after a while he came to the surface again with the ball in his mouth, and he threw it on the grass.

The King's daughter was overjoyed to see her pretty plaything again, and she caught it up and ran off with it.

"Stop, stop!" cried the frog; "take me up too; I cannot run as fast as you!"

But it was of no use, for croak, croak after her as he might, she would not listen to him, but made haste home, and very soon forgot all about the poor frog, who had to betake himself to his well again.

The next day, when the King's daughter was sitting at table with the King and all the court, and eating from her golden plate, there came something pitter patter up the marble stairs, and then there came a knocking at the door, and a voice crying "Youngest King's daughter, let me in!"

And she got up and ran to see who it could be, but when she opened the door, there was the frog sitting outside. Then she shut the door hastily and went back to her seat, feeling very uneasy. The King noticed how quickly her heart was beating, and said,

"My child, what are you afraid of? is there a giant standing at the door ready to carry you away?"

"Oh no," answered she; "no giant, but a horrid frog."

"And what does the frog want?" asked the King.

"O dear father," answered she, "when I was sitting by the well yesterday, and playing with my golden ball, it fell into the water, and while I was crying for the loss of it, the frog came and got it again for me on condition I would let him be my companion, but I never thought that he could leave the water and come after me; but now there he is outside the door, and he wants to come in to me."

And then they all heard him knocking the second time and crying,

> "Youngest King's daughter,
> Open to me!
> By the well water
> What promised you me?
> Youngest King's daughter
> Now open to me!"

"That which thou hast promised must thou perform," said the King; "so go now and let him in."

So she went and opened the door, and the frog hopped in, following at her heels, till she reached her chair. Then he stopped and cried,

"Lift me up to sit by you."

But she delayed doing so until the King ordered her. When once the frog was on the chair, he wanted to get on the table, and there he sat and said,

"Now push your golden plate a little nearer, so that we may eat together."

And so she did, but everybody might see how unwilling she was, and the frog feasted heartily, but every morsel seemed to stick in her throat.

"I have had enough now," said the frog at last, "and as I am tired, you must carry me to your room, and make ready your silken bed, and we will lie down and go to sleep."

Then the King's daughter began to weep, and was afraid of the cold frog, that nothing would satisfy him but he must sleep in her pretty clean bed. Now the King grew angry with her, saying,

"That which thou hast promised in thy time of necessity, must thou now perform."

So she picked up the frog with her finger and thumb, carried him upstairs and put him in a corner, and when she had lain down to sleep, he came creeping up, saying, "I am tired and want sleep as much as you; take me up, or I will tell your father."

Then she felt beside herself with rage, and picking him up, she threw him with all her strength against the wall, crying,

"Now will you be quiet, you horrid frog!"

But as he fell, he ceased to be a frog, and became all at once a prince with beautiful kind eyes. And it came to pass that, with her father's consent, they became bride and bridegroom. And he told her how a wicked witch had bound him by her spells, and how no one but she alone could have released him, and that they two would go together to his father's kingdom. And there came to the door a carriage drawn by eight white horses, with white plumes on their heads, and with golden harness, and behind the carriage was standing faithful Henry, the servant of the young prince. Now, faithful Henry had suffered such care and pain when his master was turned into a frog, that he had been obliged to wear three iron bands over his heart, to keep it from breaking with trouble and anxiety. When the carriage started to take the prince to his kingdom, and faithful Henry had helped them both in, he got up behind, and was full of joy at his master's deliverance. And when they had gone a part of the way, the prince heard a sound at the back of the carriage, as if something had broken, and he turned round and cried,

"Henry, the wheel must be breaking!" but Henry answered,

> " The wheel does not break,
> 'Tis the band round my heart
> That, to lessen its ache,
> When I grieved for your sake,
> I bound round my heart."

Again, and yet once again there was the same sound, and the prince thought it must be the wheel breaking, but it was the breaking of the other bands from faithful Henry's heart, because it was now so relieved and happy.

CAT & MOUSE in PARTNERSHIP.

A CAT having made acquaintance with a mouse, professed such great love and friendship for her, that the mouse at last agreed that they should live and keep house together.

"We must make provision for the winter," said the cat, "or we shall suffer hunger, and you, little mouse, must not stir out, or you will be caught in a trap."

So they took counsel together and bought a little pot of fat. And then they could not tell where to put it for safety, but after long consideration the cat said there could not be a better place than the church, for nobody would steal there; and they would put it under the altar and not touch it until they were really in want. So this was done, and the little pot placed in safety.

But before long the cat was seized with a great wish to taste it.

"Listen to me, little mouse," said he; "I have been asked by my cousin to stand god-father to a little son she has brought into the world; he is white with brown spots; and they want to have the christening to-day, so let me go to it, and you stay at home and keep house."

"Oh yes, certainly," answered the mouse, "pray go by all means; and when you are feasting on all the good things, think of me; I should so like a drop of the sweet red wine."

But there was not a word of truth in all this; the cat had no cousin, and had not been asked to stand god-father: he

went to the church, straight up to the little pot, and licked the
fat off the top; then he took a walk over the roofs of the town,
saw his acquaintances, stretched himself in the sun, and licked
his whiskers as often as he thought of the little pot of fat;
and then when it was evening he went home.

"Here you are at last," said the mouse; "I expect you
have had a merry time."

"Oh, pretty well," answered the cat.

"And what name did you give the child?" asked the
mouse.

"Top-off," answered the cat, drily.

"Top-off!" cried the mouse, "that is a singular and
wonderful name! is it common in your family?"

"What does it matter?" said the cat; "it's not any worse
than Crumb-picker, like your god-child."

A little time after this the cat was again seized with a
longing.

"Again I must ask you," said he to the mouse, "to do
me a favour, and keep house alone for a day. I have been
asked a second time to stand god-father; and as the little one
has a white ring round its neck, I cannot well refuse."

So the kind little mouse consented, and the cat crept
along by the town wall until he reached the church, and
going straight to the little pot of fat, devoured half of it.

"Nothing tastes so well as what one keeps to oneself,"
said he, feeling quite content with his day's work. When he
reached home, the mouse asked what name had been given to
the child.

"Half-gone," answered the cat.

"Half-gone!" cried the mouse, "I never heard such a
name in my life! I'll bet it's not to be found in the calendar."

Soon after that the cat's mouth began to water again for
the fat.

"Good things always come in threes," said he to the
mouse; "again I have been asked to stand god-father, the
little one is quite black with white feet, and not any white
hair on its body; such a thing does not happen every day, so
you will let me go, won't you?"

"Top-off, Half-gone," murmured the mouse, "they are
such curious names, I cannot but wonder at them!"

"That's because you are always sitting at home," said the cat, "in your little grey frock and hairy tail, never seeing the world, and fancying all sorts of things."

So the little mouse cleaned up the house and set it all in order. Meanwhile the greedy cat went and made an end of the little pot of fat.

"Now all is finished one's mind will be easy," said he, and came home in the evening, quite sleek and comfortable. The mouse asked at once what name had been given to the third child.

"It won't please you any better than the others," answered the cat. "It is called All-gone."

"All-gone!" cried the mouse. "What an unheard-of-name! I never met with anything like it! All-gone! whatever can it mean?" And shaking her head, she curled herself round and went to sleep. After that the cat was not again asked to stand god-father.

When the winter had come and there was nothing more to be had out of doors, the mouse began to think of their store.

"Come, cat," said she, "we will fetch our pot of fat, how good it will taste, to be sure!"

"Of course it will," said the cat, "just as good as if you stuck your tongue out of window!"

So they set out, and when they reached the place, they found the pot, but it was standing empty.

"Oh, now I know what it all meant," cried the mouse, "now I see what sort of a partner you have been! Instead of standing god-father you have devoured it all up; first Top-off, then Half-gone, then "——

"Will you hold your tongue!" screamed the cat, "another word, and I devour you too!"

And the poor little mouse, having "All-gone" on her tongue, out it came, and the cat leaped upon her and made an end of her. And that is the way of the world.

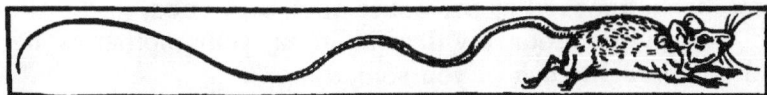

The WOLF and the SEVEN GOSLINGS.

HERE was once an old goose who had seven little ones, and was as fond of them as ever mother was of her children. One day she had to go into the wood to fetch food for them, so she called them all round her.

"Dear children," said she, "I am going out into the wood; and while I am gone, be on your guard against the wolf, for if he were once to get inside he would eat you up, skin, bones, and all. The wretch often disguises himself, but he may always be known by his hoarse voice and black paws."

"Dear mother," answered the goslings, "you need not be afraid, we will take good care of ourselves." And the mother bleated good-bye, and went on her way with an easy mind.

It was not long before some one came knocking at the house-door, and crying out,

"Open the door, my dear children, your mother is come back, and has brought each of you something."

But the little geese knew it was the wolf by the hoarse voice.

"We will not open the door," cried they; "you are not our mother, she has a delicate and sweet voice, and your voice is hoarse; you must be the wolf."

Then off went the wolf to a shop and bought a big lump of chalk, and ate it up to make his voice soft. And then he came back, knocked at the house-door, and cried,

"Open the door, my dear children, your mother is here, and has brought each of you something."

But the wolf had put up his black paws against the window, and the goslings seeing this, cried out,

"We will not open the door; our mother has no black paws like you; you must be the wolf."

The wolf then ran to a baker.

"Baker," said he, "I am hurt in the foot; pray spread some dough over the place."

And when the baker had plastered his feet, he ran to the miller.

"Miller," said he, "strew me some white meal over my paws." But the miller refused, thinking the wolf must be meaning harm to some one.

"If you don't do it," cried the wolf, "I'll eat you up!"

And the miller was afraid and did as he was told. And that just shows what men are.

And now came the rogue the third time to the door and knocked. "Open, children!" cried he. "Your dear mother has come home, and brought you each something from the wood."

"First show us your paws," said the goslings, "so that we may know if you are really our mother or not."

And he put up his paws against the window, and when they saw that they were white, all seemed right, and they opened the door; and when he was inside they saw it was the wolf, and they were terrified and tried to hide themselves. One ran under the table, the second got into the bed, the third into the oven, the fourth in the kitchen, the fifth in the cupboard, the sixth under the sink, the seventh in the clock-case. But the wolf found them all, and gave them short shrift; one after the other he swallowed down, all but the youngest, who was hid in the clock-case. And so the wolf, having got what he wanted, strolled forth into the green meadows, and laying himself down under a tree, he fell asleep.

Not long after, the mother goose came back from the wood; and, oh! what a sight met her eyes! the door was standing wide open, table, chairs, and stools, all thrown about, dishes broken, quilt and pillows torn off the bed. She sought her children, they were nowhere to be found. She called to each of them by name, but nobody answered, until she came to the name of the youngest.

"Here I am, mother," a little voice cried, "here, in the clock-case."

And so she helped him out, and heard how the wolf had come, and eaten all the rest. And you may think how she cried for the loss of her dear children. At last in her grief she wandered out of doors, and the youngest gosling with her ; and when they came into the meadow, there they saw the wolf lying under a tree, and snoring so that the branches shook. The mother goose looked at him carefully on all sides and she noticed how something inside his body was moving and struggling.

"Dear me !" thought she, "can it be that my poor children that he devoured for his evening meal are still alive ?" And she sent the little gosling back to the house for a pair of shears, and needle, and thread. Then she cut the wolf's body open, and no sooner had she made one snip than out came the head of one of the goslings, and then another snip, and then one after the other the six little goslings all jumped out alive and well, for in his greediness the rogue had swallowed them down whole. How delightful this was ! so they comforted their dear mother and hopped about like tailors at a wedding.

"Now fetch some good hard stones," said the mother, "and we will fill his body with them, as he lies asleep."

And so they fetched some in all haste, and put them inside him, and the mother sewed him up so quickly again that he was none the wiser.

When the wolf at last awoke, and got up, the stones inside him made him feel very thirsty, and as he was going to the brook to drink, they struck and rattled one against another. And so he cried out :

> "What is this I feel inside me
> Knocking hard against my bones?
> How should such a thing betide me !
> They were geese, and now they're stones."

So he came to the brook, and stooped to drink, but the heavy stones weighed him down, so he fell over into the water and was drowned. And when the seven little geese saw it they came up running.

"The wolf is dead, the wolf is dead !" they cried, and taking hands, they danced with their mother all about the place.

FAITHFUL·IOHN

"IT HAPPENED, AS THEY WERE STILL
JOURNEYING ON THE OPEN SEA, THAT
FAITHFUL IOHN, AS HE SAT IN THE FORE
PART OF THE SHIP, & MADE MUSIC, CAUGHT
SIGHT OF THREE RAVENS FLYING OVER-
HEAD.   THEN HE STOPPED PLAYING &
LISTENED TO WHAT THEY SAID TO ONE ANOTHER"

To face page 43

⁂ FAITHFUL ⁂ JOHN ⁂

HERE was once an old King, who, having fallen sick, thought to himself, "This is very likely my death-bed on which I am lying."

Then he said, "Let Faithful John be sent for."

Faithful John was his best-beloved servant, and was so called because he had served the King faithfully all his life long. When he came near the bed, the King said to him, "Faithful John, I feel my end drawing near, and my only care is for my son; he is yet of tender years, and does not always know how to shape his conduct; and unless you promise me to instruct him in all his actions and be a true foster-father to him, I shall not be able to close my eyes in peace."

Then answered Faithful John, "I will never forsake him, and will serve him faithfully, even though it should cost me my life."

And the old King said, "Then I die, being of good cheer and at peace." And he went on to say,

"After my death, you must lead him through the whole castle, into all the chambers, halls, and vaults, and show him the treasures that in them lie; but the last chamber in the long gallery, in which lies hidden the picture of the Princess of the Golden Palace, you must not show him. If he were to see that picture, he would directly fall into so great a love for her, that he would faint with the strength of it, and afterwards for her sake run into great dangers; so you must guard him well."

And as Faithful John gave him his hand upon it, the old King became still and silent, laid his head upon the pillow, and died.

When the old King was laid in the grave, Faithful John told the young King what he had promised to his father on his death-bed, and said,

"And I will certainly hold to my promise and be faithful to you, as I was faithful to him, even though it should cost me my life."

When the days of mourning were at an end, Faithful John said to the Prince,

"It is now time that you should see your inheritance; I will show you all the paternal castle."

Then he led him over all the place, upstairs and downstairs, and showed him all the treasures and the splendid chambers; one chamber only he did not open, that in which the perilous picture hung. Now the picture was so placed that when the door opened it was the first thing to be seen, and was so wonderfully painted that it seemed to breathe and move, and in the whole world was there nothing more lovely or more beautiful. The young King noticed how Faithful John always passed by this one door, and asked,

"Why do you not undo this door?"

"There is something inside that would terrify you," answered he. But the King answered,

"I have seen the whole castle, and I will know what is in here also." And he went forward and tried to open the door by force.

Then Faithful John called him back, and said, "I promised your father on his death-bed that you should not see what is in that room; it might bring great misfortune on you and me were I to break my promise."

But the young King answered, "I shall be undone if I do not go inside that room; I shall have no peace day or night until I have seen it with these eyes; and I will not move from this place until you have unlocked it."

Then Faithful John saw there was no help for it, and he chose out the key from the big bunch with a heavy heart and many sighs. When the door was opened he walked in first, and thought that by standing in front of the King he might hide the picture from him, but that was no good, the King stood on tiptoe, and looked over his shoulder. And when he saw the image of the lady that was so wonderfully beautiful, and so glittering with gold and jewels, he fell on the ground powerless. Faithful John helped him up, took him to his bed, and thought with sorrow, "Ah me! the evil has come to pass; what will become of us?"

Then he strengthened the King with wine, until he came to himself. The first words that he said were,

"Oh, the beautiful picture! whose portrait is it?"

"It is the portrait of the Princess of the Golden Palace," answered Faithful John. Then the King said,

"My love for her is so great that if all the leaves of the forest were tongues they could not utter it! I stake my life on the chance of obtaining her, and you, my Faithful John, must stand by me."

The faithful servant considered for a long time how the business should be begun; it seemed to him that it would be a difficult matter to come only at a sight of the Princess. At last he thought out a way, and said to the King,

"All that she has about her is of gold—tables, chairs, dishes, drinking-cups, bowls, and all the household furniture; in your treasury are five tons of gold, let the goldsmiths of your kingdom work it up into all kinds of vessels and implements, into all kinds of birds, and wild creatures, and wonderful beasts, such as may please her; then we will carry them off with us, and go and seek our fortune."

The King had all the goldsmiths fetched, and they worked day and night, until at last some splendid things were got ready. When a ship had been loaded with them, Faithful John put on the garb of a merchant, and so did the King, so as the more completely to disguise themselves. Then they journeyed over the sea, and went so far that at last they came to the city where the Princess of the Golden Palace dwelt.

Faithful John told the King to stay in the ship, and to wait for him.

"Perhaps," said he, "I shall bring the Princess back with me, so take care that everything is in order; let the golden vessels be placed about, and the whole ship be adorned."

Then he gathered together in his apron some of the gold

things, one of each kind, landed, and went up to the royal
castle. And when he reached the courtyard of the castle there
stood by the well a pretty maiden, who had two golden pails
in her hand, and she was drawing water with them; and as
she turned round to carry them away she saw the strange man,
and asked him who he was. He answered,

"I am a merchant," and opened his apron, and let her look
within it.

"Ah, what beautiful things!" cried she, and setting down
her pails, she turned the golden toys over, and looked at them
one after another: then she said,

"The Princess must see these; she takes so much pleasure in gold things that she will buy them all from you."

Then she took him by the hand and led him in, for she
was the chamber-maid.

When the Princess saw the golden wares she was very
pleased, and said,

"All these are so finely worked that I should like to buy
them of you."

But the faithful John said,

"I am only the servant of a rich merchant, and what I
have here is nothing to what my master has in the ship—the
cunningest and costliest things that ever were made of gold."

The Princess then wanted it all to be brought to her; but
he said,

"That would take up many days; so great is the number
of them, and so much space would they occupy that there
would not be enough room for them in your house."

But the Princess's curiosity and fancy grew so much that
at last she said,

"Lead me to the ship; I will myself go and see your
master's treasures."

Then Faithful John led her to the ship joyfully, and the
King, when he saw that her beauty was even greater than the
picture had set forth, felt his heart leap at the sight. Then
she climbed up into the ship, and the King received her.
Faithful John stayed by the steersman, and gave orders for the
ship to push off, saying, "Spread all sail, that she may fly
like a bird in the air."

So the King showed her all the golden things, each separately—the dishes, the bowls, the birds, the wild creatures, and the wonderful beasts. Many hours were passed in looking at them all, and in her pleasure the Princess never noticed that the ship was moving onwards. When she had examined the last, she thanked the merchant, and prepared to return home; but when she came to the ship's side, she saw that they were on the high seas, far from land, and speeding on under full sail.

"Ah!" cried she, full of terror, "I am betrayed and carried off by this merchant. Oh that I had died rather than have fallen into his power!"

But the King took hold of her hand, and said,

"No merchant am I, but a King, and no baser of birth than thyself; it is because of my over-mastering love for thee that I have carried thee off by cunning. The first time I saw thy picture I fell fainting to the earth."

When the Princess of the Golden Palace heard this she became more trustful, and her heart inclined favourably towards him, so that she willingly consented to become his wife.

It happened, however, as they were still journeying on the open sea, that Faithful John, as he sat in the forepart of the ship and made music, caught sight of three ravens in the air flying overhead. Then he stopped playing, and listened to what they said one to another, for he understood them quite well. The first one cried,

"Ay, there goes the Princess of the Golden Palace."

"Yes," answered the second; "but he has not got her safe yet." And the third said,

"He has her, though; she sits beside him in the ship."

Then the first one spoke again,

"What does that avail him? When they come on land a fox-red horse will spring towards them; then will the King try to mount him; and if he does, the horse will rise with him into the air, so that he will never see his bride again." The second raven asked,

"Is there no remedy?"

"Oh yes; if another man mounts quickly, and takes the pistol out of the holster and shoots the horse dead with it, he will save the young King. But who knows that? and he that knows it and does it will become stone from toe to knee."

Then said the second.

" I know further, that if the horse should be killed, the young King will not even then be sure of his bride. When they arrive at the castle there will lie a wrought bride-shirt in a dish, and it will seem all woven of gold and silver, but it is really of sulphur and pitch, and if he puts it on it will burn him to the marrow of his bones." The third raven said,

" Is there no remedy ? "

" Oh yes," answered the second; "if another man with gloves on picks up the shirt, and throws it into the fire, so that it is consumed, then is the young King delivered. But what avails that ? He who knows it and does it will be turned into stone from his heart to his knee." Then spoke the third,

" I know yet more, that even when the bride-shirt is burnt up the King is not sure of his bride ; when at the wedding the dance begins, and the young Queen dances, she will suddenly grow pale and fall to the earth as if she were dead, and unless some one lifts her up and takes three drops of blood from her right breast, she will die. But he that knows this and does this will become stone from the crown of his head to the sole of his foot."

When the ravens had spoken thus among themselves they flew away. Faithful John had understood it all, and from that time he remained quiet and sad, for he thought to himself that were he to conceal what he had heard from his master, misfortune would befall ; and were he to discover it his own life would be sacrificed. At last, however, he said within himself,

" I will save my master, though I myself should perish ! "

So when they came on land, it happened just as the ravens had foretold, there sprang forward a splendid fox-red horse.

" Come on ! " said the King, " he shall carry me to the castle," and was going to mount, when Faithful John passed before him and mounted quickly, drew the pistol out of the holster, and shot the horse dead. Then the other servants of the king cried out (for they did not wish well to Faithful John),

" How shameful to kill that beautiful animal that was to have carried the king to his castle." But the King said,

" Hold your tongues, and let him be : he is my Faithful John ; he knows what is the good of it."

Then they went up to the castle, and there stood in the

hall a dish, and the wrought bride-shirt that lay on it seemed as if of gold and silver. The young King went up to it and was going to put it on, but Faithful John pushed him away, picked it up with his gloved hands, threw it quickly on the fire, and there let it burn. The other servants began grumbling again, and said,

"Look, he is even burning up the king's bridal shirt!" But the young King said,

"Who knows but that there may be a good reason for it? let him be, he is my Faithful John."

Then the wedding feast was held; and the bride led the dance; Faithful John watched her carefully, and all at once she grew pale and fell down as if she were dead. Then he went quickly to her, and carried her into a chamber hard by, laid her down, and kneeling, took three drops of blood from her right breast. Immediately she drew breath again and raised herself up, but the young King witnessing all, and not knowing why Faithful John had done this, grew very angry, and cried out,

"Throw him into prison!"

The next morning Faithful John was condemned to death and led to the gallows, and as he stood there ready to suffer, he said,

"He who is about to die is permitted to speak once before his end; may I claim that right?"

"Yes," answered the King, "it is granted to you." Then said Faithful John,

"I have been condemned unjustly, for I have always been faithful," and he related how he had heard on the sea voyage the talk of the ravens, and how he had done everything in order to save his master. Then cried the King,

"O my Faithful John, pardon! pardon! lead him down!" But Faithful John, as he spoke the last words, fell lifeless, and became stone.

The King and Queen had great grief because of this, and the King said,

"Ah, how could I have evil-rewarded such faithfulness!" and he caused the stone image to be lifted up and put to stand in his sleeping-room by the side of his bed. And as often as he saw it he wept and said,

E

"Would that I could bring thee back to life, my Faithful John!"

After some time the Queen bore twins—two little sons—that grew and thrived, and were the joy of their parents. One day, when the Queen was in church, the two children were sitting and playing with their father, and he gazed at the stone image full of sadness, sighed, and cried,

"Oh that I could bring thee back to life, my Faithful John!" Then the stone began to speak, and said,

"Yes, thou canst bring me back to life again, if thou wilt bestow therefor thy best-beloved." Then cried the King,

"All that I have in the world will I give up for thee!" The stone went on to say,

"If thou wilt cut off the heads of thy two children with thy own hand, and besmear me with their blood, I shall receive life again."

The King was horror-struck at the thought that he must put his beloved children to death, but he remembered all John's faithfulness, and how he had died for him, and he drew his sword and cut off his children's heads with his own hand. And when he had besmeared the stone with their blood life returned to it, and Faithful John stood alive and well before him; and he said to the king,

"Thy faithfulness shall not be unrewarded," and, taking up the heads of the children, he set them on again, and besmeared the wound with their blood, upon which in a moment they were whole again, and jumped about, and went on playing as if nothing had happened to them.

Now was the King full of joy; and when he saw the Queen coming he put the Faithful John and the two children in a great chest. When she came in he said to her,

"Hast thou prayed in church?"

"Yes," answered she, "but I was thinking all the while of Faithful John, and how he came to such great misfortune through us."

"Then," said he, "dear wife, we can give him life again, but it will cost us both our little sons, whom we must sacrifice."

The Queen grew pale and sick at heart, but said,

"We owe it him, because of his great faithfulness."

Then the King rejoiced because she thought as he did, and

he went and unlocked the chest and took out the children and Faithful John, and said,

"God be praised, he is delivered, and our little sons are ours again;" and he related to her how it had come to pass.

After that they all lived together in happiness to their lives' end.

·THE·WONDERFUL·MUSICIAN·

HERE was once a wonderful musician, and he was one day walking through a wood all alone, thinking of this and that : and when he had nothing more left to think about, he said to himself,

"I shall grow tired of being in this wood, so I will bring out a good companion."

So he took the fiddle that hung at his back and fiddled so that the wood echoed. Before long a wolf came through the thicket and trotted up to him.

"Oh, here comes a wolf ! I had no particular wish for such company," said the musician : but the wolf drew nearer, and said to him,

"Ho, you musician, how finely you play ! I must learn how to play too."

"That is easily done," answered the musician, "you have only to do exactly as I tell you."

"O musician," said the wolf, "I will obey you, as a scholar does his master."

The musician told him to come with him. As they went a part of the way together they came to an old oak tree, which was hollow within and cleft through the middle.

"Look here," said the musician, "if you want to learn how to fiddle, you must put your fore feet in this cleft."

The wolf obeyed, but the musician took up a stone and quickly wedged both his paws with one stroke, so fast, that the wolf was a prisoner, and there obliged to stop.

"Stay there until I come back again," said the musician, and went his way.

After a while he said again to himself,

"I shall grow weary here in this wood; I will bring out another companion," and he took his fiddle and fiddled away in the wood. Before long a fox came slinking through the trees.

"Oh, here comes a fox!" said the musician; "I had no particular wish for such company."

The fox came up to him and said,

"O my dear musician, how finely you play! I must learn how to play too."

"That is easily done," said the musician, "you have only to do exactly as I tell you."

"O musician," answered the fox, "I will obey you, as a scholar his master."

"Follow me," said the musician; and as they went a part of the way together they came to a footpath with a high hedge on each side. Then the musician stopped, and taking hold of a hazel-branch bent it down to the earth, and put his foot on the end of it; then he bent down a branch from the other side, and said: "Come on, little fox, if you wish to learn something, reach me your left fore foot."

The fox obeyed, and the musician bound the foot to the left hand branch.

"Now, little fox," said he, "reach me the right one;" then he bound it to the right hand branch. And when he had seen that the knots were fast enough he let go, and the branches flew back and caught up the fox, shaking and struggling, in the air.

"Wait there until I come back again," said the musician, and went his way.

By and by he said to himself: "I shall grow weary in this wood; I will bring out another companion."

So he took his fiddle, and the sound echoed through the wood. Then a hare sprang out before him.

"Oh, here comes a hare!" said he, "that's not what I want."

"Ah, my dear musician," said the hare, "how finely you play! I should like to learn how to play too."

" That is soon done," said the musician, " only you must do whatever I tell you."

" O musician," answered the hare, " I will obey you, as a scholar his master."

So they went a part of the way together, until they came to a clear place in the wood where there stood an aspen tree. The musician tied a long string round the neck of the hare, and knotted the other end of it to the tree.

" Now then, courage, little hare ! run twenty times round the tree ! " cried the musician, and the hare obeyed : as he ran round the twentieth time the string had wound twenty times round the tree trunk and the hare was imprisoned, and pull and tug as he would he only cut his tender neck with the string. "Wait there until I come back again," said the musician, and walked on.

The wolf meanwhile had struggled, and pulled, and bitten, at the stone, and worked away so long, that at last he made his paws free and got himself out of the cleft. Full of anger and fury he hastened after the musician to tear him to pieces. When the fox saw him run by he began groaning, and cried out with all his might,

" Brother wolf, come and help me ! the musician has betrayed me." The wolf then pulled the branches down, bit the knots in two, and set the fox free, and he went with him to take vengeance on the musician. They found the imprisoned hare, and set him likewise free, and then they all went on together to seek their enemy.

The musician had once more played his fiddle, and this time he had been more fortunate. The sound had reached the ears of a poor woodcutter, who immediately, and in spite of himself, left his work, and, with his axe under his arm, came to listen to the music.

" At last here comes the right sort of companion," said the musician ; " it was a man I wanted, and not wild animals." And then he began to play so sweetly that the poor man stood as if enchanted, and his heart was filled with joy. And as he was standing there up came the wolf, the fox, and the hare, and he could easily see that they meant mischief. Then he raised his shining axe, and stood in front of the musician, as if to say,

"Whoever means harm to him had better take care of himself, for he will have to do with me!"

Then the animals were frightened, and ran back into the wood, and the musician, when he had played once more to the man to show his gratitude, went on his way.

NCE upon a time there lived a King and Queen very peacefully together ; they had twelve children, all boys. Now the King said to the Queen one day,

"If our thirteenth child should be a girl the twelve boys shall die, so that her riches may be the greater, and the kingdom fall to her alone."

Then he caused twelve coffins to be made ; and they were filled with shavings, and a little pillow laid in each, and they were brought and put in a locked-up room ; and the King gave the key to the Queen, and told her to say nothing about it to any one.

But the mother sat the whole day sorrowing, so that her youngest son, who never left her, and to whom she had given the Bible name Benjamin, said to her,

" Dear mother, why are you so sad ? "

" Dearest child," answered she, " I dare not tell you."

But he let her have no peace until she went and unlocked the room, and showed him the twelve coffins with the shavings and the little pillows. Then she said,

" My dear Benjamin, your father has caused these coffins to be made for you and your eleven brothers, and if I bring a little girl into the world you are all to be put to death together and buried therein." And she wept as she spoke, and her little son comforted her and said,

" Weep not, dear mother, we will save ourselves and go far away." Then she answered,

" Yes, go with your eleven brothers out into the world, and let one of you always sit on the top of the highest tree that can be found, and keep watch upon the tower of this castle. If a little son is born I will put out a white flag, and then you may safely venture back again; but if it is a little daughter I will put out a red flag, and then flee away as fast as you can, and the dear God watch over you. Every night will I arise and pray for you—in winter that you may have a fire to warm yourselves by, and in summer that you may not languish in the heat."

After that, when she had given her sons her blessing, they went away out into the wood. One after another kept watch, sitting on the highest oak tree, looking towards the tower. When eleven days had passed, and Benjamin's turn came, he saw a flag put out, but it was not white, but blood red, to warn them that they were to die. When the brothers knew this they became angry, saying,

" Shall we suffer death because of a girl! we swear to be revenged; wherever we find a girl we will shed her blood."

Then they went deeper into the wood; and in the middle, where it was darkest, they found a little enchanted house, standing empty. Then they said,

" Here will we dwell; and you, Benjamin, the youngest and weakest, shall stay at home and keep house; we others will go abroad and purvey food."

Then they went into the wood and caught hares, wild roes, birds, and pigeons, and whatever else is good to eat, and brought them to Benjamin for him to cook and make ready to satisfy their hunger. So they lived together in the little house for ten years, and the time did not seem long.

By this time the Queen's little daughter was growing up; she had a kind heart and a beautiful face, and a golden star on her forehead. Once when there was a great wash she saw among the clothes twelve shirts, and she asked her mother,

" Whose are these twelve shirts? they are too small to be my father's." Then the mother answered with a sore heart,

" Dear child, they belong to your twelve brothers." The little girl said,

" Where are my twelve brothers? I have never heard of them." And her mother answered,

"God only knows where they are wandering about in the world." Then she led the little girl to the secret room and unlocked it, and showed her the twelve coffins with the shavings and the little pillows.

"These coffins," said she, "were intended for your twelve brothers, but they went away far from home when you were born," and she related how everything had come to pass. Then said the little girl,

"Dear mother, do not weep, I will go and seek my brothers."

So she took the twelve shirts and went far and wide in the great forest. The day sped on, and in the evening she came to the enchanted house. She went in and found a youth, who asked,

"Whence do you come, and what do you want?" and he marvelled at her beauty, her royal garments, and the star on her forehead. Then she answered,

"I am a king's daughter, and I seek my twelve brothers, and I will go everywhere under the blue sky until I find them." And she showed him the twelve shirts which belonged to them. Then Benjamin saw that it must be his sister, and said,

"I am Benjamin, your youngest brother."

And she began weeping for joy, and Benjamin also, and they kissed and cheered each other with great love. After a while he said,

"Dear sister, there is still a hindrance; we have sworn that any maiden that we meet must die, as it was because of a maiden that we had to leave our kingdom." Then she said,

"I will willingly die, if so I may benefit my twelve brothers."

"No," answered he, "you shall not die; sit down under this tub until the eleven brothers come, and I agree with them about it." She did so; and as night came on they returned from hunting, and supper was ready. And as they were sitting at table and eating, they asked,

"What news?" And Benjamin said,

"Don't you know any?"

"No," answered they. So he said,

"You have been in the wood, and I have stayed at home, and yet I know more than you."

· " Tell us !" cried they. He answered,

" Promise me that the first maiden we see shall not be put to death."

" Yes, we promise," cried they all, " she shall have mercy; tell us now." Then he said,

" Our sister is here," and lifted up the tub, and the king's daughter came forth in her royal garments with her golden star on her forehead, and she seemed so beautiful, delicate, and sweet, that they all rejoiced, and fell on her neck and kissed her, and loved her with all their hearts.

After this she remained with Benjamin in the house and helped him with the work. The others went forth into the woods to catch wild animals, does, birds, and pigeons, for food for them all, and their sister and Benjamin took care that all was made ready for them. She fetched the wood for cooking, and the vegetables, and watched the pots on the fire, so that supper was always ready when the others came in. She kept also great order in the house, and the beds were always beautifully white and clean, and the brothers were contented, and lived in unity.

One day the two got ready a fine feast, and when they were all assembled they sat down and ate and drank, and were full of joy. Now there was a little garden belonging to the enchanted house, in which grew twelve lilies; the maiden, thinking to please her brothers, went out to gather the twelve flowers, meaning to give one to each as they sat at meat. But as she broke off the flowers, in the same moment the brothers were changed into twelve ravens, and flew over the wood far away, and the house with the garden also disappeared. So the poor maiden stood alone in the wild wood, and as she was looking around her she saw an old woman standing by her, who said,

" My child, what hast thou done ! why couldst thou not leave the twelve flowers standing? they were thy twelve brothers, who are now changed to ravens for ever." The maiden said, weeping,

" Is there no means of setting them free ? "

" No," said the old woman, " there is in the whole world no way but one, and that is difficult; thou canst not release them but by being dumb for seven years: thou must neither speak nor laugh ; and wert thou to speak one single word, and it wanted but one hour of the seven years, all would be in vain, and thy brothers would perish because of that one word."

Then the maiden said in her heart, " I am quite sure that I can set my brothers free," and went and sought a tall tree, climbed up, and sat there spinning, and never spoke or laughed. Now it happened that a King, who was hunting in the wood, had with him a large greyhound, who ran to the tree where the maiden was, sprang up at it, and barked loudly. Up came the King and saw the beautiful Princess with the golden star on her forehead, and he was so charmed with her beauty that he prayed her to become his wife. She gave no answer, only a little nod of her head. Then he himself climbed the tree and brought her down, set her on his horse and took her home. The wedding was held with great splendour and rejoicing, but the bride neither spoke nor laughed. After they had lived pleasantly together for a few years, the King's mother, who was a wicked woman, began to slander the young Queen, and said to the King,

" She is only a low beggar-maid that you have taken to yourself; who knows what mean tricks she is playing ? Even if she is really dumb and cannot speak she might at least laugh ; not to laugh is the sign of a bad conscience."

At first the King would believe nothing of it, but the old woman talked so long, and suggested so many bad things, that he at last let himself be persuaded, and condemned the Queen to death.

Now a great fire was kindled in the courtyard, and she was to be burned in it; and the King stood above at the window, and watched it all with weeping eyes, for he had held her very dear. And when she was already fast bound to the stake, and the fire was licking her garments with red tongues, the last moment of the seven years came to an end. Then a rushing sound was heard in the air, and twelve ravens came flying and sank downwards; and as they touched the earth they became her twelve brothers that she had lost. They rushed through the fire and quenched the flames, and set their dear sister free, kissing and consoling her. And now that her mouth was opened, and that she might venture to speak, she told the King the reason of her dumbness, and why she had never laughed. The King rejoiced when he heard of her innocence, and they all lived together in happiness until their death.

But the wicked mother-in-law was very unhappy, and died miserably.

·THE·VAGABONDS·

HE cock said to the hen, "It is nutting time, let us go together to the mountains and have a good feast for once, before the squirrels come and carry all away."

"Yes," answered the hen, "come along ; we will have a jolly time together."

Then they set off together to the mountains, and as it was a fine day they stayed there till the evening. Now whether it was that they had eaten so much, or because of their pride and haughtiness, I do not know, but they would not go home on foot; so the cock set to work to make a little carriage out of nutshells. When it was ready, the hen seated herself in it, and said to the cock,

"Now you can harness yourself to it."

"That's all very fine," said the cock, "I would sooner go home on foot than do such a thing : and I never agreed to it. I don't mind being coachman, and sitting on the box ; but as to drawing it myself, it's quite out of the question."

As they were wrangling, a duck came quacking,

"You thieving vagabonds, who told you you might go to my mountain? Look out, or it will be the worse for you!" and flew at the cock with bill wide open. But the cock was not backward, and he gave the duck a good dig in the body, and hacked at her with his spurs so valiantly that she begged for mercy, and willingly allowed herself to be harnessed to the carriage. Then the cock seated himself on the box and was coachman ; so off they went at a great pace, the cock crying out " Run, duck, as fast as you can !"

When they had gone a part of the way they met two foot-passengers, a pin and a needle. They cried "Stop ! stop !" and said that it would soon be blindman's holiday ; that they could not go a step farther ; that the ways were very muddy ; might they just get in for a little ? they had been standing at the door of the tailors' house of call and had been delayed because of beer.

The cock, seeing they were slender folks that would not take up a great deal of room, let them both step in, only they must promise not to tread on his toes nor on the hen's.

Late in the evening they came to an inn, and there they found that they could not go any farther that night, as the duck's paces were not good, she waddled so much from side to side ; so they turned in. The landlord at first made some difficulty ; his house was full already, and he thought they had no very distinguished appearance ; at last, however, when they had made many fine speeches, and had promised him the egg that the hen had laid on the way, and that he should keep the duck, who laid one every day, he agreed to let them stay the night ; and so they had a very gay time.

Early in the morning, when it was beginning to grow light, and everybody was still asleep, the cock waked up the hen, fetched the egg, and made a hole in it, and they ate it up between them, and put the eggshell on the hearth. Then they went up to the needle, who was still sleeping, picked him up by his head, and stuck him in the landlord's chair-cushion, and having also placed the pin in his towel, off they flew over the hills and far away. The duck, who had chosen to sleep in the open air, and had remained in the yard, heard the rustling of their wings, and, waking up, looked about till she found a brook, down which she swam a good deal faster than she had drawn the carriage.

A few hours later the landlord woke, and, leaving his feather-bed, began washing himself ; but when he took the towel to dry himself he drew the pin all across his face, and made a red streak from ear to ear. Then he went into the kitchen to light his pipe, but when he stooped towards the hearth to take up a coal the eggshell flew in his eyes.

"Everything goes wrong this morning," said he, and let himself drop, full of vexation, into his grandfather's chair; but up he jumped in a moment, crying, "Oh dear!" for the needle had gone into him.

Now he became angry, and had his suspicions of the guests who had arrived so late the evening before; and when he looked round for them they were nowhere to be seen.

Then he swore that he would never more harbour such vagabonds, that consumed so much, paid nothing, and played such nasty tricks into the bargain.

·THE·BROTHER·AND·SISTER·

THE brother took his sister's hand and said to her,

"Since our mother died we have had no good days; our stepmother beats us every day, and if we go near her she kicks us away; we have nothing to eat but hard crusts of bread left over; the dog under the table fares better; he gets a good piece every now and then. If our mother only knew, how she would pity us! Come, let us go together out into the wide world!"

So they went, and journeyed the whole day through fields and meadows and stony places, and if it rained the sister said,

"The skies and we are weeping together."

In the evening they came to a great wood, and they were so weary with hunger and their long journey, that they climbed up into a high tree and fell asleep.

The next morning, when they awoke, the sun was high in heaven, and shone brightly through the leaves. Then said the brother,

"Sister, I am thirsty; if I only knew where to find a brook, that I might go and drink! I almost think that I hear one rushing." So the brother got down and led his sister by the hand, and they went to seek the brook. But their wicked stepmother was a witch, and had known quite well that the two children had run away, and had sneaked after them, as only witches can, and had laid a spell on all the brooks in the

F

forest. So when they found a little stream flowing smoothly over its pebbles, the brother was going to drink of it; but the sister heard how it said in its rushing,

"He a tiger will be who drinks of me,
Who drinks of me a tiger will be!"

Then the sister cried,

"Pray, dear brother, do not drink, or you will become a wild beast, and will tear me in pieces."

So the brother refrained from drinking, though his thirst was great, and he said he would wait till he came to the next brook. When they came to a second brook the sister heard it say,

"He a wolf will be who drinks of me,
Who drinks of me a wolf will be!"

Then the sister cried,

"Pray, dear brother, do not drink, or you will be turned into a wolf, and will eat me up!"

So the brother refrained from drinking, and said,

"I will wait until we come to the next brook, and then I must drink, whatever you say; my thirst is so great."

And when they came to the third brook the sister heard how in its rushing it said,

"Who drinks of me a fawn will be,
He a fawn will be who drinks of me!"

Then the sister said,

"O my brother, I pray drink not, or you will be turned into a fawn, and run away far from me."

But he had already kneeled by the side of the brook and stooped and drunk of the water, and as the first drops passed his lips he became a fawn.

And the sister wept over her poor lost brother, and the fawn wept also, and stayed sadly beside her. At last the maiden said,

"Be comforted, dear fawn, indeed I will never leave you."

Then she untied her golden girdle and bound it round the fawn's neck, and went and gathered rushes to make a soft cord, which she fastened to him; and then she led him on, and they went deeper into the forest. And when they had

gone a long long way, they came at last to a little house, and
the maiden looked inside, and as it was empty she thought,

" We might as well live here."

And she fetched leaves and moss to make a soft bed for
the fawn, and every morning she went out and gathered roots
and berries and nuts for herself, and fresh grass for the fawn,
who ate out of her hand with joy, frolicking round her. At
night, when the sister was tired, and had said her prayers, she
laid her head on the fawn's back, which served her for a pillow,
and softly fell asleep. And if only the brother could have
got back his own shape again, it would have been a charming
life. So they lived a long while in the wilderness alone.

Now it happened that the King of that country held a great
hunt in the forest. The blowing of the horns, the barking of
the dogs, and the lusty shouts of the huntsmen sounded
through the wood, and the fawn heard them and was eager
to be among them.

" Oh," said he to his sister, " do let me go to the hunt ;
I cannot stay behind any longer," and begged so long that at
last she consented.

" But mind," said she to him, " come back to me at night.
I must lock my door against the wild hunters, so, in order
that I may know you, you must knock and say, ' Little sister,
let me in,' and unless I hear that I shall not unlock the
door."

Then the fawn sprang out, and felt glad and merry in the
open air. The King and his huntsmen saw the beautiful
animal, and began at once to pursue him, but they could not
come within reach of him, for when they thought they were
certain of him he sprang away over the bushes and disappeared.
As soon as it was dark he went back to the little house,
knocked at the door, and said,

" Little sister, let me in."

Then the door was opened to him, and he went in, and
rested the whole night long on his soft bed. The next morning the hunt began anew, and when the fawn heard the hunting-
horns and the tally-ho of the huntsmen he could rest no
longer, and said,

" Little sister, let me out, I must go." The sister opened
the door and said,

"Now, mind you must come back at night and say the same words."

When the King and his hunters saw the fawn with the golden collar again, they chased him closely, but he was too nimble and swift for them. This lasted the whole day, and at last the hunters surrounded him, and one of them wounded his foot a little, so that he was obliged to limp and to go slowly. Then a hunter slipped after him to the little house, and heard how he called out, "Little sister, let me in," and saw the door open and shut again after him directly. The hunter noticed all this carefully, went to the King, and told him all he had seen and heard. Then said the King,

"To-morrow we will hunt again."

But the sister was very terrified when she saw that her fawn was wounded. She washed his foot, laid cooling leaves round it, and said, "Lie down on your bed, dear fawn, and rest, that you may be soon well." The wound was very slight, so that the fawn felt nothing of it the next morning. And when he heard the noise of the hunting outside, he said,

"I cannot stay in, I must go after them; I shall not be taken easily again!" The sister began to weep, and said,

"I know you will be killed, and I left alone here in the forest, and forsaken of everybody. I cannot let you go!"

"Then I shall die here with longing," answered the fawn; "when I hear the sound of the horn I feel as if I should leap out of my skin."

Then the sister, seeing there was no help for it, unlocked the door with a heavy heart, and the fawn bounded away into the forest, well and merry. When the King saw him, he said to his hunters,

"Now, follow him up all day long till the night comes, and see that you do him no hurt."

So as soon as the sun had gone down, the King said to the huntsmen : "Now, come and show me the little house in the wood."

And when he got to the door he knocked at it, and cried,

"Little sister, let me in!"

Then the door opened, and the King went in, and there stood a maiden more beautiful than any he had seen before.

The maiden shrieked out when she saw, instead of the fawn, a man standing there with a gold crown on his head. But the King looked kindly on her, took her by the hand, and said,

"Will you go with me to my castle, and be my dear wife?"

"Oh yes," answered the maiden, "but the fawn must come too. I could not leave him." And the King said,

"He shall remain with you as long as you live, and shall lack nothing." Then the fawn came bounding in, and the sister tied the cord of rushes to him, and led him by her own hand out of the little house.

The King put the beautiful maiden on his horse, and carried her to his castle, where the wedding was held with great pomp ; so she became lady Queen, and they lived together happily for a long while ; the fawn was well tended and cherished, and he gambolled about the castle garden.

Now the wicked stepmother, whose fault it was that the children were driven out into the world, never dreamed but that the sister had been eaten up by wild beasts in the forest, and that the brother, in the likeness of a fawn, had been slain by the hunters. But when she heard that they were so happy, and that things had gone so well with them, jealousy and envy arose in her heart, and left her no peace, and her chief thought was how to bring misfortune upon them.

Her own daughter, who was as ugly as sin, and had only one eye, complained to her, and said,

"I never had the chance of being a Queen."

"Never mind," said the old woman, to satisfy her ; "when the time comes, I shall be at hand."

After a while the Queen brought a beautiful baby-boy into the world, and that day the King was out hunting. The old witch took the shape of the bedchamber woman, and went into the room where the Queen lay, and said to her,

"Come, the bath is ready; it will give you refreshment and new strength. Quick, or it will be cold."

Her daughter was within call, so they carried the sick Queen into the bath-room, and left her there. And in the bath-room they had made a great fire, so as to suffocate the beautiful young Queen.

When that was managed, the old woman took her daughter, put a cap on her, and laid her in the bed in the Queen's place, gave her also the Queen's form and countenance, only she could not restore the lost eye. So, in order that the King might not remark it, she had to lie on the side where there was no eye. In the evening, when the King came home and heard that a little son was born to him, he rejoiced with all his heart, and was going at once to his dear wife's bedside to see how she did. Then the old woman cried hastily,

" For your life, do not draw back the curtains, to let in the light upon her; she must be kept quiet." So the King went away, and never knew that a false Queen was lying in the bed.

Now, when it was midnight, and every one was asleep, the nurse, who was sitting by the cradle in the nursery and watching there alone, saw the door open, and the true Queen come in. She took the child out of the cradle, laid it in her bosom, and fed it. Then she shook out its little pillow, put the child back again, and covered it with the coverlet. She did not forget the fawn either : she went to him where he lay in the corner, and stroked his back tenderly. Then she went in perfect silence out at the door, and the nurse next morning asked the watchmen if any one had entered the castle during the night, but they said they had seen no one. And the Queen came many nights, and never said a word ; the nurse saw her always, but she did not dare speak of it to any one.

After some time had gone by in this manner, the Queen seemed to find voice, and said one night,

" My child my fawn twice more I come to see,
Twice more I come, and then the end must be."

The nurse said nothing, but as soon as the Queen had disappeared she went to the King and told him all. The King said,

" Ah, heaven ! what do I hear ! I will myself watch by the child to-morrow night."

So at evening he went into the nursery, and at midnight the Queen appeared, and said,

" My child my fawn once more I come to see,
Once more I come, and then the end must be."

And she tended the child, as she was accustomed to do,

before she vanished. The King dared not speak to her, but he watched again the following night, and heard her say,

" My child my fawn this once I come to see,
   This once I come, and now the end must be."

Then the King could contain himself no longer, but rushed towards her, saying,

" You are no other than my dear wife ! " Then she answered,

" Yes, I am your dear wife," and in that moment, by the grace of heaven, her life returned to her, and she was once more well and strong. Then she told the King the snare that the wicked witch and her daughter had laid for her. The King had them both brought to judgment, and sentence was passed upon them. The daughter was sent away into the wood, where she was devoured by the wild beasts, and the witch was burned, and ended miserably. And as soon as her body was in ashes the spell was removed from the fawn, and he took human shape again ; and then the sister and brother lived happily together until the end.

·RAPUNZEL·

THERE once lived a man and his wife, who had long wished for a child, but in vain. Now there was at the back of their house a little window which overlooked a beautiful garden full of the finest vegetables and flowers; but there was a high wall all round it, and no one ventured into it, for it belonged to a witch of great might, and of whom all the world was afraid. One day that the wife was standing at the window, and looking into the garden, she saw a bed filled with the finest rampion; and it looked so fresh and green that she began to wish for some; and at length she longed for it greatly. This went on for days, and as she knew she could not get the rampion, she pined away, and grew pale and miserable. Then the man was uneasy, and asked,

" What is the matter, dear wife ? "

" Oh," answered she, " I shall die unless I can have some of that rampion to eat that grows in the garden at the back of our house." The man, who loved her very much, thought to himself,

" Rather than lose my wife I will get some rampion, cost what it will."

So in the twilight he climbed over the wall into the witch's garden, plucked hastily a handful of rampion and brought it to his wife. She made a salad of it at once, and ate of it to her heart's content. But she liked it so much, and it tasted so good, that the next day she longed for it

RAPUNZEL

"O RAPUNZEL, RAPUNZEL!
LET DOWN THINE HAIR."

thrice as much as she had done before; if she was to have any rest the man must climb over the wall once more. So he went in the twilight again; and as he was climbing back, he saw, all at once, the witch standing before him, and was terribly frightened, as she cried, with angry eyes,

"How dare you climb over into my garden like a thief, and steal my rampion! it shall be the worse for you!"

"Oh," answered he, "be merciful rather than just, I have only done it through necessity; for my wife saw your rampion out of the window, and became possessed with so great a longing that she would have died if she could not have had some to eat." Then the witch said,

"If it is all as you say you may have as much rampion as you like, on one condition—the child that will come into the world must be given to me. It shall go well with the child, and I will care for it like a mother."

In his distress of mind the man promised everything; and when the time came when the child was born the witch appeared, and, giving the child the name of Rapunzel (which is the same as rampion), she took it away with her.

Rapunzel was the most beautiful child in the world. When she was twelve years old the witch shut her up in a tower in the midst of a wood, and it had neither steps nor door, only a small window above. When the witch wished to be let in, she would stand below and would cry,

"Rapunzel, Rapunzel! let down your hair!"

Rapunzel had beautiful long hair that shone like gold. When she heard the voice of the witch she would undo the fastening of the upper window, unbind the plaits of her hair, and let it down twenty ells below, and the witch would climb up by it.

After they had lived thus a few years it happened that as the King's son was riding through the wood, he came to the tower; and as he drew near he heard a voice singing so sweetly that he stood still and listened. It was Rapunzel in her loneliness trying to pass away the time with sweet songs. The King's son wished to go in to her, and sought to find a door in the tower, but there was none. So he rode home, but the song had entered into his heart, and every day he went into the wood and listened to it. Once, as he was stand-

ing there under a tree, he saw the witch come up, and listened while she called out,

"O Rapunzel, Rapunzel! let down your hair."

Then he saw how Rapunzel let down her long tresses, and
how the witch climbed up by it and went in to her, and he
said to himself,

"Since that is the ladder I will climb it, and seek my
fortune." And the next day, as soon as it began to grow dusk,
he went to the tower and cried,

"O Rapunzel, Rapunzel! let down your hair."

And she let down her hair, and the King's son climbed up
by it.

Rapunzel was greatly terrified when she saw that a man
had come in to her, for she had never seen one before ; but
the King's son began speaking so kindly to her, and told how
her singing had entered into his heart, so that he could have
no peace until he had seen her herself. Then Rapunzel forgot her terror, and when he asked her to take him for her
husband, and she saw that he was young and beautiful, she
thought to herself,

"I certainly like him much better than old mother Gothel,"
and she put her hand into his hand, saying,

"I would willingly go with thee, but I do not know how I
shall get out. When thou comest, bring each time a silken
rope, and I will make a ladder, and when it is quite ready I
will get down by it out of the tower, and thou shalt take me
away on thy horse." They agreed that he should come to her
every evening, as the old woman came in the day-time. So
the witch knew nothing of all this until once Rapunzel said
to her unwittingly,

"Mother Gothel, how is it that you climb up here so
slowly, and the King's son is with me in a moment?"

"O wicked child," cried the witch, "what is this I hear !
I thought I had hidden thee from all the world, and thou hast
betrayed me !"

In her anger she seized Rapunzel by her beautiful hair,
struck her several times with her left hand, and then grasping
a pair of shears in her right—snip, snap—the beautiful locks
lay on the ground. And she was so hard-hearted that she
took Rapunzel and put her in a waste and desert place, where
she lived in great woe and misery.

The same day on which she took Rapunzel away she went back to the tower in the evening and made fast the severed locks of hair to the window-hasp, and the King's son came and cried,

"Rapunzel, Rapunzel! let down your hair."

Then she let the hair down, and the King's son climbed up, but instead of his dearest Rapunzel he found the witch looking at him with wicked glittering eyes.

"Aha!" cried she, mocking him, "you came for your darling, but the sweet bird sits no longer in the nest, and sings no more; the cat has got her, and will scratch out your eyes as well! Rapunzel is lost to you; you will see her no more."

The King's son was beside himself with grief, and in his agony he sprang from the tower : he escaped with life, but the thorns on which he fell put out his eyes. Then he wandered blind through the wood, eating nothing but roots and berries, and doing nothing but lament and weep for the loss of his dearest wife.

So he wandered several years in misery until at last he came to the desert place where Rapunzel lived with her twin-children that she had borne, a boy and a girl. At first he heard a voice that he thought he knew, and when he reached the place from which it seemed to come Rapunzel knew him, and fell on his neck and wept. And when her tears touched his eyes they became clear again, and he could see with them as well as ever.

Then he took her to his kingdom, where he was received with great joy, and there they lived long and happily.

The THREE·LITTLE·MEN·in·the·WOOD·

HERE was once a man, whose wife was dead, and a woman, whose husband was dead; and the man had a daughter, and so had the woman. The girls were acquainted with each other, and used to play together sometimes in the woman's house. So the woman said to the man's daughter,

"Listen to me, tell your father that I will marry him, and then you shall have milk to wash in every morning and wine to drink, and my daughter shall have water to wash in and water to drink."

The girl went home and told her father what the woman had said. The man said,

"What shall I do! Marriage is a joy, and also a torment."

At last, as he could come to no conclusion, he took off his boot, and said to his daughter,

"Take this boot, it has a hole in the sole; go up with it into the loft, hang it on the big nail and pour water in it. If it holds water, I will once more take to me a wife; if it let out the water, so will I not."

The girl did as she was told, but the water held the hole together, and the boot was full up to the top. So she went and told her father how it was. And he went up to see with his own eyes, and as there was no mistake about it, he went to the widow and courted her, and then they had the wedding.

The next morning, when the two girls awoke, there stood by the bedside of the man's daughter milk to wash in and wine to drink, and by the bedside of the woman's daughter there stood water to wash in and water to drink.

On the second morning there stood water to wash in and water to drink for both of them alike.   On the third morning there stood water to wash in and water to drink for the man's daughter, and milk to wash in and wine to drink for the woman's daughter; and so it remained ever after.   The woman hated her step-daughter, and never knew how to treat her badly enough from one day to another.   And she was jealous because her step-daughter was pleasant and pretty, and her real daughter was ugly and hateful.

Once in winter, when it was freezing hard, and snow lay deep on hill and valley, the woman made a frock out of paper, called her step-daughter, and said,

"Here, put on this frock, go out into the wood and fetch me a basket of strawberries; I have a great wish for some."

"Oh dear," said the girl, "there are no strawberries to be found in winter; the ground is frozen, and the snow covers everything.   And why should I go in the paper frock? it is so cold out of doors that one's breath is frozen; the wind will blow through it, and the thorns will tear it off my back!"

"How dare you contradict me!" cried the step-mother, "be off, and don't let me see you again till you bring me a basket of strawberries."

Then she gave her a little piece of hard bread, and said,

"That will do for you to eat during the day," and she thought to herself, "She is sure to be frozen or starved to death out of doors, and I shall never set eyes on her again."

So the girl went obediently, put on the paper frock, and started out with the basket.   The snow was lying everywhere, far and wide, and there was not a blade of green to be seen. When she entered the wood she saw a little house with three little men peeping out of it.   She wished them good day, and knocked modestly at the door.   They called her in, and she came into the room and sat down by the side of the oven to warm herself and eat her breakfast.   The little men said,

"Give us some of it."

"Willingly," answered she, breaking her little piece of bread in two, and giving them half.   They then said,

"What are you doing here in the wood this winter time in your little thin frock?"

"Oh," answered she, "I have to get a basket of strawberries, and I must not go home without them."

When she had eaten her bread they gave her a broom, and told her to go and sweep the snow away from the back door. When she had gone outside to do it the little men talked among themselves about what they should do for her, as she was so good and pretty, and had shared her bread with them. Then the first one said,

"She shall grow prettier every day."   The second said,

"Each time she speaks a piece of gold shall fall from her mouth."   The third said,

"A king shall come and take her for his wife."

In the meanwhile the girl was doing as the little men had told her, and had cleared the snow from the back of the little house, and what do you suppose she found? fine ripe strawberries, showing dark red against the snow!   Then she joyfully filled her little basket full, thanked the little men, shook hands with them all, and ran home in haste to bring her step-mother the thing she longed for.   As she went in and said, "Good evening," a piece of gold fell from her mouth at once.   Then she related all that had happened to her in the wood, and at each word that she spoke gold pieces fell out of her mouth, so that soon they were scattered all over the room.

"Just look at her pride and conceit!" cried the step-sister, "throwing money about in this way!" but in her heart she was jealous because of it, and wanted to go too into the wood to fetch strawberries.   But the mother said,

"No, my dear little daughter, it is too cold, you will be frozen to death."

But she left her no peace, so at last the mother gave in, got her a splendid fur coat to put on, and gave her bread and butter and cakes to eat on the way.

The girl went into the wood and walked straight up to the little house.   The three little men peeped out again, but she gave them no greeting, and without looking round or taking any notice of them she came stumping into the room, sat herself down by the oven, and began to eat her bread and butter and cakes.

"Give us some of that," cried the little men, but she answered,

"I've not enough for myself; how can I give away any?"

Now when she had done with her eating, they said,

"Here is a broom, go and sweep all clean by the back door."

"Oh, go and do it yourselves," answered she; "I am not your housemaid."

But when she saw that they were not going to give her anything, she went out to the door.   Then the three little men said among themselves,

"What shall we do to her, because she is so unpleasant, and has such a wicked jealous heart, grudging everybody everything?"   The first said,

"She shall grow uglier every day."   The second said,

"Each time she speaks a toad shall jump out of her mouth at every word."   The third said,

"She shall die a miserable death."

The girl was looking outside for strawberries, but as she found none, she went sulkily home.   And directly she opened her mouth to tell her mother what had happened to her in the wood a toad sprang out of her mouth at each word, so that every one who came near her was quite disgusted.

The step-mother became more and more set against the man's daughter, whose beauty increased day by day, and her only thought was how to do her some injury.   So at last she took a kettle, set it on the fire, and scalded some yarn in it. When it was ready she hung it over the poor girl's shoulder, and gave her an axe, and she was to go to the frozen river and break a hole in the ice, and there to rinse the yarn.   She obeyed, and went and hewed a hole in the ice, and as she was about it there came by a splendid coach, in which the King sat.   The coach stood still, and the King said,

"My child, who art thou, and what art thou doing there?" She answered,

"I am a poor girl, and am rinsing yarn."

Then the King felt pity for her, and as he saw that she was very beautiful, he said,

"Will you go with me?"

"Oh yes, with all my heart," answered she; and she felt very glad to be out of the way of her mother and sister.

So she stepped into the coach and went off with the King; and when they reached his castle the wedding was celebrated with great splendour, as the little men in the wood had foretold.

At the end of a year the young Queen had a son; and as the step-mother had heard of her great good fortune she came with her daughter to the castle, as if merely to pay the King and Queen a visit. One day, when the King had gone out, and when nobody was about, the bad woman took the Queen by the head, and her daughter took her by the heels, and dragged her out of bed, and threw her out of the window into a stream that flowed beneath it. Then the old woman put her ugly daughter in the bed, and covered her up to her chin. When the King came back, and wanted to talk to his wife a little, the old woman cried,

"Stop, stop! she is sleeping nicely; she must be kept quiet to-day."

The King dreamt of nothing wrong, and came again the next morning; and as he spoke to his wife, and she answered him, there jumped each time out of her mouth a toad instead of the piece of gold as heretofore. Then he asked why that should be, and the old woman said it was because of her great weakness, and that it would pass away.

But in the night, the boy who slept in the kitchen saw how something in the likeness of a duck swam up the gutter, and said,—

"My King, what mak'st thou?
Sleepest thou, or wak'st thou?"

But there was no answer. Then it said,

"What cheer my two guests keep they?"

So the kitchen-boy answered,

"In bed all soundly sleep they."

It asked again,

"And my little baby, how does *he?*"

And he answered,

"He sleeps in his cradle quietly."

Then the duck took the shape of the Queen, and went to the child, and gave him to drink, smoothed his little bed, covered him up again, and then, in the likeness of a duck, swam back down the gutter. In this way she came two nights, and on the third she said to the kitchen-boy,

"Go and tell the King to brandish his sword three times over me on the threshold!"

Then the kitchen-boy ran and told the King, and he came with his sword and brandished it three times over the duck, and at the third time his wife stood before him living, and hearty, and sound, as she had been before.

The King was greatly rejoiced, but he hid the Queen in a chamber until the Sunday came when the child was to be baptized. And after the baptism he said,

"What does that person deserve who drags another out of bed and throws him in the water?"

And the old woman answered,

"No better than to be put into a cask with iron nails in it, and to be rolled in it down the hill into the water."

Then said the King,

"You have spoken your own sentence;" and he ordered a cask to be fetched, and the old woman and her daughter were put into it, and the top hammered down, and the cask was rolled down the hill into the river.

·THE·THREE·SPINSTERS·

HERE was once a girl who was lazy and would not spin, and her mother could not persuade her to it, do what she would. At last the mother became angry and out of patience, and gave her a good beating, so that she cried out loudly. At that moment the Queen was going by; as she heard the crying, she stopped; and, going into the house, she asked the mother why she was beating her daughter, so that every one outside in the street could hear her cries.

The woman was ashamed to tell of her daughter's laziness, so she said,

"I cannot stop her from spinning; she is for ever at it, and I am poor and cannot furnish her with flax enough."

Then the Queen answered,

"I like nothing better than the sound of the spinning-wheel, and always feel happy when I hear its humming; let me take your daughter with me to the castle—I have plenty of flax, she shall spin there to her heart's content."

The mother was only too glad of the offer, and the Queen took the girl with her. When they reached the castle the Queen showed her three rooms which were filled with the finest flax as full as they could hold.

"Now you can spin me this flax," said she, "and when you can show it me all done you shall have my eldest son for bridegroom; you may be poor, but I make nothing of that—your industry is dowry enough."

The girl was inwardly terrified, for she could not have spun the flax, even if she were to live to be a hundred years old, and were to sit spinning every day of her life from morning to evening. And when she found herself alone she began to weep, and sat so for three days without putting her hand to it. On the third day the Queen came, and when she saw that nothing had been done of the spinning she was much surprised; but the girl excused herself by saying that she had not been able to begin because of the distress she was in at leaving her home and her mother. The excuse contented the Queen, who said, however, as she went away,

" To-morrow you must begin to work."

When the girl found herself alone again she could not tell how to help herself or what to do, and in her perplexity she went and gazed out of the window. There she saw three women passing by, and the first of them had a broad flat foot, the second had a big under-lip that hung down over her chin, and the third had a remarkably broad thumb. They all of them stopped in front of the window, and called out to know what it was that the girl wanted. She told them all her need, and they promised her their help, and said,

" Then will you invite us to your wedding, and not be ashamed of us, and call us your cousins, and let us sit at your table; if you will promise this, we will finish off your flax-spinning in a very short time."

" With all my heart," answered the girl; " only come in now, and begin at once."

Then these same women came in, and she cleared a space in the first room for them to sit and carry on their spinning. The first one drew out the thread and moved the treddle that turned the wheel, the second moistened the thread, the third twisted it, and rapped with her finger on the table, and as often as she rapped a heap of yarn fell to the ground, and it was most beautifully spun. But the girl hid the three spinsters out of the Queen's sight, and only showed her, as often as she came, the heaps of well-spun yarn; and there was no end to the praises she received. When the first room was empty they went on to the second, and then to the third, so that at last all was finished. Then the three women took their leave, saying to the girl,

"Do not forget what you have promised, and it will be all the better for you."

So when the girl took the Queen and showed her the empty rooms, and the great heaps of yarn, the wedding was at once arranged, and the bridegroom rejoiced that he should have so clever and diligent a wife, and praised her exceedingly.

"I have three cousins," said the girl, "and as they have shown me a great deal of kindness, I would not wish to forget them in my good fortune ; may I be allowed to invite them to the wedding, and to ask them to sit at the table with us?"

The Queen and the bridegroom said at once,

"There is no reason against it."

So when the feast began in came the three spinsters in strange guise, and the bride said,

"Dear cousins, you are welcome."

"Oh," said the bridegroom, "how come you to have such dreadfully ugly relations?"

And then he went up to the first spinster and said,

"How is it that you have such a broad flat foot?"

"With treading," answered she, "with treading."

Then he went up to the second and said,

"How is it that you have such a great hanging lip?"

"With licking," answered she, "with licking."

Then he asked the third,

"How is it that you have such a broad thumb?"

"With twisting thread," answered she, "with twisting thread."

Then the bridegroom said that from that time forward his beautiful bride should never touch a spinning-wheel.

And so she escaped that tiresome flax-spinning.

·HANSEL·AND·GRETHEL·

NEAR a great forest there lived a poor woodcutter and his wife, and his two children; the boy's name was Hansel and the girl's Grethel. They had very little to bite or to sup, and once, when there was great dearth in the land, the man could not even gain the daily bread. As he lay in bed one night thinking of this, and turning and tossing, he sighed heavily, and said to his wife,

"What will become of us? we cannot even feed our children; there is nothing left for ourselves."

"I will tell you what, husband," answered the wife; "we will take the children early in the morning into the forest, where it is thickest; we will make them a fire, and we will give each of them a piece of bread, then we will go to our work and leave them alone; they will never find the way home again, and we shall be quit of them."

"No, wife," said the man, "I cannot do that; I cannot find in my heart to take my children into the forest and to leave them there alone; the wild animals would soon come and devour them."

"O you fool," said she, "then we will all four starve; you had better get the coffins ready,"—and she left him no peace until he consented.

"But I really pity the poor children," said the man.

The two children had not been able to sleep for hunger, and had heard what their step-mother had said to their father. Grethel wept bitterly, and said to Hansel,

" It is all over with us."

" Do be quiet, Grethel," said Hansel, " and do not fret; I will manage something." And when the parents had gone to sleep he got up, put on his little coat, opened the back door, and slipped out. The moon was shining brightly, and the white flints that lay in front of the house glistened like pieces of silver. Hansel stooped and filled the little pocket of his coat as full as it would hold. Then he went back again, and said to Grethel,

" Be easy, dear little sister, and go to sleep quietly; God will not forsake us," and laid himself down again in his bed.

When the day was breaking, and before the sun had risen, the wife came and awakened the two children, saying,

" Get up, you lazy bones; we are going into the forest to cut wood."

Then she gave each of them a piece of bread, and said,

" That is for dinner, and you must not eat it before then, for you will get no more."

Grethel carried the bread under her apron, for Hansel had his pockets full of the flints. Then they set off all together on their way to the forest. When they had gone a little way Hansel stood still and looked back towards the house, and this he did again and again, till his father said to him,

" Hansel, what are you looking at? take care not to forget your legs."

" O father," said Hansel, " I am looking at my little white kitten, who is sitting up on the roof to bid me good-bye."

" You young fool," said the woman, " that is not your kitten, but the sunshine on the chimney-pot."

Of course Hansel had not been looking at his kitten, but had been taking every now and then a flint from his pocket and dropping it on the road.

When they reached the middle of the forest the father told the children to collect wood to make a fire to keep them warm; and Hansel and Grethel gathered brushwood enough for a little mountain; and it was set on fire, and when the flame was burning quite high the wife said,

" Now lie down by the fire and rest yourselves, you children, and we will go and cut wood; and when we are ready we will come and fetch you."

So Hansel and Grethel sat by the fire, and at noon they each ate their pieces of bread. They thought their father was in the wood all the time, as they seemed to hear the strokes of the axe : but really it was only a dry branch hanging to a withered tree that the wind moved to and fro. So when they had stayed there a long time their eyelids closed with weariness, and they fell fast asleep. When at last they woke it was night, and Grethel began to cry, and said,

" How shall we ever get out of this wood ? " But Hansel comforted her, saying,

"Wait a little while longer, until the moon rises, and then we can easily find the way home."

And when the full moon got up Hansel took his little sister by the hand, and followed the way where the flint stones shone like silver, and showed them the road. They walked on the whole night through, and at the break of day they came to their father's house. They knocked at the door, and when the wife opened it and saw that it was Hansel and Grethel she said,

" You naughty children, why did you sleep so long in the wood ? we thought you were never coming home again ! "

But the father was glad, for it had gone to his heart to leave them both in the woods alone.

Not very long after that there was again great scarcity in those parts, and the children heard their mother say at night in bed to their father,

" Everything is finished up ; we have only half a loaf, and after that the tale comes to an end. The children must be off ; we will take them farther into the wood this time, so that they shall not be able to find the way back again ; there is no other way to manage."

The man felt sad at heart, and he thought,

" It would better to share one's last morsel with one's children."

But the wife would listen to nothing that he said, but scolded and reproached him. He who says A must say B too, and when a man has given in once he has to do it a second time.

But the children were not asleep, and had heard all the talk. When the parents had gone to sleep Hansel got up to

go out and get more flint stones, as he did before, but the wife
had locked the door, and Hansel could not get out; but he
comforted his little sister, and said,

"Don't cry, Grethel, and go to sleep quietly, and God will
help us."

Early the next morning the wife came and pulled the
children out of bed. She gave them each a little piece of bread
—less than before; and on the way to the wood Hansel
crumbled the bread in his pocket, and often stopped to throw
a crumb on the ground.

"Hansel, what are you stopping behind and staring for?"
said the father.

"I am looking at my little pigeon sitting on the roof, to say
good-bye to me," answered Hansel.

"You fool," said the wife, "that is no pigeon, but the
morning sun shining on the chimney pots."

Hansel went on as before, and strewed bread crumbs all
along the road.

The woman led the children far into the wood, where they
had never been before in all their lives. And again there was
a large fire made, and the mother said,

"Sit still there, you children, and when you are tired you
can go to sleep; we are going into the forest to cut wood, and
in the evening, when we are ready to go home we will come
and fetch you."

So when noon came Grethel shared her bread with
Hansel, who had strewed his along the road. Then they went
to sleep, and the evening passed, and no one came for the
poor children. When they awoke it was dark night, and
Hansel comforted his little sister, and said,

"Wait a little, Grethel, until the moon gets up, then we
shall be able to see the way home by the crumbs of bread
that I have scattered along it."

So when the moon rose they got up, but they could find
no crumbs of bread, for the birds of the woods and of the
fields had come and picked them up. Hansel thought they
might find the way all the same, but they could not. They
went on all that night, and the next day from the morning until
the evening, but they could not find the way out of the wood,
and they were very hungry, for they had nothing to eat but the

few berries they could pick up. And when they were so tired that they could no longer drag themselves along, they lay down under a tree and fell asleep.

It was now the third morning since they had left their father's house. They were always trying to get back to it, but instead of that they only found themselves farther in the wood, and if help had not soon come they would have been starved. About noon they saw a pretty snow-white bird sitting on a bough, and singing so sweetly that they stopped to listen. And when he had finished the bird spread his wings and flew before them, and they followed after him until they came to a little house, and the bird perched on the roof, and when they came nearer they saw that the house was built of bread, and roofed with cakes; and the window was of transparent sugar.

"We will have some of this," said Hansel, "and make a fine meal. I will eat a piece of the roof, Grethel, and you can have some of the window—that will taste sweet."

So Hansel reached up and broke off a bit of the roof, just to see how it tasted, and Grethel stood by the window and gnawed at it. Then they heard a thin voice call out from inside,

> " Nibble, nibble, like a mouse,
> Who is nibbling at my house?"

And the children answered,

> " Never mind,
> It is the wind."

And they went on eating, never disturbing themselves. Hansel, who found that the roof tasted very nice, took down a great piece of it, and Grethel pulled out a large round window-pane, and sat her down and began upon it. Then the door opened, and an aged woman came out, leaning upon a crutch. Hansel and Grethel felt very frightened, and let fall what they had in their hands. The old woman, however, nodded her head, and said,

"Ah, my dear children, how come you here? you must come indoors and stay with me, you will be no trouble."

So she took them each by the hand, and led them into her little house. And there they found a good meal laid out, of milk and pancakes, with sugar, apples, and nuts. After that she showed them two little white beds, and Hansel and Grethel laid themselves down on them, and thought they were in heaven.

The old woman, although her behaviour was so kind, was a wicked witch, who lay in wait for children, and had built the little house on purpose to entice them. When they were once inside she used to kill them, cook them, and eat them, and then it was a feast-day with her. The witch's eyes were red, and she could not see very far, but she had a keen scent, like the beasts, and knew very well when human creatures were near. When she knew that Hansel and Grethel were coming, she gave a spiteful laugh, and said triumphantly,

" I have them, and they shall not escape me !"

Early in the morning, before the children were awake, she got up to look at them, and as they lay sleeping so peacefully with round rosy cheeks, she said to herself,

" What a fine feast I shall have !"

Then she grasped Hansel with her withered hand, and led him into a little stable, and shut him up behind a grating ; and call and scream as he might, it was no good. Then she went back to Grethel and shook her, crying,

" Get up, lazy bones ; fetch water, and cook something nice for your brother ; he is outside in the stable, and must be fattened up. And when he is fat enough I will eat him."

Grethel began to weep bitterly, but it was of no use, she had to do what the wicked witch bade her.

And so the best kind of victuals was cooked for poor Hansel, while Grethel got nothing but crab-shells. Each morning the old woman visited the little stable, and cried,

" Hansel, stretch out your finger, that I may tell if you will soon be fat enough."

Hansel, however, used to hold out a little bone, and the old woman, who had weak eyes, could not see what it was, and supposing it to be Hansel's finger, wondered very much that it was not getting fatter. When four weeks had passed and Hansel seemed to remain so thin, she lost patience and could wait no longer.

" Now then, Grethel," cried she to the little girl ; " be quick and draw water ; be Hansel fat or be he lean, to-morrow I must kill and cook him."

Oh what a grief for the poor little sister to have to fetch water, and how the tears flowed down over her cheeks !

" Dear God, pray help us !" cried she ; "if we had been devoured by wild beasts in the wood at least we should have died together."

"Spare me your lamentations," said the old woman ; " they are of no avail."

Early next morning Grethel had to get up, make the fire, and fill the kettle.

" First we will do the baking," said the old woman ; " I have heated the oven already, and kneaded the dough."

She pushed poor Grethel towards the oven, out of which the flames were already shining.

" Creep in," said the witch, "and see if it is properly hot, so that the bread may be baked."

And Grethel once in, she meant to shut the door upon her and let her be baked, and then she would have eaten her. But Grethel perceived her intention, and said,

" I don't know how to do it : how shall I get in ?"

" Stupid goose," said the old woman, " the opening is big enough, do you see ? I could get in myself !" and she stooped down and put her head in the oven's mouth. Then Grethel gave her a push, so that she went in farther, and she shut the iron door upon her, and put up the bar. Oh how frightfully she howled ! but Grethel ran away, and left the wicked witch to burn miserably. Grethel went straight to Hansel, opened the stable-door, and cried,

" Hansel, we are free ! the old witch is dead !"

Then out flew Hansel like a bird from its cage as soon as the door is opened. How rejoiced they both were ! how they fell each on the other's neck ! and danced about, and kissed each other ! And as they had nothing more to fear they went over all the old witch's house, and in every corner there stood chests of pearls and precious stones.

" This is something better than flint stones," said Hansel, as he filled his pockets, and Grethel, thinking she also would like to carry something home with her, filled her apron full.

" Now, away we go," said Hansel ;—" if we only can get out of the witch's wood."

When they had journeyed a few hours they came to a great piece of water.

"We can never get across this," said Hansel, "I see no stepping-stones and no bridge."

"And there is no boat either," said Grethel; "but here comes a white duck; if I ask her she will help us over." So she cried,

> "Duck, duck, here we stand,
> Hansel and Grethel, on the land,
> Stepping-stones and bridge we lack,
> Carry us over on your nice white back."

And the duck came accordingly, and Hansel got upon her and told his sister to come too.

"No," answered Grethel, "that would be too hard upon the duck; we can go separately, one after the other."

And that was how it was managed, and after that they went on happily, until they came to the wood, and the way grew more and more familiar, till at last they saw in the distance their father's house. Then they ran till they came up to it, rushed in at the door, and fell on their father's neck. The man had not had a quiet hour since he left his children in the wood; but the wife was dead. And when Grethel opened her apron the pearls and precious stones were scattered all over the room, and Hansel took one handful after another out of his pocket. Then was all care at an end, and they lived in great joy together.

Sing every one,
My story is done,
And look! round the house
There runs a little mouse,
He that can catch her before she scampers in,
May make himself a very very large fur-cap
out of her skin.

THE WHITE·SNAKE

"THEY·DIVIDED·THE·APPLE·OF·
·LIFE·AND·ATE·IT·TOGETHER·"

SWAIN, SC

·THE·WHITE·SNAKE·

LONG time ago there lived a King whose wisdom was noised abroad in all the country. Nothing remained long unknown to him, and it was as if the knowledge of hidden things was brought to him in the air. However, he had one curious custom. Every day at dinner, after the table had been cleared and every one gone away, a trusty servant had to bring in one other dish. But it was covered up, and the servant himself did not know what was in it, and no one else knew, for the King waited until he was quite alone before he uncovered it. This had gone on a long time, but at last there came a day when the servant could restrain his curiosity no longer, but as he was carrying the dish away he took it into his own room. As soon as he had fastened the door securely, he lifted the cover, and there he saw a white snake lying on the dish. After seeing it he could not resist the desire to taste it, and so he cut off a small piece and put it in his mouth. As soon as it touched his tongue he heard outside his window a strange chorus of delicate voices. He went and listened, and found that it was the sparrows talking together, and telling each other all they had seen in the fields and woods. The virtue of the snake had given him power to understand the speech of animals.

Now it happened one day that the Queen lost her most splendid ring, and suspicion fell upon the trusty servant, who had the general superintendence, and he was accused of steal-

ing it.   The King summoned him to his presence, and after
many reproaches told him that if by the next day he was not
able to name the thief he should be considered guilty, and
punished.   It was in vain that he protested his innocence; he
could get no better sentence.   In his uneasiness and anxiety
he went out into the courtyard, and began to consider what
he could do in so great a necessity.   There sat the ducks by
the running water and rested themselves, and plumed themselves with their flat bills, and held a comfortable chat.   The
servant stayed where he was and listened to them.   They told
how they had waddled about all yesterday morning and found
good food; and then one of them said pitifully,

"Something lies very heavy in my craw,—it is the ring
that was lying under the Queen's window; I swallowed it down
in too great a hurry."

Then the servant seized her by the neck, took her into the
kitchen, and said to the cook,

"Kill this one, she is quite ready for cooking."

"Yes," said the cook, weighing it in her hand; "there
will be no trouble of fattening this one—it has been ready ever
so long."

She then slit up its neck, and when it was opened the
Queen's ring was found in its craw.   The servant could now
clearly prove his innocence, and in order to make up for the
injustice he had suffered the King permitted him to ask some
favour for himself, and also promised him the place of greatest
honour in the royal household.

But the servant refused it, and only asked for a horse and
money for travelling, for he had a fancy to see the world, and
look about him a little.   So his request was granted, and he
set out on his way; and one day he came to a pool of water,
by which he saw three fishes who had got entangled in the
rushes, and were panting for water.   Although fishes are
usually considered dumb creatures, he understood very well
their lament that they were to perish so miserably; and as
he had a compassionate heart he dismounted from his horse,
and put the three fishes back again into the water.   They
quivered all over with joy, stretched out their heads, and
called out to him,

"We will remember and reward thee, because thou hast

delivered us." He rode on, and after a while he heard a small voice come up from the sand underneath his horse's feet. He listened, and understood how an ant-king was complaining,

" If only these men would keep off, with their great awkward beasts ! here comes this stupid horse treading down my people with his hard hoofs ! "

The man then turned his horse to the side-path, and the ant-king called out to him,

" We will remember and reward thee ! "

The path led him through a wood, and there he saw a father-raven and mother-raven standing by their nest and throwing their young ones out.

" Off with you ! young gallows-birds ! " cried they ; " we cannot stuff you any more ; you are big enough to fend for yourselves ! " The poor young ravens lay on the ground, fluttering, and beating the air with their pinions, and crying,

" We are poor helpless things, we cannot fend for ourselves, we cannot even fly ! we can only die of hunger ! "

Then the kind young man dismounted, killed his horse with his dagger, and left it to the young ravens for food. They came hopping up, feasted away at it, and cried,

" We will remember and reward thee ! "

So now he had to use his own legs, and when he had gone a long way he came to a great town. There was much noise and thronging in the streets, and there came a man on a horse, who proclaimed,

" That the King's daughter seeks a husband, but he who wishes to marry her must perform a difficult task, and if he cannot carry it through successfully, he must lose his life."

Many had already tried, but had lost their lives, in vain. The young man, when he saw the King's daughter, was so dazzled by her great beauty, that he forgot all danger, went to the King and offered himself as a wooer.

Then he was led to the sea-side, and a gold ring was thrown into the water before his eyes. Then the King told him that he must fetch the ring up again from the bottom of the sea, saying,

" If you come back without it, you shall be put under the waves again and again until you are drowned."

Every one pitied the handsome young man, but they went,

and left him alone by the sea. As he was standing on the shore and thinking of what he should do, there came three fishes swimming by, none other than those he had set free. The middle one had a mussel in his mouth, and he laid it on the strand at the young man's feet; and when he took it up and opened it there was the gold ring inside! Full of joy he carried it to the King, and expected the promised reward; but the King's daughter, proud of her high birth, despised him, and set him another task to perform. She went out into the garden, and strewed about over the grass ten sacks full of millet seed.

"By the time the sun rises in the morning you must have picked up all these," she said, "and not a grain must be wanting."

The young man sat down in the garden and considered how it was possible to do this task, but he could contrive nothing, and stayed there, feeling very sorrowful, and expecting to be led to death at break of day. But when the first beams of the sun fell on the garden he saw that the ten sacks were all filled, standing one by the other, and not even a grain was missing. The ant-king had arrived in the night with his thousands of ants, and the grateful creatures had picked up all the millet seed, and filled the sacks with great industry. The King's daughter came herself into the garden and saw with astonishment that the young man had performed all that had been given him to do. But she could not let her proud heart melt, but said,

"Although he has completed the two tasks, he shall not be my bridegroom unless he brings me an apple from the tree of life."

The young man did not know where the tree of life was to be found, but he set out and went on and on, as long as his legs could carry him, but he had no hope of finding it. When he had gone through three kingdoms he came one evening to a wood, and seated himself under a tree to go to sleep; but he heard a rustling in the boughs, and a golden apple fell into his hand. Immediately three ravens flew towards him, perched on his knee, and said,

"We are the three young ravens that you delivered from starving; when we grew big, and heard that you were seeking the golden apple, we flew over the sea to the end of the earth, where the tree of life stands, and we fetched the apple."

Full of joy the young man set off on his way home, and brought the golden apple to the King's beautiful daughter, who was without any further excuse.

So they divided the apple of life, and ate it together; and their hearts were filled with love, and they lived in undisturbed happiness to a great age.

The STRAW, The COAL, and the BEAN

THERE lived in a certain village a poor old woman who had collected a mess of beans, and was going to cook them. So she made a fire on her hearth, and, in order to make it burn better, she put in a handful of straw. When the beans began to bubble in the pot, one of them fell out and lay, never noticed, near a straw which was already there; soon a red-hot coal jumped out of the fire and joined the pair. The straw began first, and said,

"Dear friends, how do you come here?" The coal answered,

"I jumped out of the fire by great good luck, or I should certainly have met with my death. I should have been burned to ashes." The bean said,

"I too have come out of it with a whole skin, but if the old woman had kept me in the pot I should have been cooked into a soft mass like my comrades."

"Nor should I have met with a better fate," said the straw; "the old woman has turned my brothers into fire and smoke, sixty of them she took up at once and deprived of life. Very luckily I managed to slip through her fingers."

"What had we better do now?" said the coal.

"I think," answered the bean, "that as we have been so lucky as to escape with our lives, we will join in good fellowship together, and, lest any more bad fortune should happen to us here, we will go abroad into foreign lands."

The proposal pleased the two others, and forthwith they started on their travels.   Soon they came to a little brook, and as there was no stepping-stone, and no bridge, they could not tell how they were to get to the other side.   The straw was struck with a good idea, and said,

" I will lay myself across, so that you can go over me as if I were a bridge ! "

So the straw stretched himself from one bank to the other, and the coal, who was of an ardent nature, quickly trotted up to go over the new-made bridge.   When, however, she reached the middle, and heard the water rushing past beneath her, she was struck with terror, and stopped, and could get no farther.   So the straw began to get burnt, broke in two pieces, and fell in the brook, and the coal slipped down, hissing as she touched the water, and gave up the ghost.   The bean, who had prudently remained behind on the bank, could not help laughing at the sight, and not being able to contain herself, went on laughing so excessively that she burst.   And now would she certainly have been undone for ever, if a tailor on his travels had not by good luck stopped to rest himself by the brook.   As he had a compassionate heart, he took out needle and thread and stitched her together again.   The bean thanked him in the most elegant manner, but as he had sewn her up with black stitches, all beans since then have a black seam.

·The FISHERMAN and his WIFE·

HERE was once a fisherman and his wife who lived together in a hovel by the sea-shore, and the fisherman went out every day with his hook and line to catch fish, and he angled and angled.

One day he was sitting with his rod and looking into the clear water, and he sat and sat.

At last down went the line to the bottom of the water, and when he drew it up he found a great flounder on the hook. And the flounder said to him,

"Fisherman, listen to me; let me go, I am not a real fish but an enchanted prince. What good shall I be to you if you land me? I shall not taste well; so put me back into the water again, and let me swim away."

"Well," said the fisherman, "no need of so many words about the matter, as you can speak I had much rather let you swim away."

Then he put him back into the clear water, and the flounder sank to the bottom, leaving a long streak of blood behind him. Then the fisherman got up and went home to his wife in their hovel.

"Well, husband," said the wife, "have you caught nothing to-day?"

"No," said the man—"that is, I did catch a flounder, but as he said he was an enchanted prince, I let him go again."

"Then, did you wish for nothing?" said the wife.

"No," said the man; "what should I wish for?"

"Oh dear!" said the wife; "and it is so dreadful always to live in this evil-smelling hovel; you might as well have wished for a little cottage; go again and call him; tell him we want a little cottage, I daresay he will give it us; go, and be quick."

And when he went back, the sea was green and yellow, and not nearly so clear. So he stood and said,

> " O man, O man!—if man you be,
> Or flounder, flounder, in the sea—
> Such a tiresome wife I've got,
> For she wants what I do not."

Then the flounder came swimming up, and said,

"Now then, what does she want?"

"Oh," said the man, "you know when I caught you my wife says I ought to have wished for something. She does not want to live any longer in the hovel, and would rather have a cottage.

"Go home with you," said the flounder, "she has it already."

So the man went home, and found, instead of the hovel, a little cottage, and his wife was sitting on a bench before the door. And she took him by the hand, and said to him,

"Come in and see if this is not a great improvement."

So they went in, and there was a little house-place and a beautiful little bedroom, a kitchen and larder, with all sorts of furniture, and iron and brass ware of the very best. And at the back was a little yard with fowls and ducks, and a little garden full of green vegetables and fruit.

"Look," said the wife, "is not that nice?"

"Yes," said the man, "if this can only last we shall be very well contented."

"We will see about that," said the wife. And after a meal they went to bed.

So all went well for a week or fortnight, when the wife said,

"Look here, husband, the cottage is really too confined, and the yard and garden are so small; I think the flounder had better get us a larger house; I should like very much to live in a large stone castle; so go to your fish and he will send us a castle."

"O my dear wife," said the man, "the cottage is good enough; what do we want a castle for?"

"We want one," said the wife; "go along with you; the flounder can give us one."

"Now, wife," said the man, "the flounder gave us the cottage; I do not like to go to him again, he may be angry."

"Go along," said the wife, "he might just as well give us it as not; do as I say!"

The man felt very reluctant and unwilling; and he said to himself,

"It is not the right thing to do;" nevertheless he went.

So when he came to the seaside, the water was purple and dark blue and grey and thick, and not green and yellow as before.   And he stood and said,

> " O man, O man !—if man you be,
> Or flounder, flounder, in the sea—
> Such a tiresome wife I've got,
> For she wants what I do not."

"Now then, what does she want?" said the flounder.

"Oh," said the man, half frightened, "she wants to live in a large stone castle."

"Go home with you, she is already standing before the door," said the flounder.

Then the man went home, as he supposed, but when he got there, there stood in the place of the cottage a great castle of stone, and his wife was standing on the steps, about to go in; so she took him by the hand, and said,

"Let us enter."

With that he went in with her, and in the castle was a great hall with a marble pavement, and there were a great many servants, who led them through large doors, and the passages were decked with tapestry, and the rooms with golden chairs and tables, and crystal chandeliers hanging from the ceiling; and all the rooms had carpets.   And the tables were covered with eatables and the best wine for any one who wanted them.   And at the back of the house was a great stable-yard for horses and cattle, and carriages of the finest; besides, there was a splendid large garden, with the most beautiful flowers and fine fruit trees, and a pleasance full half a mile long, with deer and oxen and sheep, and everything that heart could wish for.

"There!" said the wife, "is not this beautiful?"

"Oh yes," said the man, "if it will only last we can live in this fine castle and be very well contented."

"We will see about that," said the wife, "in the meanwhile we will sleep upon it." With that they went to bed.

The next morning the wife was awake first, just at the break of day, and she looked out and saw from her bed the beautiful country lying all round. The man took no notice of it, so she poked him in the side with her elbow, and said,

"Husband, get up and just look out of the window. Look, just think if we could be king over all this country! Just go to your fish and tell him we should like to be king."

"Now, wife," said the man, "what should we be kings for? I don't want to be king."

"Well," said the wife, "if you don't want to be king, I will be king."

"Now, wife," said the man, "what do you want to be king for? I could not ask him such a thing."

"Why not?" said the wife, "you must go directly all the same; I must be king."

So the man went, very much put out that his wife should want to be king.

"It is not the right thing to do—not at all the right thing," thought the man. He did not at all want to go, and yet he went all the same.

And when he came to the sea the water was quite dark grey, and rushed far inland, and had an ill smell. And he stood and said,

> "O man, O man!—if man you be,
> Or flounder, flounder, in the sea—
> Such a tiresome wife I've got,
> For she wants what I do not."

"Now then, what does she want?" said the fish.

"Oh dear!" said the man, "she wants to be king."

"Go home with you, she is so already," said the fish.

So the man went back, and as he came to the palace he saw it was very much larger, and had great towers and splendid gateways; the herald stood before the door, and a number of soldiers with kettle-drums and trumpets.

And when he came inside everything was of marble and gold, and there were many curtains with great golden tassels. Then he went through the doors of the saloon to where the great throne-room was, and there was his wife sitting upon a throne of gold and diamonds, and she had a great golden crown on, and the sceptre in her hand was of pure gold and jewels, and on each side stood six pages in a row, each one a head shorter than the other. So the man went up to her and said,

"Well, wife, so now you are king!"

"Yes," said the wife, "now I am king."

So then he stood and looked at her, and when he had gazed at her for some time he said,

"Well, wife, this is fine for you to be king! now there is nothing more to wish for."

"O husband!" said the wife, seeming quite restless, "I am tired of this already. Go to your fish and tell him that now I am king I must be emperor."

"Now, wife," said the man," "what do you want to be emperor for?"

"Husband," said she, "go and tell the fish I want to be emperor."

"Oh dear!" said the man, "he could not do it—I cannot ask him such a thing. There is but one emperor at a time; the fish can't possibly make any one emperor—indeed he can't."

"Now, look here," said the wife, "I am king, and you are only my husband, so will you go at once? Go along! for if he was able to make me king he is able to make me emperor; and I will and must be emperor, so go along!"

So he was obliged to go; and as he went he felt very uncomfortable about it, and he thought to himself,

"It is not at all the right thing to do; to want to be emperor is really going too far; the flounder will soon be beginning to get tired of this."

With that he came to the sea, and the water was quite

black and thick, and the foam flew, and the wind blew, and the man was terrified.   But he stood and said,

"O man, O man!—if man you be,
Or flounder, flounder, in the sea—
Such a tiresome wife I've got,
For she wants what I do not."

" What is it now ? " said the fish.

" Oh dear ! " said the man, " my wife wants to be emperor."

" Go home with you," said the fish, " she is emperor already."

So the man went home, and found the castle adorned with polished marble and alabaster figures, and golden gates.   The troops were being marshalled before the door, and they were blowing trumpets and beating drums and cymbals ; and when he entered he saw barons and earls and dukes waiting about like servants ; and the doors were of bright gold.   And he saw his wife sitting upon a throne made of one entire piece of gold, and it was about two miles high ; and she had a great golden crown on, which was about three yards high, set with brilliants and carbuncles ; and in one hand she held the sceptre, and in the other the globe ; and on both sides of her stood pages in two rows, all arranged according to their size, from the most enormous giant of two miles high to the tiniest dwarf of the size of my little finger ; and before her stood earls and dukes in crowds.   So the man went up to her and said,

" Well, wife, so now you are emperor."

" Yes," said she, " now I am emperor."

Then he went and sat down and had a good look at her, and then he said,

" Well now, wife, there is nothing left to be, now you are emperor."

" What are you talking about, husband ? " said she ; " I am emperor, and next I will be pope ! so go and tell the fish so."

" Oh dear !" said the man, " what is it that you don't want ? You can never become pope ; there is but one pope in Christendom, and the fish can't possibly do it."

" Husband," said she, " no more words about it ; I must and will be pope ; so go along to the fish."

"Now, wife," said the man, "how can I ask him such a thing? it is too bad—it is asking a little too much; and, besides, he could not do it."

"What rubbish!" said the wife; "if he could make me emperor he can make me pope. Go along and ask him; I am emperor, and you are only my husband, so go you must."

So he went, feeling very frightened, and he shivered and shook, and his knees trembled; and there arose a great wind, and the clouds flew by, and it grew very dark, and the sea rose mountains high, and the ships were tossed about, and the sky was partly blue in the middle, but at the sides very dark and red, as in a great tempest. And he felt very desponding, and stood trembling and said,

> "O man, O man!—if man you be,
> Or flounder, flounder, in the sea—
> Such a tiresome wife I've got,
> For she wants what I do not."

"Well, what now?" said the fish.

"Oh dear!" said the man, "she wants to be pope."

"Go home with you, she is pope already," said the fish.

So he went home, and he found himself before a great church, with palaces all round. He had to make his way through a crowd of people; and when he got inside he found the place lighted up with thousands and thousands of lights; and his wife was clothed in a golden garment, and sat upon a very high throne, and had three golden crowns on, all in the greatest priestly pomp; and on both sides of her there stood two rows of lights of all sizes—from the size of the longest tower to the smallest rushlight, and all the emperors and kings were kneeling before her and kissing her foot.

"Well, wife," said the man, and sat and stared at her, "so you are pope."

"Yes," said she, "now I am pope!"

And he went on gazing at her till he felt dazzled, as if he were sitting in the sun. And after a little time he said,

"Well, now, wife, what is there left to be, now you are pope?"

And she sat up very stiff and straight, and said nothing.

And he said again, "Well, wife, I hope you are contented at last with being pope; you can be nothing more."

"We will see about that," said the wife. With that they both went to bed; but she was as far as ever from being contented, and she could not get to sleep for thinking of what she should like to be next.

The husband, however, slept as fast as a top after his busy day; but the wife tossed and turned from side to side the whole night through, thinking all the while what she could be next, but nothing would occur to her; and when she saw the red dawn she slipped off the bed, and sat before the window to see the sun rise, and as it came up she said,

"Ah, I have it! what if I should make the sun and moon to rise—husband!" she cried, and stuck her elbow in his ribs, "wake up, and go to your fish, and tell him I want power over the sun and moon."

The man was so fast asleep that when he started up he fell out of bed. Then he shook himself together, and opened his eyes and said,

"Oh,—wife, what did you say?"

"Husband," said she, "if I cannot get the power of making the sun and moon rise when I want them, I shall never have another quiet hour. Go to the fish and tell him so."

"O wife!" said the man, and fell on his knees to her, "the fish can really not do that for you. I grant you he could make you emperor and pope; do be contented with that, I beg of you."

And she became wild with impatience, and screamed out,

"I can wait no longer, go at once!"

And so off he went as well as he could for fright. And a dreadful storm arose, so that he could hardly keep his feet; and the houses and trees were blown down, and the mountains trembled, and rocks fell in the sea; the sky was quite black, and it thundered and lightened; and the waves, crowned with foam, ran mountains high. So he cried out, without being able to hear his own words,

> "O man, O man!—if man you be,
> Or flounder, flounder, in the sea—
> Such a tiresome wife I've got,
> For she wants what I do not."

"Well, what now?" said the flounder.

"Oh dear!" said the man, "she wants to order about the sun and moon."

"Go home with you!" said the flounder, "you will find her in the old hovel."

And there they are sitting to this very day.

· THE · GALLANT · TAILOR ·

ONE summer morning a little tailor was sitting on his board near the window, and working cheerfully with all his might, when an old woman came down the street crying,

"Good jelly to sell! good jelly to sell!"

The cry sounded pleasant in the little tailor's ears, so he put his head out of the window, and called out,

"Here, my good woman—come here, if you want a customer."

So the poor woman climbed the steps with her heavy basket, and was obliged to unpack and display all her pots to the tailor. He looked at every one of them, and lifting all the lids, applied his nose to each, and said at last,

"The jelly seems pretty good; you may weigh me out four half ounces, or I don't mind having a quarter of a pound."

The woman, who had expected to find a good customer, gave him what he asked for, but went off angry and grumbling.

"This jelly is the very thing for me," cried the little tailor; "it will give me strength and cunning;" and he took down the bread from the cupboard, cut a whole round of the loaf, and spread the jelly on it, laid it near him, and went on stitching more gallantly than ever. All the while the scent of the sweet jelly was spreading throughout the room, where there were quantities of flies, who were attracted by it and flew to partake.

" Now then, who asked you to come ? " said the tailor, and drove the unbidden guests away. But the flies, not understanding his language, were not to be got rid of like that, and returned in larger numbers than before. Then the tailor, not being able to stand it any longer, took from his chimney-corner a ragged cloth, and saying,

" Now, I'll let you have it ! " beat it among them unmercifully. When he ceased, and counted the slain, he found seven lying dead before him.

" This is indeed somewhat," he said, wondering at his own gallantry ; " the whole town shall know this."

So he hastened to cut out a belt, and he stitched it, and put on it in large capitals " Seven at one blow ! "

" — The town, did I say ! " said the little tailor ; " the whole world shall know it ! " And his heart quivered with joy, like a lamb's tail.

The tailor fastened the belt round him, and began to think of going out into the world, for his workshop seemed too small for his worship. So he looked about in all the house for something that it would be useful to take with him, but he found nothing but an old cheese, which he put in his pocket. Outside the door he noticed that a bird had got caught in the bushes, so he took that and put it in his pocket with the cheese. Then he set out gallantly on his way, and as he was light and active he felt no fatigue. The way led over a mountain, and when he reached the topmost peak he saw a terrible giant sitting there, and looking about him at his ease. The tailor went bravely up to him, called out to him, and said,

" Comrade, good day ! there you sit looking over the wide world ! I am on the way thither to seek my fortune : have you a fancy to go with me ? "

The giant looked at the tailor contemptuously, and said,

" You little rascal ! you miserable fellow ! "

" That may be ! " answered the little tailor, and undoing his coat he showed the giant his belt ; " you can read there whether I am a man or not ! "

The giant read : " Seven at one blow ! " and thinking it meant men that the tailor had killed, felt at once more respect for the little fellow. But as he wanted to prove him, he took up a stone and squeezed it so hard that water came out of it.

"Now you can do that," said the giant,—"that is, if you have the strength for it."

"That's not much," said the little tailor, "I call that play," and he put his hand in his pocket and took out the cheese and squeezed it, so that the whey ran out of it.

"Well," said he, "what do you think of that?"

The giant did not know what to say to it, for he could not have believed it of the little man. Then the giant took up a stone and threw it so high that it was nearly out of sight.

"Now, little fellow, suppose you do that!"

"Well thrown," said the tailor; "but the stone fell back to earth again,—I will throw you one that will never come back." So he felt in his pocket, took out the bird, and threw it into the air. And the bird, when it found itself at liberty, took wing, flew off, and returned no more.

"What do you think of that, comrade?" asked the tailor.

"There is no doubt that you cán throw," said the giant; "but we will see if you can carry."

He led the little tailor to a mighty oak-tree which had been felled, and was lying on the ground, and said,

"Now, if you are strong enough, help me to carry this tree out of the wood."

"Willingly," answered the little man; "you take the trunk on your shoulders, I will take the branches with all their foliage, that is much the most difficult."

So the giant took the trunk on his shoulders, and the tailor seated himself on a branch, and the giant, who could not see what he was doing, had the whole tree to carry, and the little man on it as well. And the little man was very cheerful and merry, and whistled the tune: "*There were three tailors riding by,*" as if carrying the tree was mere child's play. The giant, when he had struggled on under his heavy load a part of the way, was tired out, and cried,

"Look here, I must let go the tree!"

The tailor jumped off quickly, and taking hold of the tree with both arms, as if he were carrying it, said to the giant,

"You see you can't carry the tree though you are such a big fellow!"

They went on together a little farther, and presently they came to a cherry-tree, and the giant took hold of the topmost

branches, where the ripest fruit hung, and pulling them downwards, gave them to the tailor to hold, bidding him eat.   But
the little tailor was much too weak to hold the tree, and as
the giant let go, the tree sprang back, and the tailor was
caught up into the air.   And when he dropped down again
without any damage, the giant said to him,

"How is this? haven't you strength enough to hold such
a weak sprig as that?"

"It is not strength that is lacking," answered the little
tailor ; "how should it to one who has slain seven at one blow!
I just jumped over the tree because the hunters are shooting
down there in the bushes.   You jump it too, if you can."

The giant made the attempt, and not being able to vault
the tree, he remained hanging in the branches, so that once
more the little tailor got the better of him.   Then said the
giant,

"As you are such a gallant fellow, suppose you come with
me to our den, and stay the night."

The tailor was quite willing, and he followed him.   When
they reached the den there sat some other giants by the fire,
and each had a roasted sheep in his hand, and was eating it.
The little tailor looked round and thought,

"There is more elbow-room here than in my workshop."

And the giant showed him a bed, and told him he had
better lie down upon it and go to sleep.   The bed was, however, too big for the tailor, so he did not stay in it, but crept
into a corner to sleep.   As soon as it was midnight the giant
got up, took a great staff of iron and beat the bed through
with one stroke, and supposed he had made an end of that
grasshopper of a tailor.   Very early in the morning the giants
went into the wood and forgot all about the little tailor, and
when they saw him coming after them alive and merry, they
were terribly frightened, and, thinking he was going to kill
them, they ran away in all haste.

So the little tailor marched on, always following his nose.
And after he had gone a great way he entered the courtyard
belonging to a King's palace, and there he felt so overpowered
with fatigue that he lay down and fell asleep.   In the meanwhile came various people, who looked at him very curiously,
and read on his belt, "Seven at one blow!"

"Oh !" said they, "why should this great lord come here in time of peace? what a mighty champion he must be."

Then they went and told the King about him, and they thought that if war should break out what a worthy and useful man he would be, and that he ought not to be allowed to depart at any price. The King then summoned his council, and sent one of his courtiers to the little tailor to beg him, so soon as he should wake up, to consent to serve in the King's army. So the messenger stood and waited at the sleeper's side until his limbs began to stretch, and his eyes to open, and then he carried his answer back. And the answer was,

"That was the reason for which I came," said the little tailor, "I am ready to enter the King's service."

So he was received into it very honourably, and a separate dwelling set apart for him.

But the rest of the soldiers were very much set against the little tailor, and they wished him a thousand miles away.

"What shall be done about it?" they said among themselves ; "if we pick a quarrel and fight with him then seven of us will fall at each blow. That will be of no good to us."

So they came to a resolution, and went all together to the King to ask for their discharge.

"We never intended," said they, "to serve with a man who kills seven at a blow."

The King felt sorry to lose all his faithful servants because of one man, and he wished that he had never seen him, and would willingly get rid of him if he might. But he did not dare to dismiss the little tailor for fear he should kill all the King's people, and place himself upon the throne. He thought a long while about it, and at last made up his mind what to do. He sent for the little tailor, and told him that as he was so great a warrior he had a proposal to make to him. He told him that in a wood in his dominions dwelt two giants, who did great damage by robbery, murder, and fire, and that no man durst go near them for fear of his life. But that if the tailor should overcome and slay both these giants the King would give him his only daughter in marriage, and half his kingdom as dowry, and that a hundred horsemen should go with him to give him assistance.

"That would be something for a man like me!" thought

I

the little tailor, "a beautiful princess and half a kingdom are not to be had every day," and he said to the King,

"Oh yes, I can soon overcome the giants, and yet have no need of the hundred horsemen; he who can kill seven at one blow has no need to be afraid of two."

So the little tailor set out, and the hundred horsemen followed him. When he came to the border of the wood he said to his escort,

"Stay here while I go to attack the giants."

Then he sprang into the wood, and looked about him right and left. After a while he caught sight of the two giants; they were lying down under a tree asleep, and snoring so that all the branches shook. The little tailor, all alive, filled both his pockets with stones and climbed up into the tree, and made his way to an overhanging bough, so that he could seat himself just above the sleepers; and from there he let one stone after another fall on the chest of one of the giants. For a long time the giant was quite unaware of this, but at last he waked up and pushed his comrade, and said,

"What are you hitting me for?"

"You are dreaming," said the other, "I am not touching you." And they composed themselves again to sleep, and the tailor let fall a stone on the other giant.

"What can that be?" cried he, "what are you casting at me?"

"I am casting nothing at you," answered the first, grumbling.

They disputed about it for a while, but as they were tired, they gave it up at last, and their eyes closed once more. Then the little tailor began his game anew, picked out a heavier stone and threw it down with force upon the first giant's chest.

"This is too much!" cried he, and sprang up like a madman and struck his companion such a blow that the tree shook above them. The other paid him back with ready coin, and they fought with such fury that they tore up trees by their roots to use for weapons against each other, so that at last they both of them lay dead upon the ground. And now the little tailor got down.

"Another piece of luck!" said he,—"that the tree I was

sitting in did not get torn up too, or else I should have had to jump like a squirrel from one tree to another."

Then he drew his sword and gave each of the giants a few hacks in the breast, and went back to the horsemen and said,

"The deed is done, I have made an end of both of them: but it went hard with me, in the struggle they rooted up trees to defend themselves, but it was of no use, they had to do with a man who can kill seven at one blow."

"Then are you not wounded?" asked the horsemen.

"Nothing of the sort!" answered the tailor, "I have not turned a hair."

The horsemen still would not believe it, and rode into the wood to see, and there they found the giants wallowing in their blood, and all about them lying the uprooted trees.

The little tailor then claimed the promised boon, but the King repented him of his offer, and he sought again how to rid himself of the hero.

"Before you can possess my daughter and the half of my kingdom," said he to the tailor, "you must perform another heroic act. In the wood lives a unicorn who does great damage; you must secure him."

"A unicorn does not strike more terror into me than two giants. Seven at one blow!—that is my way," was the tailor's answer.

So, taking a rope and an axe with him, he went out into the wood, and told those who were ordered to attend him to wait outside. He had not far to seek, the unicorn soon came out and sprang at him, as if he would make an end of him without delay. "Softly, softly," said he, "most haste, worst speed," and remained standing until the animal came quite near, then he slipped quietly behind a tree. The unicorn ran with all his might against the tree and stuck his horn so deep into the trunk that he could not get it out again, and so was taken.

"Now I have you," said the tailor, coming out from behind the tree, and, putting the rope round the unicorn's neck, he took the axe, set free the horn, and when all his party were assembled he led forth the animal and brought it to the King.

The King did not yet wish to give him the promised reward, and set him a third task to do. Before the wedding could take place the tailor was to secure a wild boar which had done a great deal of damage in the wood.

The huntsmen were to accompany him.

"All right," said the tailor, "this is child's play."

But he did not take the huntsmen into the wood, and they were all the better pleased, for the wild boar had many a time before received them in such a way that they had no fancy to disturb him. When the boar caught sight of the tailor he ran at him with foaming mouth and gleaming tusks to bear him to the ground, but the nimble hero rushed into a chapel which chanced to be near, and jumped quickly out of a window on the other side. The boar ran after him, and when he got inside the door shut after him, and there he was imprisoned, for the creature was too big and unwieldy to jump out of the window too. Then the little tailor called the huntsmen that they might see the prisoner with their own eyes; and then he betook himself to the king, who now, whether he liked it or not, was obliged to fulfil his promise, and give him his daughter and the half of his kingdom. But if he had known that the great warrior was only a little tailor he would have taken it still more to heart. So the wedding was celebrated with great splendour and little joy, and the tailor was made into a king.

One night the young queen heard her husband talking in his sleep and saying,

"Now boy, make me that waistcoat and patch me those breeches, or I will lay my yard measure about your shoulders!"

And so, as she perceived of what low birth her husband was, she went to her father the next morning and told him all, and begged him to set her free from a man who was nothing better than a tailor. The king bade her be comforted, saying,

"To-night leave your bedroom door open, my guard shall stand outside, and when he is asleep they shall come in and bind him and carry him off to a ship, and he shall be sent to the other side of the world."

So the wife felt consoled, but the king's water-bearer, who had been listening all the while, went to the little tailor and disclosed to him the whole plan.

"I shall put a stop to all this," said he.

At night he lay down as usual in bed, and when his wife thought that he was asleep, she got up, opened the door and lay down again. The little tailor, who only made believe to be asleep, began to murmur plainly,

"Now, boy, make me that waistcoat and patch me those breeches, or I will lay my yard measure about your shoulders! I have slain seven at one blow, killed two giants, caught a unicorn, and taken a wild boar, and shall I be afraid of those who are standing outside my room door?"

And when they heard the tailor say this, a great fear seized them; they fled away as if they had been wild hares, and none of them would venture to attack him.

And so the little tailor all his lifetime remained a king.

✝ ASCHENPUTTEL ✝

HERE was once a rich man whose wife lay sick, and when she felt her end drawing near she called to her only daughter to come near her bed, and said,

"Dear child, be pious and good, and God will always take care of you, and I will look down upon you from heaven, and will be with you."

And then she closed her eyes and expired. The maiden went every day to her mother's grave and wept, and was always pious and good. When the winter came the snow covered the grave with a white covering, and when the sun came in the early spring and melted it away, the man took to himself another wife.

The new wife brought two daughters home with her, and they were beautiful and fair in appearance, but at heart were black and ugly. And then began very evil times for the poor step-daughter.

"Is the stupid creature to sit in the same room with us?" said they; "those who eat food must earn it. Out upon her for a kitchen-maid!"

They took away her pretty dresses, and put on her an old gray kirtle, and gave her wooden shoes to wear.

"Just look now at the proud princess, how she is decked out!" cried they laughing, and then they sent her into the kitchen. There she was obliged to do heavy work from morning to night, get up early in the morning, draw water

make the fires, cook, and wash.   Besides that, the sisters did
their utmost to torment her,—mocking her, and strewing peas
and lentils among the ashes, and setting her to pick them up.
In the evenings, when she was quite tired out with her hard
day's work, she had no bed to lie on, but was obliged to rest
on the hearth among the cinders.   And as she always looked
dusty and dirty, they named her Aschenputtel.

It happened one day that the father went to the fair, and
he asked his two step-daughters what he should bring back for
them.

"Fine clothes!" said one.

"Pearls and jewels!" said the other.

"But what will you have, Aschenputtel?" said he.

"The first twig, father, that strikes against your hat on the
way home; that is what I should like you to bring me."

So he bought for the two step-daughters fine clothes,
pearls, and jewels, and on his way back, as he rode through a
green lane, a hazel-twig struck against his hat; and he broke
it off and carried it home with him.   And when he reached
home he gave to the step-daughters what they had wished for,
and to Aschenputtel he gave the hazel-twig.   She thanked
him, and went to her mother's grave, and planted this twig
there, weeping so bitterly that the tears fell upon it and
watered it, and it flourished and became a fine tree.   Aschenputtel went to see it three times a day, and wept and prayed,
and each time a white bird rose up from the tree, and if she
uttered any wish the bird brought her whatever she had
wished for.

Now it came to pass that the king ordained a festival that
should last for three days, and to which all the beautiful young
women of that country were bidden, so that the king's son
might choose a bride from among them.   When the two step-
daughters heard that they too were bidden to appear, they felt
very pleased, and they called Aschenputtel, and said,

"Comb our hair, brush our shoes, and make our buckles
fast, we are going to the wedding feast at the king's castle."

Aschenputtel, when she heard this, could not help crying,
for she too would have liked to go to the dance, and she begged
her step-mother to allow her.

"What, you Aschenputtel!" said she, "in all your dust

and dirt, you want to go to the festival! you that have no dress and no shoes! you want to dance!"

But as she persisted in asking, at last the step-mother said,

"I have strewed a dish-full of lentils in the ashes, and if you can pick them all up again in two hours you may go with us."

Then the maiden went to the back-door that led into the garden, and called out,

> " O gentle doves, O turtle-doves,
> And all the birds that be,
> The lentils that in ashes lie
> Come and pick up for me !
>   The good must be put in the dish,
>   The bad you may eat if you wish."

Then there came to the kitchen-window two white doves, and after them some turtle-doves, and at last a crowd of all the birds under heaven, chirping and fluttering, and they alighted among the ashes; and the doves nodded with their heads, and began to pick, peck, pick, peck, and then all the others began to pick, peck, pick, peck, and put all the good grains into the dish. Before an hour was over all was done, and they flew away. Then the maiden brought the dish to her step-mother, feeling joyful, and thinking that now she should go to the feast; but the step-mother said,

"No, Aschenputtel, you have no proper clothes, and you do not know how to dance, and you would be laughed at!"

And when Aschenputtel cried for disappointment, she added,

"If you can pick two dishes full of lentils out of the ashes, nice and clean, you shall go with us," thinking to herself, "for that is not possible." When she had strewed two dishes full of lentils among the ashes the maiden went through the back-door into the garden, and cried,

> " O gentle doves, O turtle-doves,
> And all the birds that be,
> The lentils that in ashes lie
> Come and pick up for me !
>   The good must be put in the dish,
>   The bad you may eat if you wish."

So there came to the kitchen-window two white doves, and then some turtle-doves, and at last a crowd of all the other birds under heaven, chirping and fluttering, and they alighted among the ashes, and the doves nodded with their heads and began to pick, peck, pick, peck, and then all the others began to pick, peck, pick, peck, and put all the good grains into the dish. And before half-an-hour was over it was all done, and they flew away. Then the maiden took the dishes to the step-mother, feeling joyful, and thinking that now she should go with them to the feast; but she said " All this is of no good to you; you cannot come with us, for you have no proper clothes, and cannot dance ; you would put us to shame."

Then she turned her back on poor Aschenputtel, and made haste to set out with her two proud daughters.

And as there was no one left in the house, Aschenputtel went to her mother's grave, under the hazel bush, and cried,

> " Little tree, little tree, shake over me,
> That silver and gold may come down and cover me."

Then the bird threw down a dress of gold and silver, and a pair of slippers embroidered with silk and silver. And in all haste she put on the dress and went to the festival. But her step-mother and sisters did not know her, and thought she must be a foreign princess, she looked so beautiful in her golden dress. Of Aschenputtel they never thought at all, and supposed that she was sitting at home, and picking the lentils out of the ashes. The King's son came to meet her, and took her by the hand and danced with her, and he refused to stand up with any one else, so that he might not be obliged to let go her hand ; and when any one came to claim it he answered,

"She is my partner."

And when the evening came she wanted to go home, but the prince said he would go with her to take care of her, for he wanted to see where the beautiful maiden lived. But she escaped him, and jumped up into the pigeon-house. Then the prince waited until the father came, and told him the strange maiden had jumped into the pigeon-house. The father thought to himself,

"It cannot surely be Aschenputtel," and called for axes and hatchets, and had the pigeon-house cut down, but there was no one in it. And when they entered the house there sat Aschenputtel in her dirty clothes among the cinders, and a little oil-lamp burnt dimly in the chimney; for Aschenputtel had been very quick, and had jumped out of the pigeon-house again, and had run to the hazel bush; and there she had taken off her beautiful dress and had laid it on the grave, and the bird had carried it away again, and then she had put on her little gray kirtle again, and had sat down in the kitchen among the cinders.

The next day, when the festival began anew, and the parents and step-sisters had gone to it, Aschenputtel went to the hazel bush and cried,

" Little tree, little tree, shake over me,
That silver and gold may come down and cover me."

Then the bird cast down a still more splendid dress than on the day before. And when she appeared in it among the guests every one was astonished at her beauty. The prince had been waiting until she came, and he took her hand and danced with her alone. And when any one else came to invite her he said,

" She is my partner."

And when the evening came she wanted to go home, and the prince followed her, for he wanted to see to what house she belonged; but she broke away from him, and ran into the garden at the back of the house. There stood a fine large tree, bearing splendid pears; she leapt as lightly as a squirrel among the branches, and the prince did not know what had become of her. So he waited until the father came, and then he told him that the strange maiden had rushed from him, and that he thought she had gone up into the pear-tree. The father thought to himself,

" It cannot surely be Aschenputtel," and called for an axe, and felled the tree, but there was no one in it. And when they went into the kitchen there sat Aschenputtel among the cinders, as usual, for she had got down the other side of the tree, and had taken back her beautiful clothes to the bird on the hazel bush, and had put on her old gray kirtle again.

On the third day, when the parents and the step-children had set off, Aschenputtel went again to her mother's grave, and said to the tree,

" Little tree, little tree, shake over me,
    That silver and gold may come down and cover me."

Then the bird cast down a dress, the like of which had never been seen for splendour and brilliancy, and slippers that were of gold.

And when she appeared in this dress at the feast nobody knew what to say for wonderment. The prince danced with her alone, and if any one else asked her he answered,

" She is my partner."

And when it was evening Aschenputtel wanted to go home, and the prince was about to go with her, when she ran past him so quickly that he could not follow her. But he had laid a plan, and had caused all the steps to be spread with pitch, so that as she rushed down them the left shoe of the maiden remained sticking in it. The prince picked it up, and saw that it was of gold, and very small and slender. The next morning he went to the father and told him that none should be his bride save the one whose foot the golden shoe should fit. Then the two sisters were very glad, because they had pretty feet. The eldest went to her room to try on the shoe, and her mother stood by. But she could not get her great toe into it, for the shoe was too small; then her mother handed her a knife, and said,

" Cut the toe off, for when you are queen you will never have to go on foot." So the girl cut her toe off, squeezed her foot into the shoe, concealed the pain, and went down to the prince. Then he took her with him on his horse as his bride, and rode off. They had to pass by the grave, and there sat the two pigeons on the hazel bush, and cried,

" There they go, there they go !
    There is blood on her shoe ;
    The shoe is too small,
    —Not the right bride at all !"

Then the prince looked at her shoe, and saw the blood flowing. And he turned his horse round and took the false bride home again, saying she was not the right one, and that the other sister must try on the shoe. So she went into her room to do so, and got her toes comfortably in, but her heel was too large. Then her mother handed her the knife, saying, " Cut a piece off your heel; when you are queen you will never have to go on foot."

So the girl cut a piece off her heel, and thrust her foot into the shoe, concealed the pain, and went down to the prince, who took his bride before him on his horse and rode off. When they passed by the hazel bush the two pigeons sat there and cried,

> " There they go, there they go!
> There is blood on her shoe;
> The shoe is too small,
> —Not the right bride at all!"

Then the prince looked at her foot, and saw how the blood was flowing from the shoe, and staining the white stocking. And he turned his horse round and brought the false bride home again.

"This is not the right one," said he, "have you no other daughter?"

"No," said the man, "only my dead wife left behind her a little stunted Aschenputtel; it is impossible that she can be the bride." But the King's son ordered her to be sent for, but the mother said,

"Oh no! she is much too dirty, I could not let her be seen."

But he would have her fetched, and so Aschenputtel had to appear.

First she washed her face and hands quite clean, and went in and curtseyed to the prince, who held out to her the golden shoe. Then she sat down on a stool, drew her foot out of the heavy wooden shoe, and slipped it into the golden one, which fitted it perfectly. And when she stood up, and the prince looked in her face, he knew again the beautiful maiden that had danced with him, and he cried,

"This is the right bride!"

The step-mother and the two sisters were thunderstruck, and grew pale with anger; but he put Aschenputtel before him on his horse and rode off. And as they passed the hazel bush, the two white pigeons cried,

> " There they go, there they go!
> No blood on her shoe;

> The shoe's not too small,
> The right bride is she after all."

And when they had thus cried, they came flying after and perched on Aschenputtel's shoulders, one on the right, the other on the left, and so remained.

And when her wedding with the prince was appointed to be held the false sisters came, hoping to curry favour, and to take part in the festivities. So as the bridal procession went to the church, the eldest walked on the right side and the younger on the left, and the pigeons picked out an eye of each of them. And as they returned the elder was on the left side and the younger on the right, and the pigeons picked out the other eye of each of them. And so they were condemned to go blind for the rest of their days because of their wickedness and falsehood.

·The MOUSE, the BIRD, and the SAUSAGE·

ONCE on a time, a mouse and a bird and a sausage lived and kept house together in perfect peace among themselves, and in great prosperity. It was the bird's business to fly to the forest every day and bring back wood. The mouse had to draw the water, make the fire, and set the table; and the sausage had to do the cooking. Nobody is content in this world: much will have more! One day the bird met another bird on the way, and told him of his excellent condition in life. But the other bird called him a poor simpleton to do so much work, while the two others led easy lives at home.

When the mouse had made up her fire and drawn water, she went to rest in her little room until it was time to lay the cloth. The sausage stayed by the saucepans, looked to it that the victuals were well cooked, and just before dinner-time he stirred the broth or the stew three or four times well round himself, so as to enrich and season and flavour it. Then the bird used to come home and lay down his load, and they sat down to table, and after a good meal they would go to bed and sleep their fill till the next morning. It really was a most satisfactory life.

But the bird came to the resolution next day never again to fetch wood: he had, he said, been their slave long enough, now they must change about and make a new arrangement. So in spite of all the mouse and the sausage could say, the

bird was determined to have his own way.   So they drew lots
to settle it, and it fell so that the sausage was to fetch wood, the
mouse was to cook, and the bird was to draw water.

Now see what happened.   The sausage went away after
wood, the bird made up the fire, and the mouse put on the
pot, and they waited until the sausage should come home,
bringing the wood for the next day.   But the sausage was
absent so long, that they thought something must have
happened to him, and the bird went part of the way to see if
he could see anything of him.   Not far off he met with a dog
on the road, who, looking upon the sausage as lawful prey,
had picked him up, and made an end of him.   The bird then
lodged a complaint against the dog as an open and flagrant
robber, but it was all no good, as the dog declared that he had
found forged letters upon the sausage, so that he deserved to
lose his life.

The bird then very sadly took up the wood and carried it
home himself, and related to the mouse all he had seen and
heard.   They were both very troubled, but determined to look
on the bright side of things, and still to remain together.   And
so the bird laid the cloth, and the mouse prepared the food, and
finally got into the pot, as the sausage used to do, to stir and
flavour the broth, but then she had to part with fur and skin,
and lastly with life !

And when the bird came to dish up the dinner, there
was no cook to be seen ; and he turned over the heap of
wood, and looked and looked, but the cook never appeared
again.   By accident the wood caught fire, and the bird
hastened to fetch water to put it out, but he let fall the
bucket in the well, and himself after it, and as he could not
get out again, he was obliged to be drowned.

·MOTHER· HULDA·

A WIDOW had two daughters; one was pretty and industrious, the other was ugly and lazy. And as the ugly one was her own daughter, she loved her much the best, and the pretty one was made to do all the work, and be the drudge of the house. Every day the poor girl had to sit by a well on the high road and spin until her fingers bled. Now it happened once that as the spindle was bloody, she dipped it into the well to wash it; but it slipped out of her hand and fell in. Then she began to cry, and ran to her step-mother, and told her of her misfortune; and her step-mother scolded her without mercy, and said in her rage,

"As you have let the spindle fall in, you must go and fetch it out again!"

Then the girl went back again to the well, not knowing what to do, and in the despair of her heart she jumped down into the well the same way the spindle had gone. After that she knew nothing; and when she came to herself she was in a beautiful meadow, and the sun was shining on the flowers that grew round her. And she walked on through the meadow until she came to a baker's oven that was full of bread; and the bread called out to her,

"Oh, take me out, take me out, or I shall burn; I am baked enough already!"

Then she drew near, and with the baker's peel she took out all the loaves one after the other. And she went farther

MOTHER HULDA

"THEN THE GIRL WENT BACK AGAIN
TO THE WELL NOT KNOWING WHAT
TO DO, AND IN THE DESPAIR OF HER
HEART SHE JUMPED DOWN INTO
THE WELL THE SAME WAY THE
SPINDLE HAD GONE."

on till she came to a tree weighed down with apples, and it called out to her,

"Oh, shake me, shake me, we apples are all of us ripe!"

Then she shook the tree until the apples fell like rain, and she shook until there were no more to fall; and when she had gathered them together in a heap, she went on farther. At last she came to a little house, and an old woman was peeping out of it, but she had such great teeth that the girl was terrified and about to run away, only the old woman called her back.

"What are you afraid of, my dear child? Come and live with me, and if you do the house-work well and orderly, things shall go well with you. You must take great pains to make my bed well, and shake it up thoroughly, so that the feathers fly about, and then in the world it snows, for I am Mother Hulda." *

As the old woman spoke so kindly, the girl took courage, consented, and went to her work. She did everything to the old woman's satisfaction, and shook the bed with such a will that the feathers flew about like snow-flakes: and so she led a good life, had never a cross word, but boiled and roast meat every day. When she had lived a long time with Mother Hulda, she began to feel sad, not knowing herself what ailed her; at last she began to think she must be home-sick; and although she was a thousand times better off than at home where she was, yet she had a great longing to go home. At last she said to her mistress,

"I am home-sick, and although I am very well off here, I cannot stay any longer; I must go back to my own home."

Mother Hulda answered,

"It pleases me well that you should wish to go home, and, as you have served me faithfully, I will undertake to send you there!"

She took her by the hand and led her to a large door standing open, and as she was passing through it there fell upon her a heavy shower of gold, and the gold hung all about her, so that she was covered with it.

"All this is yours, because you have been so industrious," said Mother Hulda; and, besides that, she returned to her her

* In Hesse, when it snows, they say, "Mother Hulda is making her bed."

K

spindle, the very same that she had dropped in the well. And then the door was shut again, and the girl found herself back again in the world, not far from her mother's house ; and as she passed through the yard the cock stood on the top of the well and cried,

> " Cock-a-doodle doo !
> Our golden girl has come home too ! "

Then she went in to her mother, and as she had returned covered with gold she was well received.

So the girl related all her history, and what had happened to her, and when the mother heard how she came to have such great riches she began to wish that her ugly and idle daughter might have the same good fortune. So she sent her to sit by the well and spin ; and in order to make her spindle bloody she put her hand into the thorn hedge. Then she threw the spindle into the well, and jumped in herself. She found herself, like her sister, in the beautiful meadow, and followed the same path, and when she came to the baker's oven, the bread cried out,

"Oh, take me out, take me out, or I shall burn ; I am quite done already ! "

But the lazy-bones answered,

"I have no desire to black my hands," and went on farther. Soon she came to the apple-tree, who called out,

"Oh, shake me, shake me, we apples are all of us ripe ! "

But she answered,

"That is all very fine ; suppose one of you should fall on my head," and went on farther. When she came to Mother Hulda's house she did not feel afraid, as she knew beforehand of her great teeth, and entered into her service at once. The first day she put her hand well to the work, and was industrious, and did everything Mother Hulda bade her, because of the gold she expected ; but the second day she began to be idle, and the third day still more so, so that she would not get up in the morning. Neither did she make Mother Hulda's bed as it ought to have been made, and did not shake it for the feathers to fly about. So that Mother Hulda soon grew tired of her, and gave her warning, at which the lazy thing was well pleased, and thought that now the shower of gold was coming; so Mother Hulda led her to the door, and as she stood in the doorway, instead of the shower of gold a great kettle full of pitch was emptied over her.

"That is the reward for your service," said Mother Hulda, and shut the door. So the lazy girl came home all covered with pitch, and the cock on the top of the well seeing her, cried,

> " Cock-a-doodle doo!
> Our dirty girl has come home too!"

And the pitch remained sticking to her fast, and never, as long as she lived, could it be got off.

·LITTLE·RED·CAP·

HERE was once a sweet little maid, much beloved by everybody, but most of all by her grandmother, who never knew how to make enough of her. Once she sent her a little cap of red velvet, and as it was very becoming to her, and she never wore anything else, people called her Little Red-cap. One day her mother said to her,

"Come, Little Red-cap, here are some cakes and a flask of wine for you to take to grandmother; she is weak and ill, and they will do her good. Make haste and start before it grows hot, and walk properly and nicely, and don't run, or you might fall and break the flask of wine, and there would be none left for grandmother. And when you go into her room, don't forget to say, Good morning, instead of staring about you."

"I will be sure to take care," said Little Red-cap to her mother, and gave her hand upon it. Now the grandmother lived away in the wood, half-an-hour's walk from the village; and when Little Red-cap had reached the wood, she met the wolf; but as she did not know what a bad sort of animal he was, she did not feel frightened.

"Good day, Little Red-cap," said he.

"Thank you kindly, Wolf," answered she.

"Where are you going so early, Little Red-cap?"

"To my grandmother's."

"What are you carrying under your apron?"

"Cakes and wine; we baked yesterday; and my grandmother is very weak and ill, so they will do her good, and strengthen her."

"Where does your grandmother live, Little Red-cap?"

"A quarter of an hour's walk from here; her house stands beneath the three oak trees, and you may know it by the hazel bushes," said Little Red-cap. The wolf thought to himself,

"That tender young thing would be a delicious morsel, and would taste better than the old one; I must manage somehow to get both of them."

Then he walked by Little Red-cap a little while, and said,

"Little Red-cap, just look at the pretty flowers that are growing all round you, and I don't think you are listening to the song of the birds; you are posting along just as if you were going to school, and it is so delightful out here in the wood."

Little Red-cap glanced round her, and when she saw the sunbeams darting here and there through the trees, and lovely flowers everywhere, she thought to herself,

"If I were to take a fresh nosegay to my grandmother she would be very pleased, and it is so early in the day that I shall reach her in plenty of time;" and so she ran about in the wood, looking for flowers. And as she picked one she saw a still prettier one a little farther off, and so she went farther and farther into the wood. But the wolf went straight to the grandmother's house and knocked at the door.

"Who is there?" cried the grandmother.

"Little Red-cap," he answered, "and I have brought you some cake and wine. Please open the door."

"Lift the latch," cried the grandmother; "I am too feeble to get up."

So the wolf lifted the latch, and the door flew open, and he fell on the grandmother and ate her up without saying one word. Then he drew on her clothes, put on her cap, lay down in her bed, and drew the curtains.

Little Red-cap was all this time running about among the flowers, and when she had gathered as many as she could hold, she remembered her grandmother, and set off to go to her. She was surprised to find the door standing open, and when she came inside she felt very strange, and thought to herself,

"Oh dear, how uncomfortable I feel, and I was so glad this morning to go to my grandmother!"

And when she said, "Good morning," there was no answer. Then she went up to the bed and drew back the curtains; there lay the grandmother with her cap pulled over her eyes, so that she looked very odd.

"O grandmother, what large ears you have got!"

"The better to hear with."

"O grandmother, what great eyes you have got!"

"The better to see with."

"O grandmother, what large hands you have got!"

"The better to take hold of you with."

"But, grandmother, what a terrible large mouth you have got!"

"The better to devour you!" And no sooner had the wolf said it than he made one bound from the bed, and swallowed up poor Little Red-cap.

Then the wolf, having satisfied his hunger, lay down again in the bed, went to sleep, and began to snore loudly. The huntsman heard him as he was passing by the house, and thought,

"How the old woman snores—I had better see if there is anything the matter with her."

Then he went into the room, and walked up to the bed, and saw the wolf lying there.

"At last I find you, you old sinner!" said he; "I have been looking for you a long time." And he made up his mind that the wolf had swallowed the grandmother whole, and that she might yet be saved. So he did not fire, but took a pair of shears and began to slit up the wolf's body. When he made a few snips Little Red-cap appeared, and after a few more snips she jumped out and cried, "Oh dear, how frightened I have been! it is so dark inside the wolf." And then out came the old grandmother, still living and breathing. But Little Red-cap went and quickly fetched some large stones, with which she filled the wolf's body, so that when he waked up, and was going to rush away, the stones were so heavy that he sank down and fell dead.

They were all three very pleased. The huntsman took off the wolf's skin, and carried it home. The grandmother ate the cakes, and drank the wine, and held up her head again, and Little Red-cap said to herself that she would never more stray about in the wood alone, but would mind what her mother told her.

It must also be related how a few days afterwards, when Little Red-cap was again taking cakes to her grandmother, another wolf spoke to her, and wanted to tempt her to leave the path; but she was on her guard, and went straight on her way, and told her grandmother how that the wolf had met her, and wished her good-day, but had looked so wicked about the eyes that she thought if it had not been on the high road he would have devoured her.

"Come," said the grandmother, "we will shut the door, so that he may not get in."

Soon after came the wolf knocking at the door, and calling out, "Open the door, grandmother, I am Little Red-cap, bringing you cakes." But they remained still, and did not open the door. After that the wolf slunk by the house, and got at last upon the roof to wait until Little Red-cap should return home in the evening; then he meant to spring down upon her, and devour her in the darkness. But the grandmother discovered his plot. Now there stood before the house a great stone trough, and the grandmother said to the child, "Little Red-cap, I was boiling sausages yesterday, so take the bucket, and carry away the water they were boiled in, and pour it into the trough."

And Little Red-cap did so until the great trough was quite full. When the smell of the sausages reached the nose of the wolf he snuffed it up, and looked round, and stretched out his neck so far that he lost his balance and began to slip, and he slipped down off the roof straight into the great trough, and was drowned. Then Little Red-cap went cheerfully home, and came to no harm.

·THE·BREMEN·TOWN·MUSICIANS·

HERE was once an ass whose master had made him carry sacks to the mill for many a long year, but whose strength began at last to fail, so that each day as it came found him less capable of work. Then his master began to think of turning him out, but the ass, guessing that something was in the wind that boded him no good, ran away, taking the road to Bremen; for there he thought he might get an engagement as town musician. When he had gone a little way he found a hound lying by the side of the road panting, as if he had run a long way.

"Now, Holdfast, what are you so out of breath about?" said the ass.

"Oh dear!" said the dog, "now I am old, I get weaker every day, and can do no good in the hunt, so, as my master was going to have me killed, I have made my escape; but now, how am I to gain a living?"

"I will tell you what," said the ass, "I am going to Bremen to become town musician. You may as well go with me, and take up music too. I can play the lute, and you can beat the drum."

And the dog consented, and they walked on together. It was not long before they came to a cat sitting in the road, looking as dismal as three wet days.

"Now then, what is the matter with you, old shaver?" said the ass.

"I should like to know who would be cheerful when his neck is in danger?" answered the cat. "Now that I am old my teeth are getting blunt, and I would rather sit by the oven and purr than run about after mice, and my mistress wanted to drown me; so I took myself off; but good advice is scarce, and I do not know what is to become of me."

"Go with us to Bremen," said the ass, "and become town musician. You understand serenading."

The cat thought well of the idea, and went with them accordingly. After that the three travellers passed by a yard, and a cock was perched on the gate crowing with all his might.

"Your cries are enough to pierce bone and marrow," said the ass; "what is the matter?"

"I have foretold good weather for Lady-day, so that all the shirts may be washed and dried; and now on Sunday morning company is coming, and the mistress has told the cook that I must be made into soup, and this evening my neck is to be wrung, so that I am crowing with all my might while I can."

"You had much better go with us, Chanticleer," said the ass. "We are going to Bremen. At any rate that will be better than dying. You have a powerful voice, and when we are all performing together it will have a very good effect."

So the cock consented, and they went on all four together.

But Bremen was too far off to be reached in one day, and towards evening they came to a wood, where they determined to pass the night. The ass and the dog lay down under a large tree; the cat got up among the branches, and the cock flew up to the top, as that was the safest place for him. Before he went to sleep he looked all round him to the four points of the compass, and perceived in the distance a little light shining, and he called out to his companions that there must be a house not far off, as he could see a light, so the ass said,

"We had better get up and go there, for these are uncomfortable quarters." The dog began to fancy a few bones, not quite bare, would do him good. And they all set off in the direction of the light, and it grew larger and brighter, until at last it led them to a robber's house, all lighted up. The ass, being the biggest, went up to the window, and looked in.

"Well, what do you see?" asked the dog.

"What do I see?" answered the ass; "here is a table set out with splendid eatables and drinkables, and robbers sitting at it and making themselves very comfortable."

"That would just suit us," said the cock.

"Yes, indeed, I wish we were there," said the ass. Then they consulted together how it should be managed so as to get the robbers out of the house, and at last they hit on a plan. The ass was to place his forefeet on the window-sill, the dog was to get on the ass's back, the cat on the top of the dog, and lastly the cock was to fly up and perch on the cat's head. When that was done, at a given signal they all began to perform their music. The ass brayed, the dog barked, the cat mewed, and the cock crowed; then they burst through into the room, breaking all the panes of glass. The robbers fled at the dreadful sound; they thought it was some goblin, and fled to the wood in the utmost terror. Then the four companions sat down to table, made free with the remains of the meal, and feasted as if they had been hungry for a month. And when they had finished they put out the lights, and each sought out a sleeping-place to suit his nature and habits. The ass laid himself down outside on the dunghill, the dog behind the door, the cat on the hearth by the warm ashes, and the cock settled himself in the cockloft, and as they were all tired with their long journey they soon fell fast asleep.

When midnight drew near, and the robbers from afar saw that no light was burning, and that everything appeared quiet, their captain said to them that he thought that they had run away without reason, telling one of them to go and reconnoitre. So one of them went, and found everything quite quiet; he went into the kitchen to strike a light, and taking the glowing fiery eyes of the cat for burning coals, he held a match to them in order to kindle it. But the cat, not seeing the joke, flew into his face, spitting and scratching. Then he cried out in terror, and ran to get out at the back door, but the dog, who was lying there, ran at him and bit his leg; and as he was rushing through the yard by the dunghill the ass struck out and gave him a great kick with his hindfoot; and the cock, who had been wakened with the noise, and felt quite brisk, cried out, "Cock-a-doodle-doo!"

Then the robber got back as well as he could to his captain, and said, "Oh dear! in that house there is a grewsome witch, and I felt her breath and her long nails in my face; and by the door there stands a man who stabbed me in the leg with a knife; and in the yard there lies a black spectre, who beat me with his wooden club; and above, upon the roof, there sits the justice, who cried, 'Bring that rogue here!' And so I ran away from the place as fast as I could."

From that time forward the robbers never ventured to that house, and the four Bremen town musicians found themselves so well off where they were, that there they stayed. And the person who last related this tale is still living, as you see.

·PRUDENT·HANS·

NE day, Hans's mother said,
   "Where are you going, Hans?"
Hans answered,
   "To Grethel's, mother."
   "Manage well, Hans."
   "All right!   Good-bye, mother."
   "Good-bye, Hans."
Then Hans came to Grethel's.
   "Good morning, Grethel."

"Good morning, Hans.   What have you brought me to-day?"

"I have brought nothing, but I want something."

So Grethel gave Hans a needle; and then he said,

"Good-bye, Grethel," and she said, "Good-bye, Hans."

Hans carried the needle away with him, and stuck it in a hay-cart that was going along, and he followed it home.

"Good evening, mother."

"Good evening, Hans.   Where have you been?"

"To Grethel's, mother."

"What did you take her?"

"I took nothing, but I brought away something."

"What did Grethel give you?"

"A needle, mother."

"What did you do with it, Hans?"

"Stuck it in the hay-cart."

"That was very stupid of you, Hans.   You should have stuck it in your sleeve."

"All right, mother!   I'll do better next time."

When next time came, Hans's mother said,
" Where are you going, Hans ? "
" To Grethel's, mother."
" Manage well, Hans."
" All right !   Good-bye, mother."
" Good-bye, Hans."
Then Hans came to Grethel.
" Good morning, Grethel."
" Good morning, Hans.   What have you brought me to-day ? "
" I've brought nothing, but I want something."
So Grethel gave Hans a knife, and then he said, " Good-bye, Grethel," and she said, " Good-bye, Hans."
Hans took the knife away with him, and stuck it in his sleeve, and went home.
" Good evening, mother."
" Good evening, Hans.   Where have you been ? "
" To Grethel's."
" What did you take her ? "
" I took nothing, but I brought away something."
" What did Grethel give you, Hans ? "
" A knife, mother."
" What did you do with it, Hans ? "
" Stuck it in my sleeve, mother."
" That was very stupid of you, Hans.   You should have put it in your pocket."
" All right, mother !   I'll do better next time."
When next time came, Hans's mother said,
" Where to, Hans ? "
" To Grethel's, mother."
" Manage well, Hans."
" All right !   Good-bye, mother."
" Good-bye, Hans."
So Hans came to Grethel's.   " Good morning, Grethel."
" Good morning, Hans.   What have you brought me to-day ? "
" I've brought nothing, but I want to take away something."
So Grethel gave Hans a young goat ; then he said,
" Good-bye, Grethel," and she said, " Good-bye, Hans."

So Hans carried off the goat, and tied its legs together, and put it in his pocket, and by the time he got home it was suffocated.

"Good evening, mother."

"Good evening, Hans.   Where have you been?"

"To Grethel's, mother."

"What did you take her, Hans?"

"I took nothing, but I brought away something."

"What did Grethel give you, Hans?"

"A goat, mother."

"What did you do with it, Hans?"

"Put it in my pocket, mother."

"That was very stupid of you, Hans.   You should have tied a cord round its neck, and led it home."

"All right, mother!   I'll do better next time."

Then when next time came,

"Where to, Hans?"

"To Grethel's, mother."

"Manage well, Hans."

"All right!   Good-bye, mother."

"Good-bye, Hans."

Then Hans came to Grethel's.

"Good morning, Grethel."

"Good morning, Hans.   What have you brought me to-day?"

"I've brought nothing, but I want to take away something."

So Grethel gave Hans a piece of bacon.   Then he said, "Good-bye, Grethel."

She said, "Good-bye, Hans."

Hans took the bacon, and tied a string round it, and dragged it after him on his way home, and the dogs came and ate it up, so that when he got home he had the string in his hand, and nothing at the other end of it.

"Good evening, mother."

"Good evening, Hans.   Where have you been?"

"To Grethel's, mother."

"What did you take her, Hans?"

"I took her nothing, but I brought away something."

"What did Grethel give you, Hans?"

" A piece of bacon, mother."

" What did you do with it, Hans? "

" I tied a piece of string to it, and led it home, but the dogs ate it, mother."

" That was very stupid of you, Hans. You ought to have carried it on your head."

" All right ! I'll do better next time, mother."

When next time came,

" Where to, Hans? "

" To Grethel's, mother."

" Manage well, Hans."

" All right ! Good-bye, mother."

" Good-bye, Hans."

Then Hans came to Grethel's.

" Good morning, Grethel."

" Good morning, Hans. What have you brought me? "

" I have brought nothing, but I want to take away something."

So Grethel gave Hans a calf.

" Good-bye, Grethel."

" Good-bye, Hans."

Hans took the calf, and set it on his head, and carried it home, and the calf scratched his face.

" Good evening, mother."

" Good evening, Hans. Where have you been? "

" To Grethel's, mother."

" What did you take her? "

" I took nothing, but I brought away something."

" What did Grethel give you, Hans? "

" A calf, mother."

" What did you do with the calf, Hans? "

" I carried it home on my head, but it scratched my face."

" That was very stupid of you, Hans. You ought to have led home the calf, and tied it to the manger."

" All right ! I'll do better next time, mother."

When next time came,

" Where to, Hans? "

" To Grethel's, mother."

" Manage well, Hans."

" All right, mother !   Good-bye."

" Good-bye, Hans."

Then Hans came to Grethel's.

" Good morning, Grethel."

" Good morning, Hans.   What have you brought me to-day ? "

" I have brought nothing, but I want to take away something."

Then Grethel said to Hans,

" You shall take away me."

Then Hans took Grethel, and tied a rope round her neck, and led her home, and fastened her up to the manger, and went to his mother.

" Good evening, mother."

" Good evening, Hans.   Where have you been ? "

" To Grethel's, mother."

" What did you take her, Hans ? "

" Nothing, mother."

" What did Grethel give you, Hans ? "

" Nothing but herself, mother."

" Where have you left Grethel, Hans ? "

" I led her home with a rope, and tied her up to the manger to eat hay, mother."

" That was very stupid of you, Hans.   You should have cast sheep's eyes at her."

" All right, mother !   I'll do better next time."

Then Hans went into the stable, and taking all the eyes out of the sheep, he threw them in Grethel's face.   Then Grethel was angry, and getting loose, she ran away and became the bride of another.

·CLEVER·ELSE·

THERE was once a man who had a daughter who was called "Clever Else," and when she was grown up, her father said she must be married, and her mother said,

"Yes, if we could only find some one that she would consent to have."

At last one came from a distance, and his name was Hans, and when he proposed to her, he made it a condition that Clever Else should be very careful as well.

"Oh," said the father, "she does not want for brains."

"No, indeed," said the mother, "she can see the wind coming up the street and hear the flies cough."

"Well," said Hans, "if she does not turn out to be careful too, I will not have her."

Now when they were all seated at table, and had well eaten, the mother said,

"Else, go into the cellar and draw some beer."

Then Clever Else took down the jug from the hook in the wall, and as she was on her way to the cellar she rattled the lid up and down so as to pass away the time. When she got there, she took a stool and stood it in front of the cask, so that she need not stoop and make her back ache with needless trouble. Then she put the jug under the tap and turned it, and while the beer was running, in order that her eyes should not be idle, she glanced hither and thither, and finally caught sight of a pickaxe that the workmen had left sticking

in the ceiling just above her head. Then Clever Else began
to cry, for she thought,

"If I marry Hans, and we have a child, and it grows big,
and we send it into the cellar to draw beer, that pickaxe might
fall on his head and kill him."

So there she sat and cried with all her might, lamenting
the anticipated misfortune. All the while they were waiting
upstairs for something to drink, and they waited in vain. At
last the mistress said to the maid,

"Go down to the cellar and see why Else does not come."

So the maid went, and found her sitting in front of the
cask crying with all her might.

"What are you crying for?" said the maid.

"Oh dear me," answered she, "how can I help crying?
if I marry Hans, and we have a child, and it grows big, and
we send it here to draw beer, perhaps the pickaxe may fall on
its head and kill it."

"Our Else is clever indeed!" said the maid, and directly
sat down to bewail the anticipated misfortune. After a while,
when the people upstairs found that the maid did not return,
and they were becoming more and more thirsty, the master
said to the boy,

"You go down into the cellar, and see what Else and the
maid are doing."

The boy did so, and there he found both Clever Else and
the maid sitting crying together. Then he asked what was
the matter.

"Oh dear me," said Else, "how can we help crying? if I
marry Hans, and we have a child, and it grows big, and we
send it here to draw beer, the pickaxe might fall on its head
and kill it."

"Our Else is clever indeed!" said the boy, and sitting
down beside her, he began howling with a good will. Upstairs
they were all waiting for him to come back, but as he did not
come, the master said to the mistress,

"You go down to the cellar and see what Else is doing."

So the mistress went down and found all three in great
lamentations, and when she asked the cause, then Else told
her how the future possible child might be killed as soon as
it was big enough to be sent to draw beer, by the pickaxe
falling on it. Then the mother at once exclaimed,

"Our Else is clever indeed!" and, sitting down, she wept with the rest.

Upstairs the husband waited a little while, but as his wife did not return, and as his thirst constantly increased, he said,

"I must go down to the cellar myself, and see what has become of Else." And when he came into the cellar, and found them all sitting and weeping together, he was told that it was all owing to the child that Else might possibly have, and the possibility of its being killed by the pickaxe so happening to fall just at the time the child might be sitting underneath it drawing beer; and when he heard all this, he cried,

"How clever is our Else!" and sitting down, he joined his tears to theirs.

The intended bridegroom stayed upstairs by himself a long time, but as nobody came back to him, he thought he would go himself and see what they were all about. And there he found all five lamenting and crying most pitifully, each one louder than the other.

"What misfortune has happened?" cried he.

"O my dear Hans," said Else, "if we marry and have a child, and it grows big, and we send it down here to draw beer, perhaps that pickaxe which has been left sticking up there might fall down on the child's head and kill it; and how can we help crying at that!"

"Now," said Hans, "I cannot think that greater sense than that could be wanted in my household; so as you are so clever, Else, I will have you for my wife," and taking her by the hand he led her upstairs, and they had the wedding at once.

A little while after they were married, Hans said to his wife,

"I am going out to work, in order to get money; you go into the field and cut the corn, so that we may have bread."

"Very well, I will do so, dear Hans," said she. And after Hans was gone she cooked herself some nice stew, and took it with her into the field. And when she got there, she said to herself,

"Now, what shall I do? shall I reap first, or eat first? All right, I will eat first." Then she ate her fill of stew, and when she could eat no more, she said to herself,

"Now, what shall I do? shall I reap first, or sleep first? All right, I will sleep first." Then she lay down in the corn and went to sleep.   And Hans got home, and waited there a long while, and Else did not come, so he said to himself,

"My clever Else is so industrious that she never thinks of coming home and eating."

But when evening drew near and still she did not come, Hans set out to see how much corn she had cut; but she had cut no corn at all, but there she was lying in it asleep.   Then Hans made haste home, and fetched a bird-net with little bells and threw it over her; and still she went on sleeping.   And he ran home again and locked himself in, and sat him down on his bench to work.   At last, when it was beginning to grow dark, Clever Else woke, and when she got up and shook herself, the bells jingled at each movement that she made.   Then she grew frightened, and began to doubt whether she were really Clever Else or not, and said to herself,

"Am I, or am I not?"   And, not knowing what answer to make, she stood for a long while considering; at last she thought,

"I will go home to Hans and ask him if I am I or not; he is sure to know."

So she ran up to the door of her house, but it was locked; then she knocked at the window, and cried,

"Hans, is Else within?"

"Yes," answered Hans, "she is in."

Then she was in a greater fright than ever, and crying,

"Oh dear, then I am not I," she went to inquire at another door, but the people hearing the jingling of the bells would not open to her, and she could get in nowhere.   So she ran away beyond the village, and since then no one has seen her.

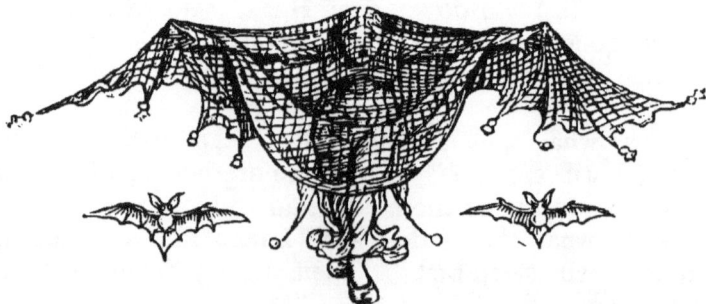

The TABLE, the ASS, and the STICK.

HERE was once a tailor who had three sons and one goat. And the goat, as she nourished them all with her milk, was obliged to have good food, and so she was led every day down to the willows by the water-side; and this business the sons did in turn. One day the eldest took the goat to the churchyard, where the best sprouts are, that she might eat her fill, and gambol about.

In the evening, when it was time to go home, he said,

"Well, goat, have you had enough?"

The goat answered,

> "I am so full,
> I cannot pull
> Another blade of grass—ba! baa!"

"Then come home," said the youth, and fastened a string to her, led her to her stall, and fastened her up.

"Now," said the old tailor, "has the goat had her proper food?"

"Oh," answered the son, "she is so full, she no more can pull."

But the father, wishing to see for himself, went out to the stall, stroked his dear goat, and said,

"My dear goat, are you full?" And the goat answered,

> "How can I be full?
> There was nothing to pull,
> Though I looked all about me—ba! baa!"

"What is this that I hear?" cried the tailor, and he ran and called out to the youth,

"O you liar, to say that the goat was full, and she has been hungry all the time!" And in his wrath he took up his yard-measure and drove his son out of the house with many blows.

The next day came the turn of the second son, and he found a fine place in the garden hedge, where there were good green sprouts, and the goat ate them all up. In the evening, when he came to lead her home, he said,

"Well, goat, have you had enough?" And the goat answered,

> "I am so full,
>   I could not pull
> Another blade of grass—ba! baa!"

"Then come home," said the youth, and led her home, and tied her up.

"Now," said the old tailor, "has the goat had her proper food?"

"Oh," answered the son, "she is so full, she no more can pull."

The tailor, not feeling satisfied, went out to the stall, and said,

"My dear goat, are you really full?" And the goat answered,

> "How can I be full?
>   There was nothing to pull,
> Though I looked all about me—ba! baa!"

"The good-for-nothing rascal," cried the tailor, "to let the dear creature go fasting!" and, running back, he chased the youth with his yard-wand out of the house.

Then came the turn of the third son, who, meaning to make all sure, found some shrubs with the finest sprouts possible, and left the goat to devour them. In the evening, when he came to lead her home, he said,

"Well, goat, are you full?" And the goat answered,

> "I am so full,
>   I could not pull
> Another blade of grass—ba! baa!"

"Then come home," said the youth; and he took her to her stall, and fastened her up.

"Now," said the old tailor, "has the goat had her proper food?"

"Oh," answered the son, "she is so full, she no more can pull."

But the tailor, not trusting his word, went to the goat and said,

"My dear goat, are you really full?" The malicious animal answered,

> "How can I be full?
> There was nothing to pull,
> Though I looked all about me—ba! baa!"

"Oh, the wretches!" cried the tailor. "The one as good-for-nothing and careless as the other. I will no longer have such fools about me;" and rushing back, in his wrath he laid about him with his yard-wand, and belaboured his son's back so unmercifully that he ran away out of the house.

So the old tailor was left alone with the goat. The next day he went out to the stall, and let out the goat, saying,

"Come, my dear creature, I will take you myself to the willows."

So he led her by the string, and brought her to the green hedges and pastures where there was plenty of food to her taste, and saying to her,

"Now, for once, you can eat to your heart's content," he left her there till the evening. Then he returned, and said,

"Well, goat, are you full?"
She answered,

> "I am so full,
> I could not pull,
> Another blade of grass—ba! baa!"

"Then come home," said the tailor, and leading her to her stall, he fastened her up.

Before he left her he turned once more, saying,

"Now then, for once you are full." But the goat actually cried,

" How can I be full?
There was nothing to pull,
Though I looked all about me—ba! baa!"

When the tailor heard that he marvelled, and saw at once that his three sons had been sent away without reason.

" Wait a minute," cried he, " you ungrateful creature! It is not enough merely to drive you away—I will teach you to show your face again among honourable tailors."

So in haste he went and fetched his razor, and seizing the goat he shaved her head as smooth as the palm of his hand. And as the yard-measure was too honourable a weapon, he took the whip and fetched her such a crack that with many a jump and spring she ran away.

The tailor felt very sad as he sat alone in his house, and would willingly have had his sons back again, but no one knew where they had gone.

The eldest son, when he was driven from home, apprenticed himself to a joiner, and he applied himself diligently to his trade, and when the time came for him to travel his master gave him a little table, nothing much to look at, and made of common wood; but it had one great quality. When any one set it down and said, " Table, be covered!" all at once the good little table had a clean cloth on it, and a plate, and knife, and fork, and dishes with roast and boiled, and a large glass of red wine sparkling so as to cheer the heart. The young apprentice thought he was set up for life, and he went merrily out into the world, and never cared whether an inn were good or bad, or whether he could get anything to eat there or not. When he was hungry, it did not matter where he was, whether in the fields, in the woods, or in a meadow, he set down his table and said, " Be covered!" and there he was provided with everything that heart could wish. At last it occurred to him that he would go back to his father, whose wrath might by this time have subsided, and perhaps because of the wonderful table he might receive him again gladly. It happened that one evening during his journey home he came to an inn that was quite full of guests, who bade him welcome, and asked him to sit down with them and eat, as otherwise he would have found some difficulty in getting anything.

" No," answered the young joiner, " I could not think of depriving you ; you had much better be my guests."

Then they laughed, and thought he must be joking.   But he brought his little wooden table, and put it in the middle of the room, and said, " Table, be covered ! "   Immediately it was set out with food much better than the landlord had been able to provide, and the good smell of it greeted the noses of the guests very agreeably.   " Fall to, good friends," said the joiner ; and the guests, when they saw how it was, needed no second asking, but taking up knife and fork fell to valiantly. And what seemed most wonderful was that when a dish was empty immediately a full one stood in its place.   All the while the landlord stood in a corner, and watched all that went on.   He could not tell what to say about it ; but he thought " such cooking as that would make my inn prosper." The joiner and his fellowship kept it up very merrily until late at night.   At last they went to sleep, and the young joiner, going to bed, left his wishing-table standing against the wall. The landlord, however, could not sleep for thinking of the table, and he remembered that there was in his lumber room an old table very like it, so he fetched it, and taking away the joiner's table, he left the other in its place.   The next morn- ing the joiner paid his reckoning, took up the table, not dreaming that he was carrying off the wrong one, and went on his way.   About noon he reached home, and his father re- ceived him with great joy.

" Now, my dear son, what have you learned ? " said he to him.

" I have learned to be a joiner, father," he answered.

" That is a good trade," returned the father ; " but what have you brought back with you from your travels ? "

" The best thing I've got, father, is this little table," said he.

The tailor looked at it on all sides, and said,

" You have certainly produced no masterpiece.   It is a rubbishing old table."

" But it is a very wonderful one," answered the son. " When I set it down, and tell it to be covered, at once the finest meats are standing on it, and wine so good that it cheers the heart.   Let us invite all the friends and neighbours, that they

may feast and enjoy themselves, for the table will provide
enough for all."

When the company was all assembled, he put his table in
the middle of the room, and said, " Table, be covered ! "

But the table never stirred, and remained just as empty as
any other table that does not understand talking.   When the
poor joiner saw that the table remained unfurnished, he felt
ashamed to stand there like a fool.   The company laughed
at him freely, and were obliged to return unfilled and un-
cheered to their houses.   The father gathered his pieces
together and returned to his tailoring, and the son went to
work under another master.

The second son had bound himself apprentice to a miller.
And when his time was up, his master said to him,

" As you have behaved yourself so well, I will give you
an ass of a remarkable kind : he will draw no cart, and carry
no sack."

" What is the good of him then ? " asked the young
apprentice.

" He spits out gold," answered the miller.   " If you put
a cloth before him and say, ' Bricklebrit,' out come gold pieces."

" That is a capital thing," said the apprentice, and, thank-
ing his master, he went out into the world.   Whenever he
wanted gold he had only to say " Bricklebrit " to his ass, and
there was a shower of gold pieces, and so he had no cares as he
travelled about.   Wherever he came he lived on the best, and
the dearer the better, as his purse was always full.   And when he
had been looking about him about the world a long time, he
thought he would go and find out his father, who would perhaps forget his anger and receive him kindly because of his
gold ass.   And it happened that he came to lodge in the same
inn where his brother's table had been exchanged.   He was
leading his ass in his hand, and the landlord was for taking
the ass from him to tie it up, but the young apprentice said,

" Don't trouble yourself, old fellow, I will take him into
the stable myself and tie him up, and then I shall know where
to find him."

The landlord thought this was very strange, and he never
supposed that a man who was accustomed to look after his ass
himself could have much to spend ; but when the stranger,

feeling in his pocket, took out two gold pieces and told him to get him something good for supper; the landlord stared, and ran and fetched the best that could be got. After supper the guest called the reckoning, and the landlord, wanting to get all the profit he could, said that it would amount to two gold pieces more. The apprentice felt in his pocket, but his gold had come to an end.

"Wait a moment, landlord," said he, "I will go and fetch some money," and he went out of the room, carrying the table-cloth with him. The landlord could not tell what to make of it, and, curious to know his proceedings, slipped after him, and as the guest shut the stable-door, he peeped in through a knot-hole. Then he saw how the stranger spread the cloth before the ass, saying, "Bricklebrit," and directly the ass spat out gold, which rained upon the ground.

"Dear me," said the landlord, "that is an easy way of getting ducats; a purse of money like that is no bad thing."

After that the guest paid his reckoning and went to bed; but the landlord slipped down to the stable in the middle of the night, led the gold-ass away, and tied up another ass in his place. The next morning early the apprentice set forth with his ass, never doubting that it was the right one. By noon he came to his father's house, who was rejoiced to see him again, and received him gladly.

"What trade have you taken up, my son?" asked the father.

"I am a miller, dear father," answered he.

"What have you brought home from your travels?" continued the father.

"Nothing but an ass," answered the son.

"We have plenty of asses here," said the father. "You had much better have brought me a nice goat!"

"Yes," answered the son, "but this is no common ass. When I say, 'Bricklebrit,' the good creature spits out a whole clothful of gold pieces. Let me call all the neighbours to-gether. I will make rich people of them all."

"That will be fine!" said the tailor. "Then I need labour no more at my needle;" and he rushed out himself and called the neighbours together. As soon as they were all assembled, the miller called out to them to make room, and brought in the ass, and spread his cloth before him.

" Now, pay attention," said he, and cried, " Bricklebrit ! " but no gold pieces came, and that showed that the animal was not more scientific than any other ass.

So the poor miller made a long face when he saw that he had been taken in, and begged pardon of the neighbours, who all went home as poor as they had come. And there was nothing for it but that the old man must take to his needle again, and that the young one should take service with a miller.

The third brother had bound himself apprentice to a turner ; and as turning is a very ingenious handicraft, it took him a long time to learn it. His brother told him in a letter how badly things had gone with them, and how on the last night of their travels the landlord deprived them of their treasures. When the young turner had learnt his trade, and was ready to travel, his master, to reward him for his good conduct, gave him a sack, and told him that there was a stick inside it.

" I can hang up the sack, and it may be very useful to me," said the young man. " But what is the good of the stick ? "

" I will tell you," answered the master. " If any one does you any harm, and you say, ' Stick, out of the sack ! ' the stick will jump out upon them, and will belabour them so soundly that they shall not be able to move or to leave the place for a week, and it will not stop until you say, ' Stick, into the sack ! ' "

The apprentice thanked him, and took up the sack and started on his travels, and when any one attacked him he would say, " Stick, out of the sack ! " and directly out jumped the stick, and dealt a shower of blows on the coat or jerkin, and the back beneath, which quickly ended the affair. One evening the young turner reached the inn where his two brothers had been taken in. He laid his knapsack on the table, and began to describe all the wonderful things he had seen in the world.

" Yes," said he, " you may talk of your self-spreading table, gold-supplying ass, and so forth ; very good things, I do not deny, but they are nothing in comparison with the treasure that I have acquired and carry with me in that sack !"

Then the landlord opened his ears.

"What in the world can it be ?" thought he. "Very likely the sack is full of precious stones ; and I have a perfect right to it, for all good things come in threes."

When bedtime came the guest stretched himself on a bench, and put his sack under his head for a pillow, and the landlord, when he thought the young man was sound asleep, came, and, stooping down, pulled gently at the sack, so as to remove it cautiously, and put another in its place. The turner had only been waiting for this to happen, and just as the landlord was giving a last courageous pull, he cried, "Stick, out of the sack !" Out flew the stick directly, and laid to heartily on the landlord's back ; and in vain he begged for mercy ; the louder he cried the harder the stick beat time on his back, until he fell exhausted to the ground. Then the turner said,

"If you do not give me the table and the ass directly, this game shall begin all over again."

"Oh dear, no !" cried the landlord, quite collapsed ; "I will gladly give it all back again if you will only make this terrible goblin go back into the sack."

Then said the young man, "I will be generous instead of just, but beware !" Then he cried, "Stick, into the sack !" and left him in peace.

The next morning the turner set out with the table and the ass on his way home to his father. The tailor was very glad, indeed, to see him again, and asked him what he had learned abroad.

"My dear father," answered he, "I am become a turner."

"A very ingenious handicraft," said the father. "And what have you brought with you from your travels ?"

"A very valuable thing, dear father," answered the son. "A stick in a sack !"

"What !" cried the father. "A stick ! The thing is not worth so much trouble when you can cut one from any tree."

"But it is not a common stick, dear father," said the young man. "When I say, 'Stick, out of the bag !' out jumps the stick upon any one who means harm to me, and

makes him dance again, and does not leave off till he is beaten
to the earth, and asks pardon.   Just look here, with this stick
I have recovered the table and the ass which the thieving landlord had taken from my two brothers.   Now, let them both
be sent for, and bid all the neighbours too, and they shall eat
and drink to their hearts' content, and I will fill their pockets
with gold."

The old tailor could not quite believe in such a thing, but
he called his sons and all the neighbours together.   Then the
turner brought in the ass, opened a cloth before him, and said
to his brother,

"Now, my dear brother, speak to him."   And the miller
said, "Bricklebrit!" and immediately the cloth was covered
with gold pieces, until they had all got more than they could
carry away.   (I tell you this because it is a pity you were not
there.)   Then the turner set down the table, and said,

"Now, my dear brother, speak to it."   And the joiner
said, "Table, be covered!" and directly it was covered, and
set forth plentifully with the richest dishes.   Then they held a
feast such as had never taken place in the tailor's house before,
and the whole company remained through the night, merry and
content.

The tailor after that locked up in a cupboard his needle
and thread, his yard-measure and goose, and lived ever after
with his three sons in great joy and splendour.

But what became of the goat, the unlucky cause of the
tailor's sons being driven out?   I will tell you.   She felt so
ashamed of her bald head that she ran into a fox's hole and
hid herself.   When the fox came home he caught sight of two
great eyes staring at him out of the darkness, and was very
frightened and ran away.   A bear met him, and seeing that he
looked very disturbed, asked him,

"What is the matter, brother fox, that you should look like
that?"

"Oh dear," answered the fox, "a grisly beast is sitting in
my hole, and he stared at me with fiery eyes!"

"We will soon drive him out," said the bear; and went to
the hole and looked in, but when he caught sight of the fiery
eyes he likewise felt great terror seize him, and not wishing to
have anything to do with so grisly a beast, he made off.   He

was soon met by a bee, who remarked that he had not a very courageous air, and said to him,

"Bear, you have a very depressed countenance, what has become of your high spirit ?"

"You may well ask," answered the bear. "In the fox's hole there sits a grisly beast with fiery eyes, and we cannot drive him out."

The bee answered, "I know you despise me, bear. I am a poor feeble little creature, but I think I can help you."

So she flew into the fox's hole, and settling on the goat's smooth-shaven head, stung her so severely that she jumped up, crying, "Ba-baa !" and ran out like mad into the world; and to this hour no one knows where she ran to.

·TOM ·THUMB·

THERE was once a poor countryman who used to sit in the chimney-corner all evening and poke the fire, while his wife sat at her spinning-wheel.

And he used to say,

" How dull it is without any children about us ; our house is so quiet, and other people's houses so noisy and merry ! "

" Yes," answered his wife, and sighed, " if we could only have one, and that one ever so little, no bigger than my thumb, how happy I should be ! It would, indeed, be having our heart's desire."

Now, it happened that after a while the woman had a child who was perfect in all his limbs, but no bigger than a thumb. Then the parents said,

" He is just what we wished for, and we will love him very much," and they named him according to his stature, " Tom Thumb." And though they gave him plenty of nourishment, he grew no bigger, but remained exactly the same size as when he was first born ; and he had very good faculties, and was very quick and prudent, so that all he did prospered.

One day his father made ready to go into the forest to cut wood, and he said, as if to himself,

" Now, I wish there was some one to bring the cart to meet me."

" O father," cried Tom Thumb, " I can bring the cart, let me alone for that, and in proper time, too ! "

Then the father laughed, and said,

" How will you manage that ? You are much too little to hold the reins."

" That has nothing to do with it, father ; while my mother goes on with her spinning I will sit in the horse's ear and tell him where to go."

" Well," answered the father, " we will try it for once."

When it was time to set off, the mother went on spinning, after setting Tom Thumb in the horse's ear ; and so he drove off, crying,

" Gee-up, gee-wo ! "

So the horse went on quite as if his master were driving him, and drew the waggon along the right road to the wood.

Now it happened just as they turned a corner, and the little fellow was calling out " Gee-up ! " that two strange men passed by.

" Look," said one of them, " how is this ? There goes a waggon, and the driver is calling to the horse, and yet he is nowhere to be seen."

" It is very strange," said the other ; " we will follow the waggon, and see where it belongs."

And the waggon went right through the wood, up to the place where the wood had been hewed. When Tom Thumb caught sight of his father, he cried out,

" Look, father, here am I with the waggon ; now, take me down."

The father held the horse with his left hand, and with the right he lifted down his little son out of the horse's ear, and Tom Thumb sat down on a stump, quite happy and content. When the two strangers saw him they were struck dumb with wonder. At last one of them, taking the other aside, said to him, " Look here, the little chap would make our fortune if we were to show him in the town for money. Suppose we buy him."

So they went up to the woodcutter, and said,

" Sell the little man to us ; we will take care he shall come to no harm."

" No," answered the father ; " he is the apple of my eye, and not for all the money in the world would I sell him."

But Tom Thumb, when he heard what was going on,

M

climbed up by his father's coat tails, and, perching himself on his shoulder, he whispered in his ear,

" Father, you might as well let me go. I will soon come back again."

Then the father gave him up to the two men for a large piece of money. They asked him where he would like to sit,

" Oh, put me on the brim of your hat," said he. " There I can walk about and view the country, and be in no danger of falling off."

So they did as he wished, and when Tom Thumb had taken leave of his father, they set off all together. And they travelled on until it grew dusk, and the little fellow asked to be set down a little while for a change, and after some difficulty they consented. So the man took him down from his hat, and set him in a field by the roadside, and he ran away directly, and, after creeping about among the furrows, he slipped suddenly into a mouse-hole, just what he was looking for.

" Good evening, my masters, you can go home without me ! " cried he to them, laughing. They ran up and felt about with their sticks in the mouse-hole, but in vain. Tom Thumb crept farther and farther in, and as it was growing dark, they had to make the best of their way home, full of vexation, and with empty purses.

When Tom Thumb found they were gone, he crept out of his hiding-place underground.

" It is dangerous work groping about these holes in the darkness," said he ; " I might easily break my neck."

But by good fortune he came upon an empty snail shell.

" That's all right," said he. " Now I can get safely through the night ;" and he settled himself down in it. Before he had time to get to sleep, he heard two men pass by, and one was saying to the other,

" How can we manage to get hold of the rich parson's gold and silver ? "

" I can tell you how," cried Tom Thumb.

" How is this ? " said one of the thieves, quite frightened, " I hear some one speak ! "

So they stood still and listened, and Tom Thumb spoke again.

" Take me with you ; I will show you how to do it ! "

" Where are you, then ? " asked they.

" Look about on the ground and notice where the voice comes from," answered he.

At last they found him, and lifted him up.

" You little elf," said they, " how can you help us ? "

" Look here," answered he, " I can easily creep between the iron bars of the parson's room and hand out to you whatever you would like to have."

" Very well," said they, " we will try what you can do."

So when they came to the parsonage-house, Tom Thumb crept into the room, but cried out with all his might,

" Will you have all that is here ? "   So the thieves were terrified, and said,

" Do speak more softly, lest any one should be awaked."

But Tom Thumb made as if he did not hear them, and cried out again,

" What would you like ? will you have all that is here ? " so that the cook, who was sleeping in a room hard by, heard it, and raised herself in bed and listened.   The thieves, however, in their fear of being discovered, had run back part of the way, but they took courage again, thinking that it was only a jest of the little fellow's.   So they came back and whispered to him to be serious, and to hand them out something.

Then Tom Thumb called out once more as loud as he could,

" Oh yes, I will give it all to you, only put out your hands."

Then the listening maid heard him distinctly that time, and jumped out of bed, and burst open the door.   The thieves ran off as if the wild huntsman were behind them ; but the maid, as she could see nothing, went to fetch a light.   And when she came back with one, Tom Thumb had taken himself off, without being seen by her, into the barn ; and the maid, when she had looked in every hole and corner and found nothing, went back to bed at last, and thought that she must have been dreaming with her eyes and ears open.

So Tom Thumb crept among the hay, and found a comfortable nook to sleep in, where he intended to remain until it was day, and then to go home to his father and mother.   But other things were to befall him ; indeed, there is nothing but

trouble and worry in this world! The maid got up at dawn
of day to feed the cows. The first place she went to was the
barn, where she took up an armful of hay, and it happened to
be the very heap in which Tom Thumb lay asleep. And he
was so fast asleep, that he was aware of nothing, and never
waked until he was in the mouth of the cow, who had taken
him up with the hay.

"Oh dear," cried he, "how is it that I have got into a
mill!" but he soon found out where he was, and he had to be
very careful not to get between the cow's teeth, and at last he
had to descend into the cow's stomach.

"The windows were forgotten when this little room was
built," said he, "and the sunshine cannot get in; there is no
light to be had."

His quarters were in every way unpleasant to him, and,
what was the worst, new hay was constantly coming in, and the
space was being filled up. At last he cried out in his
extremity, as loud as he could,

"No more hay for me! no more hay for me!"

The maid was then milking the cow, and as she heard a
voice, but could see no one, and as it was the same voice that
she had heard in the night, she was so frightened that she fell
off her stool, and spilt the milk. Then she ran in great haste
to her master, crying,

"Oh, master dear, the cow spoke!"

"You must be crazy," answered her master, and he went
himself to the cow-house to see what was the matter. No
sooner had he put his foot inside the door, than Tom Thumb
cried out again,

"No more hay for me! no more hay for me!"

Then the parson himself was frightened, supposing that a
bad spirit had entered into the cow, and he ordered her to be
put to death. So she was killed, but the stomach, where Tom
Thumb was lying, was thrown upon a dunghill. Tom Thumb
had great trouble to work his way out of it, and he had just
made a space big enough for his head to go through, when a
new misfortune happened. A hungry wolf ran up and swallowed the whole stomach at one gulp. But Tom Thumb did
not lose courage. "Perhaps," thought he, "the wolf will
listen to reason," and he cried out from the inside of the wolf,

" My dear wolf, I can tell you where to get a splendid meal ! "

" Where is it to be had ? " asked the wolf.

" In such and such a house, and you must creep into it through the drain, and there you will find cakes and bacon and broth, as much as you can eat," and he described to him his father's house. The wolf needed not to be told twice. He squeezed himself through the drain in the night, and feasted in the store-room to his heart's content. When, at last, he was satisfied, he wanted to go away again, but he had become so big, that to creep the same way back was impossible. This Tom Thumb had reckoned upon, and began to make a terrible din inside the wolf, crying and calling as loud as he could.

" Will you be quiet ? " said the wolf; " you will wake the folks up ! "

" Look here," cried the little man, " you are very well satisfied, and now I will do something for my own enjoyment," and began again to make all the noise he could. At last the father and mother were awakened, and they ran to the room-door and peeped through the chink, and when they saw a wolf in occupation, they ran and fetched weapons—the man an axe, and the wife a scythe.

" Stay behind," said the man, as they entered the room ; " when I have given him a blow, and it does not seem to have killed him, then you must cut at him with your scythe."

Then Tom Thumb heard his father's voice, and cried,

" Dear father, I am here in the wolf's inside."

Then the father called out full of joy,

" Thank heaven that we have found our dear child ! " and told his wife to keep the scythe out of the way, lest Tom Thumb should be hurt with it. Then he drew near and struck the wolf such a blow on the head that he fell down dead ; and then he fetched a knife and a pair of scissors, slit up the wolf's body, and let out the little fellow.

" Oh, what anxiety we have felt about you ! " said the father.

" Yes, father, I have seen a good deal of the world, and I am very glad to breathe fresh air again."

"And where have you been all this time?" asked his father.

"Oh, I have been in a mouse-hole and a snail's shell, in a cow's stomach and a wolf's inside: now, I think, I will stay at home."

"And we will not part with you for all the kingdoms of the world," cried the parents, as they kissed and hugged their dear little Tom Thumb. And they gave him something to eat and drink, and a new suit of clothes, as his old ones were soiled with travel.

HOW·MRS·FOX·MARRIED·AGAIN

FIRST VERSION.

HERE was once an old fox with nine tails, who wished to put his wife's affection to proof, pretended to be dead, and stretched himself under the bench quite stiff, and never moved a joint, on which Mrs. Fox retired to her room and locked herself in, while her maid, the cat, stayed by the kitchen fire and attended to the cooking.

When it became known that the old fox was dead, some suitors prepared to come forward, and presently the maid heard some one knocking at the house door ; she went and opened it, and there was a young fox, who said,

> " What is she doing, Miss Cat ?
> Is she sleeping, or waking, or what is she at ? "

And the cat answered,

> " I am not asleep, I am quite wide awake,
> Perhaps you would know what I'm going to make ;
> I'm melting some butter, and warming some beer,
> Will it please you sit down, and partake of my cheer ? "

" Thank you, miss," said the fox.   " What is Mrs. Fox doing ? "

The maid answered,

> " She is sitting upstairs in her grief,
>> And her eyes with her weeping are sore ;
> From her sorrow she gets no relief,
>> Now poor old Mr. Fox is no more ! "

" But just tell her, miss, that a young fox has come to woo her."

" Very well, young master," answered the cat.

Up went the cat pit-a-pat, pit-a-pat.

She knocks at the door, rat-a-tat, rat-a-tat !

> " Mrs. Fox, are you there ? "
> " Yes, yes, pussy dear ! "
> " There's a suitor below,
>> Shall I tell him to go ? "

" But what is he like ? " asked Mrs. Fox. " Has he nine beautiful tails, like dear Mr. Fox ? "

" Oh no," answered the cat ; " he has only one."

" Then I won't have him," said Mrs. Fox.

So the cat went down-stairs, and sent the suitor away. Soon there was another knock at the door. It was another fox come to woo. He had two tails, but he met with no better success than the first. Then there arrived more foxes, one after another, each with one more tail than the last, but they were all dismissed, until there came one with nine tails like old Mr. Fox. When the widow heard that she cried, full of joy, to the cat,

> " Now, open door and window wide,
>> And turn old Mr. Fox outside."

But before they could do so, up jumped old Mr. Fox from under the bench, and cudgelled the whole pack, driving them, with Mrs. Fox, out of the house.

SECOND VERSION.

HEN old Mr. Fox died there came a wolf to woo, and he knocked at the door, and the cat opened to him; and he made her a bow, and said,

"Good day, Miss Cat, so brisk and gay,
How is it that alone you stay?
And what is it you cook to-day?"

The cat answered,

"Bread so white, and milk so sweet,
Will it please you sit and eat?"

"Thank you very much, Miss Cat," answered the wolf; "but is Mrs. Fox at home?"

Then the cat said,

"She is sitting upstairs in her grief,
And her eyes with her weeping are sore,
From her sorrow she gets no relief,
Now poor old Mr. Fox is no more!"

The wolf answered,

"Won't she take another spouse,
To protect her and her house?"

Up went the cat, pit-a-pat, pit-a-pat.
She knocks at the door, rat-a-tat, rat-a-tat!

"Mrs. Fox, are you there?"
"Yes, yes, pussy dear!"
"There's a suitor below,
Shall I tell him to go?"

But Mrs. Fox asked, "Has the gentleman red breeches and a sharp nose?"

"No," answered the cat.

"Then I won't have him," said Mrs. Fox.

After the wolf was sent away, there came a dog, a stag, a hare, a bear, a lion, and several other wild animals. But they all of them lacked the good endowments possessed by the late Mr. Fox, so that the cat had to send them all away. At last came a young fox. And Mrs. Fox inquired whether he had red breeches and a sharp nose.

"Yes, he. has," said the cat.

"Then I will have him," said Mrs. Fox, and bade the cat make ready the wedding-feast.

> "Now, cat, sweep the parlours and bustle about,
> And open the window, turn Mr. Fox out ;
> Then, if you've a fancy for anything nice,
> Just manage to catch for yourself a few mice,
> You may eat them alone,
> I do not want one."

So she was married to young Master Fox with much dancing and rejoicing, and for anything I have heard to the contrary, they may be dancing still.

·THE·ELVES·

THERE was once a shoemaker, who, through no fault of his own, became so poor that at last he had nothing left but just enough leather to make one pair of shoes. He cut out the shoes at night, so as to set to work upon them next morning; and as he had a good conscience, he laid himself quietly down in his bed, committed himself to heaven, and fell asleep. In the morning, after he had said his prayers, and was going to get to work, he found the pair of shoes made and finished, and standing on his table. He was very much astonished, and could not tell what to think, and he took the shoes in his hand to examine them more nearly; and they were so well made that every stitch was in its right place, just as if they had come from the hand of a master-workman.

Soon after a purchaser entered, and as the shoes fitted him very well, he gave more than the usual price for them, so that the shoemaker had enough money to buy leather for two more pairs of shoes. He cut them out at night, and intended to set to work the next morning with fresh spirit; but that was not to be, for when he got up they were already finished, and a customer even was not lacking, who gave him so much money that he was able to buy leather enough for four new pairs. Early next morning he found the four pairs also finished, and so it always happened; whatever he cut out in the evening was worked up by the morning, so that he was soon in the way of making a good living, and in the end became very well to do.

One night, not long before Christmas, when the shoe-maker had finished cutting out, and before he went to bed, he said to his wife,

"How would it be if we were to sit up to-night and see who it is that does us this service?"

His wife agreed, and set a light to burn. Then they both hid in a corner of the room, behind some coats that were hanging up, and then they began to watch. As soon as it was midnight they saw come in two neatly-formed naked little men, who seated themselves before the shoemaker's table, and took up the work that was already prepared, and began to stitch, to pierce, and to hammer so cleverly and quickly with their little fingers that the shoemaker's eyes could scarcely follow them, so full of wonder was he. And they never left off until every-thing was finished and was standing ready on the table, and then they jumped up and ran off.

The next morning the shoemaker's wife said to her hus-band, "Those little men have made us rich, and we ought to show ourselves grateful. With all their running about, and having nothing to cover them, they must be very cold. I'll tell you what; I will make little shirts, coats, waistcoats, and breeches for them, and knit each of them a pair of stockings and you shall make each of them a pair of shoes."

The husband consented willingly, and at night, when every thing was finished, they laid the gifts together on the table instead of the cut-out work, and placed themselves so that they could observe how the little men would behave. When mid night came, they rushed in, ready to set to work, but when they found, instead of the pieces of prepared leather, the near little garments put ready for them, they stood a moment in surprise, and then they testified the greatest delight. With the greatest swiftness they took up the pretty garments and slipped them on, singing,

> "What spruce and dandy boys are we!
> No longer cobblers we will be."

Then they hopped and danced about, jumping over the chairs and tables, and at last they danced out at the door.

From that time they were never seen again; but it alway went well with the shoemaker as long as he lived, and whateve he took in hand prospered.

(II.)

THERE was once a poor servant maid, who was very cleanly and industrious; she swept down the house every day, and put the sweepings on a great heap by the door. One morning, before she began her work, she found a letter, and as she could not read, she laid her broom in the corner, and took the letter to her master and mistress, to see what was about; and it was an invitation from the elves, who wished the maid to come and stand godmother to one of their children. The maid did not know what to do; and as she was told that no one ought to refuse the elves anything, she made up her mind to go. So there came three little elves, who conducted her into the middle of a high mountain, where the little people lived. Here everything was of a very small size, but more fine and elegant than can be told. The mother of the child lay in a bed made of ebony, studded with pearls, the counterpane was embroidered with gold, the cradle was of ivory, and the bathing-tub of gold. So the maid stood godmother, and was then for going home, but the elves begged her to stay at least three more days with them; and so she consented, and spent the time in mirth and jollity, and the elves seemed very fond of her. At last, when she was ready to go away, they filled her pockets full of gold, and led her back again out of the mountain. When she got back to the house, she was going to begin working again, and took her broom in her hand; it was still standing in the corner where she had left it, and began to sweep. Then came up some strangers and asked her who she was, and what she was doing. And she found that instead of three days, she had been seven years with the elves in the mountain, and that during that time her master and mistress had died.

(III.)

THE elves once took a child away from its mother, and left in its place a changeling with a big head and staring eyes, who did nothing but eat and drink. The mother in her trouble went to her neighbours and asked their advice. The neighbours told her to take the changeling into the kitchen and put it near the hearth, and then to make up the fire, and boil water in two egg-shells; that would make the changeling laugh, and if he laughed, it would be all over with him. So the woman did as her neighbours advised. And when she set the egg-shells of water on the fire, the changeling said,

> " Though old I be
> As forest tree,
> Cooking in an egg-shell never did I see ! "

and began to laugh. And directly there came in a crowd of elves bringing in the right child ; and they laid it near the hearth, and carried the changeling away with them.

THE
ROBBER
BRIDEGROOM

"TURN BACK, TURN BACK, THOU PRETTY BRIDE,
WITHIN THIS HOUSE THOU MUST NOT BIDE,
FOR HERE DO EVIL THINGS BETIDE."

SWAIN sc

To face page 175

THE·ROBBER·BRIDEGROOM

THERE was once a miller who had a beautiful daughter, and when she was grown up he became anxious that she should be well married and taken care of; so he thought,

"If a decent sort of man comes and asks her in marriage, I will give her to him."

Soon after a suitor came forward who seemed very well to do, and as the miller knew nothing to his disadvantage, he promised him his daughter. But the girl did not seem to love him as a bride should love her bridegroom; she had no confidence in him; as often as she saw him or thought about him, she felt a chill at her heart. One day he said to her,

"You are to be my bride, and yet you have never·been to see me."

The girl answered,

"I do not know where your house is."

Then he said,

"My house is a long way in the wood."

She began to make excuses, and said she could not find the way to it; but the bridegroom said,

"You must come and pay me a visit next Sunday; I have already invited company, and I will strew ashes on the path through the wood, so that you will be sure to find it."

When Sunday came, and the girl set out on her way, she felt very uneasy without knowing exactly why; and she filled both pockets full of peas and lentils. There were ashes strewed on the path through the wood, but, nevertheless, at each step she cast to the right and left a few peas on the ground. So she went on the whole day until she came to the middle of the wood, where it was the darkest, and there stood a lonely house, not pleasant in her eyes, for it was dismal and unhomelike. She walked in, but there was no one there, and the greatest stillness reigned. Suddenly she heard a voice cry,

> " Turn back, turn back, thou pretty bride,
> Within this house thou must not bide,
> For here do evil things betide."

The girl glanced round, and perceived that the voice came from a bird who was hanging in a cage by the wall. And again it cried,

> " Turn back, turn back, thou pretty bride,
> Within this house thou must not bide,
> For here do evil things betide."

Then the pretty bride went on from one room into another through the whole house, but it was quite empty, and no soul to be found in it.

At last she reached the cellar, and there sat a very old woman nodding her head.

"Can you tell me," said the bride, "if my bridegroom lives here?"

"Oh, poor child," answered the old woman, "do you know what has happened to you? You are in a place of cut-throats. You thought you were a bride, and soon to be married, but death will be your spouse. Look here, I have a great kettle of water to set on, and when once they have you in their power they will cut you in pieces without mercy, cook you, and eat you, for they are cannibals. Unless I have pity on you, and save you, all is over with you!"

Then the old woman hid her behind a great cask, where she could not be seen.

"Be as still as a mouse," said she; "do not move or go away, or else you are lost. At night, when the robbers are asleep, we will escape. I have been waiting a long time for an opportunity."

No sooner was it settled than the wicked gang entered the house. They brought another young woman with them, dragging her along, and they were drunk, and would not listen to her cries and groans. They gave her wine to drink, three glasses full, one of white wine, one of red, and one of yellow, and then they cut her in pieces. The poor bride all the while shaking and trembling when she saw what a fate the robbers had intended for her. One of them noticed on the little finger of their victim a golden ring, and as he could not draw it off easily, he took an axe and chopped it off, but the finger jumped away, and fell behind the cask on the bride's lap. The robber took up a light to look for it, but he could not find it. Then said one of the others,

" Have you looked behind the great cask ? "

But the old woman cried,

" Come to supper, and leave off looking till to-morrow; the finger cannot run away."

Then the robbers said the old woman was right, and they left off searching, and sat down to eat, and the old woman dropped some sleeping stuff into their wine, so that before long they stretched themselves on the cellar floor, sleeping and snoring. When the bride heard that, she came from behind the cask, and had to make her way among the sleepers lying all about on the ground, and she felt very much afraid lest she might awaken any of them. But by good luck she passed through, and the old woman with her, and they opened the door, and they made all haste to leave that house of murderers. The wind had carried away the ashes from the path, but the peas and lentils had budded and sprung up, and the moonshine upon them showed the way. And they went on through the night, till in the morning they reached the mill. Then the girl related to her father all that had happened to her.

When the wedding-day came, the friends and neighbours assembled, the miller having invited them, and the bridegroom also appeared. When they were all seated at table, each one had to tell a story. But the bride sat still, and said nothing, till at last the bridegroom said to her,

" Now, sweetheart, do you know no story? Tell us something."

She answered,

" I will tell you my dream. I was going alone through a

wood, and I came at last to a house in which there was no living soul, but by the wall was a bird in a cage, who cried,

> ' Turn back, turn back, thou pretty bride,
> Within this house thou must not bide,
> For evil things do here betide.'

" And then again it said it. Sweetheart, the dream is not ended. Then I went through all the rooms, and they were all empty, and it was so lonely and wretched. At last I went down into the cellar, and there sat an old old woman, nodding her head. I asked her if my bridegroom lived in that house, and she answered, ' Ah, poor child, you have come into a place of cut-throats; your bridegroom does live here, but he will kill you and cut you in pieces, and then cook and eat you.' Sweetheart, the dream is not ended. But the old woman hid me behind a great cask, and no sooner had she done so than the robbers came home, dragging with them a young woman, and they gave her to drink wine thrice, white, red, and yellow. Sweetheart, the dream is not yet ended. And then they killed her, and cut her in pieces. Sweetheart, my dream is not yet ended. And one of the robbers saw a gold ring on the finger of the young woman, and as it was difficult to get off, he took an axe and chopped off the finger, which jumped upwards, and then fell behind the great cask on my lap. And here is the finger with the ring ! "

At these words she drew it forth, and showed it to the company.

The robber, who during the story had grown deadly white, sprang up, and would have escaped, but the folks held him fast, and delivered him up to justice. And he and his whole gang were, for their evil deeds, condemned and executed.

·MR·KORBES·

A COCK and a hen once wanted to go a journey together. So the cock built a beautiful carriage with four red wheels, and he harnessed four little mice to it. And the cock and the hen got into it, and were driven off. Very soon they met a cat, who asked where they were going. The cock answered,

" On Mr. Korbes a call to pay,
    And that is where we go to-day ! "

" Take me with you," said the cat.
The cock answered,
" Very well, only you must sit well back, and then you will not fall forward."

" And pray take care
    Of my red wheels there ;
    And wheels be steady,
    And mice be ready
    On Mr. Korbes a call to pay,
    For that is where we go to-day ! "

Then there came up a millstone, then an egg, then a duck, then a pin, and lastly a needle, who all got up on the carriage, and were driven along. But when they came to Mr. Korbes's house he was not at home. So the mice drew the carriage into the barn, the cock and the hen flew up and perched on a beam, the cat sat by the fireside, the duck settled on the water; but the egg wrapped itself in the towel, the pin stuck itself in

the chair cushion, the needle jumped into the bed among the
pillows, and the millstone laid itself by the door.   Then Mr.
Korbes came home, and went to the hearth to make a fire,
but the cat threw ashes in his eyes.   Then he ran quickly into the
kitchen to wash himself, but the duck splashed water in his face.
Then he was going to wipe it with the towel, but the egg broke
in it, and stuck his eyelids together.   In order to get a little
peace he sat down in his chair, but the pin ran into him, and,
starting up, in his vexation he threw himself on the bed, but as
his head fell on the pillow, in went the needle, so that he called
out with the pain, and madly rushed out.   But when he reached
the housedoor the mill-stone jumped up and struck him dead.

What a bad man Mr. Korbes must have been!

ᴣ TOM·THUMB'S·TRAVELS·

HERE was once a tailor who had a son no higher than a thumb, so he was called Tom Thumb. Notwithstanding his small size, he had plenty of spirit, and one day he said to his father,

"Father, go out into the world I must and will."

"Very well, my son," said the old man, and taking a long darning needle, he put a knob of sealing-wax on the end, saying,

"Here is a sword to take with you on your journey."

Now the little tailor wanted to have one more meal first, and so he trotted into the kitchen to see what sort of a farewell feast his mother had cooked for him. It was all ready, and the dish was standing on the hearth. Then said he,

"Mother, what is the fare to-day?"

"You can see for yourself," said the mother. Then Tom Thumb ran to the hearth and peeped into the dish, but as he stretched his neck too far over it, the steam caught him and carried him up the chimney. For a time he floated with the steam about in the air, but at last he sank down to the ground. Then the little tailor found himself out in the wide world, and he wandered about, and finally engaged himself to a master tailor, but the food was not good enough for him.

"Mistress," said Tom Thumb, "if you do not give us better victuals, I shall go out early in the morning and write with a piece of chalk on the house-door, 'Plenty of potatoes to eat, and but little meat; so good-bye, Mr. Potato.'"

" What are you after, grasshopper ? " said the mistress, and growing angry she seized a piece of rag to beat him off; but he crept underneath her thimble, and then peeped at her, and put his tongue out at her. She took up the thimble, and would have seized him, but he hopped among the rags, and as the mistress turned them over to find him, he stepped into a crack in the table. " He-hee ! Mistress ! " cried he, sticking out his head, and when she was just going to grasp him, he jumped into the table-drawer. But in the end she caught him, and drove him out of the house.

So he wandered on until he came to a great wood ; and there he met a gang of robbers that were going to rob the king's treasury. When they saw the little tailor, they thought to themselves,

" Such a little fellow might easily creep through a key-hole, and serve instead of a pick-lock."

" Holloa ! " cried one, " you giant Goliath, will you come with us to the treasure-chamber ? you can slip in, and then throw us out the money."

Tom Thumb considered a little, but at last he consented and went with them to the treasure-chamber. Then he looked all over the doors above and below, but there was no crack to be seen ; at last he found one broad enough to let him pass, and he was getting through, when one of the sentinels that stood before the door saw him, and said to the other,

" See what an ugly spider is crawling there ! I will put an end to him."

" Let the poor creature alone," said the other, " it has done you no harm."

So Tom Thumb got safely through the crack into the treasure-chamber, and he opened the window beneath which the thieves were standing, and he threw them out one dollar after another. Just as he had well settled to the work, he heard the king coming to take a look at his treasure, and so Tom Thumb had to creep away. The king presently remarked that many good dollars were wanting, but could not imagine how they could have been stolen, as the locks and bolts were in good order, and everything seemed secure. And he went away, saying to the two sentinels,

" Keep good guard ; there is some one after the money."

When Tom Thumb had set to work anew, they heard the chink, chink of the money, and hastily rushed in to catch the thief. But the little tailor, as he heard them coming, was too quick for them, and, hiding in a corner, he covered himself up with a dollar, so that nothing of him was to be seen, and then he mocked the sentinels, crying, "Here I am!" They ran about, and when they came near him, he was soon in another corner under a dollar, crying, "Here I am!" Then the sentinels ran towards him, and in a moment he was in a third corner, crying, "Here I am!" In this way he made fools of them, and dodged them so long about the treasure-chamber, that they got tired and went away. Then he set to work, and threw the dollars out of the window, one after the other, till they were all gone; and when it came to the last, as he flung it with all his might, he jumped nimbly on it, and flew with it out of the window. The robbers gave him great praise, saying,

"You are a most valiant hero; will you be our captain?"

But Tom Thumb thanked them, and said he would like to see the world first. Then they divided the spoil; but the little tailor's share was only one farthing, which was all he was able to carry.

Then binding his sword to his side, he bid the robbers good day, and started on his way. He applied to several master tailors, but they would not have anything to do with him; and at last he hired himself as indoor servant at an inn. The maid servants took a great dislike to him, for he used to see everything they did without being seen by them, and he told the master and mistress about what they took from the plates, and what they carried away out of the cellar. And they said, "Wait a little, we will pay you out," and took counsel together to play him some mischievous trick. Once when one of the maids was mowing the grass in the garden she saw Tom Thumb jumping about and creeping among the cabbages, and she mowed him with the grass, tied all together in a bundle, and threw it to the cows. Among the cows was a big black one, who swallowed him down, without doing him any harm. But he did not like his lodging, it was so dark, and there was no candle to be had. When the cow was being milked, he cried out,

"Strip, strap, strull,
Will the pail soon be full?"

But he was not understood because of the noise of the milk.
Presently the landlord came into the stable and said,

"To-morrow this cow is to be slaughtered."

At that Tom Thumb felt very terrified; and with his
shrillest voice he cried,

"Let me out first; I am sitting inside here!"

The master heard him quite plainly, but could not tell
where the voice came from.

"Where are you?" asked he.

"Inside the black one," answered Tom Thumb, but the
master, not understanding the meaning of it all, went away.

The next morning the cow was slaughtered. Happily, in
all the cutting and slashing he escaped all harm, and he slipped
among the sausage-meat. When the butcher came near to set
to work, he cried with all his might,

"Don't cut so deep, don't cut so deep, I am underneath!"

But for the sound of the butcher's knife his voice was not
heard. Now, poor Tom Thumb was in great straits, and he
had to jump nimbly out of the way of the knife, and finally he
came through with a whole skin. But he could not get quite
away, and he had to let himself remain with the lumps of fat
to be put in a black pudding. His quarters were rather
narrow, and he had to be hung up in the chimney in the
smoke, and to remain there a very long while. At last, when
winter came he was taken down, for the black pudding was to
be set before a guest. And when the landlady cut the black
pudding in slices, he had to take great care not to lift up his
head too much, or it might be shaved off at the neck. At
last he saw his opportunity, took courage, and jumped out.

But as things had gone so badly with him in that house,
Tom Thumb did not mean to stay there, but betook himself
again to his wanderings. His freedom, however, did not last
long. In the open fields there came a fox who snapped him
up without thinking.

"Oh, Mr. Fox," cries Tom Thumb, "here I am sticking
in your throat; let me out again."

"Very well," answered the fox. "It is true you are no
better than nothing; promise me the hens in your father's
yard, then I will let you go."

"With all my heart," answered Tom Thumb, "you shall
have them all, I promise you."

Then the fox let him go, and he ran home. When the father saw his dear little son again, he gave the fox willingly all the hens that he had.

" And look, besides, what a fine piece of money I've got for you ! " said Tom Thumb, and handed over the farthing which he had earned in his wanderings.

But how, you ask, could they let the fox devour all the poor chicks ?

Why, you silly child, you know that your father would rather have you than the hens in his yard !

·THE·ALMOND·TREE·

LONG time ago, perhaps as much as two thousand years, there was a rich man, and he had a beautiful and pious wife, and they loved each other very much, and they had no children, though they wished greatly for some, and the wife prayed for one day and night. Now, in the courtyard in front of their house stood an almond tree; and one day in winter the wife was standing beneath it, and paring an apple, and as she pared it she cut her finger, and the blood fell upon the snow.

"Ah," said the woman, sighing deeply, and looking down at the blood, "if only I could have a child as red as blood, and as white as snow!"

And as she said these words, her heart suddenly grew light, and she felt sure she should have her wish. So she went back to the house, and when a month had passed the snow was gone; in two months everything was green; in three months the flowers sprang out of the earth; in four months the trees were in full leaf, and the branches were thickly entwined; the little birds began to sing, so that the woods echoed, and the blossoms fell from the trees; when the fifth month had passed the wife stood under the almond tree, and it smelt so sweet that her heart leaped within her, and she fell on her knees for joy; and when the sixth month had gone, the fruit was thick and fine, and she remained still; and the seventh month she gathered the almonds, and ate them eagerly, and was sick and sorrowful; and when the eighth

THE ALMOND·TREE·

"KYWITT, KYWITT, KYWITT, I CRY,
OH WHAT A BEAUTIFUL BIRD AM I!"

month had passed she called to her husband, and said, weeping,

"If I die, bury me under the almond tree."

Then she was comforted and happy until the ninth month had passed, and then she bore a child as white as snow and as red as blood, and when she saw it her joy was so great that she died.

Her husband buried her under the almond tree, and he wept sore; time passed, and he became less sad; and after he had grieved a little more he left off, and then he took another wife.

His second wife bore him a daughter, and his first wife's child was a son, as red as blood and as white as snow. Whenever the wife looked at her daughter she felt great love for her, but whenever she looked at the little boy, evil thoughts came into her heart, of how she could get all her husband's money for her daughter, and how the boy stood in the way; and so she took great hatred to him, and drove him from one corner to another, and gave him a buffet here and a cuff there, so that the poor child was always in disgrace; when he came back after school hours there was no peace for him.

Once, when the wife went into the room upstairs, her little daughter followed her, and said,

"Mother, give me an apple."

"Yes, my child," said the mother, and gave her a fine apple out of the chest, and the chest had a great heavy lid with a strong iron lock.

"Mother," said the little girl, "shall not my brother have one too?"

That was what the mother expected, and she said,

"Yes, when he comes back from school."

And when she saw from the window that he was coming, an evil thought crossed her mind, and she snatched the apple, and took it from her little daughter, saying,

"You shall not have it before your brother."

Then she threw the apple into the chest, and shut to the lid. Then the little boy came in at the door, and she said to him in a kind tone, but with evil looks,

"My son, will you have an apple?"

"Mother," said the boy, "how terrible you look! yes, giv
me an apple!"

Then she spoke as kindly as before, holding up the cove
of the chest,

"Come here and take out one for yourself."

And as the boy was stooping over the open chest, crasl
went the lid down, so that his head flew off among the re
apples. But then the woman felt great terror, and wondere
how she could escape the blame. And she went to the ches
of drawers in her bedroom and took a white handkerchief ou
of the nearest drawer, and fitting the head to the neck, sh
bound them with the handkerchief, so that nothing should b
seen, and set him on a chair before the door with the appl
in his hand.

Then came little Marjory into the kitchen to her mother
who was standing before the fire stirring a pot of hot water.

"Mother," said Marjory, "my brother is sitting before th
door and he has an apple in his hand, and looks very pale;
asked him to give me the apple, but he did not answer me
it seems very strange."

"Go again to him," said the mother, "and if he will no
answer you, give him a box on the ear."

So Marjory went again and said,

"Brother, give me the apple."

But as he took no notice, she gave him a box on the ear
and his head fell off, at which she was greatly terrified, anc
began to cry and scream, and ran to her mother, and said,

"O mother! I have knocked my brother's head off!'
and cried and screamed, and would not cease.

"O Marjory!" said her mother, "what have you done
but keep quiet, that no one may see there is anything th
matter; it can't be helped now; we will put him out of th
way safely."

When the father came home and sat down to table, he said

"Where is my son?"

But the mother was filling a great dish full of black broth
and Marjory was crying bitterly, for she could not refrain.
Then the father said again,

"Where is my son?"

"Oh," said the mother, "he is gone into the country to his great-uncle's to stay for a little while."

"What should he go for?" said the father, "and without bidding me good-bye, too!"

"Oh, he wanted to go so much, and he asked me to let him stay there six weeks; he will be well taken care of."

"Dear me," said the father, "I am quite sad about it; it was not right of him to go without bidding me good-bye."

With that he began to eat, saying,

"Marjory, what are you crying for? Your brother will come back some time."

After a while he said,

"Well, wife, the food is very good; give me some more."

And the more he ate the more he wanted, until he had eaten it all up, and he threw the bones under the table. Then Marjory went to her chest of drawers, and took one of her best handkerchiefs from the bottom drawer, and picked up all the bones from under the table and tied them up in her handkerchief, and went out at the door crying bitterly. She laid them in the green grass under the almond tree, and immediately her heart grew light again, and she wept no more. Then the almond tree began to wave to and fro, and the boughs drew together and then parted, just like a clapping of hands for joy; then a cloud rose from the tree, and in the midst of the cloud there burned a fire, and out of the fire a beautiful bird arose, and, singing most sweetly, soared high into the air; and when he had flown away, the almond tree remained as it was before, but the handkerchief full of bones was gone. Marjory felt quite glad and light-hearted, just as if her brother were still alive. So she went back merrily into the house and had her dinner.

The bird, when it flew away, perched on the roof of a goldsmith's house, and began to sing,

> " It was my mother who murdered me ;
> It was my father who ate of me ;
> It was my sister Marjory
> Who all my bones in pieces found ;
> Them in a handkerchief she bound,
> And laid them under the almond tree.
> Kywitt, kywitt, kywitt, I cry,
> Oh what a beautiful bird am I ! "

The goldsmith was sitting in his shop making a golde
chain, and when he heard the bird, who was sitting on his ro
and singing, he started up to go and look, and as he passe
over his threshold he lost one of his slippers; and he wei
into the middle of the street with a slipper on one foot an
only a sock on the other; with his apron on, and the gol
chain in one hand and the pincers in the other; and so he
stood in the sunshine looking up at the bird.

"Bird," said he, "how beautifully you sing; do sing the
piece over again."

"No," said the bird, "I do not sing for nothing twice;
you will give me that gold chain I will sing again."

"Very well," said the goldsmith, "here is the gold chair
now do as you said."

Down came the bird and took the gold chain in his rigl
claw, perched in front of the goldsmith, and sang,

> "It was my mother who murdered me ;
> It was my father who ate of me ;
> It was my sister Marjory
> Who all my bones in pieces found ;
> Them in a handkerchief she bound,
> And laid them under the almond tree.
> Kywitt, kywitt, kywitt, I cry,
> Oh what a beautiful bird am I ! "

Then the bird flew to a shoemaker's, and perched on h
roof, and sang,

> "It was my mother who murdered me;
> It was my father who ate of me ;
> It was my sister Marjory
> Who all my bones in pieces found ;
> Them in a handkerchief she bound,
> And laid them under the almond tree.
> Kywitt, kywitt, kywitt, I cry,
> Oh what a beautiful bird am I ! "

When the shoemaker heard, he ran out of his door in h
shirt sleeves and looked up at the roof of his house, holdin
his hand to shade his eyes from the sun.

"Bird," said he, "how beautifully you sing ! "

Then he called in at his door,

"Wife, come out directly; here is a bird singing beautifully; only listen."

Then he called his daughter, all his children, and acquaintance, both young men and maidens, and they came up the street and gazed on the bird, and saw how beautiful it was with red and green feathers, and round its throat was as it were gold, and its eyes twinkled in its head like stars.

"Bird," said the shoemaker, "do sing that piece over again."

"No," said the bird, "I may not sing for nothing twice; you must give me something."

"Wife," said the man, "go into the shop; on the top shelf stands a pair of red shoes; bring them here."

So the wife went and brought the shoes.

"Now bird," said the man, "sing us that piece again."

And the bird came down and took the shoes in his left claw, and flew up again to the roof, and sang,

> "It was my mother who murdered me ;
> It was my father who ate of me ;
> It was my sister Marjory
> Who all my bones in pieces found ;
> Them in a handkerchief she bound,
> And laid them under the almond tree.
> Kywitt, kywitt, kywitt, I cry,
> Oh what a beautiful bird am I !"

And when he had finished he flew away, with the chain in his right claw and the shoes in his left claw, and he flew till he reached a mill, and the mill went "clip-clap, clip-clap, clip-clap." And in the mill sat twenty millers-men hewing a millstone— "hick-hack, hick-hack, hick-hack," while the mill was going "clip-clap, clip-clap, clip-clap." And the bird perched on a linden tree that stood in front of the mill, and sang,

> "It was my mother who murdered me ;"

Here one of the men looked up.

> "It was my father who ate of me ;"

Then two more looked up and listened.

> "It was my sister Marjory"

Here four more looked up.

" Who all my bones in pieces found ;
   Them in a handkerchief she bound,"

Now there were only eight left hewing.

" And laid them under the almond tree."

Now only five.

" Kywitt, kywitt, kywitt, I cry,"

Now only one.

" Oh what a beautiful bird am I ! "

At length the last one left off, and he only heard the end.
" Bird," said he, " how beautifully you sing ; let me hea
it all ; sing that again ! "

" No," said the bird, " I may not sing it twice for nothing
if you will give me the millstone I will sing it again."

" Indeed," said the man, " if it belonged to me alone yor
should have it."

" All right," said the others, " if he sings again he shal
have it."

Then the bird came down, and all the twenty miller
heaved up the stone with poles—"yo ! heave-hô ! yo ! heavé
ho !" and the bird stuck his head through the hole in th
middle, and with the millstone round his neck he flew up tr
the tree and sang,

" It was my mother who murdered me ;
   It was my father who ate of me ;
   It was my sister Marjory
   Who all my bones in pieces found ;
   Them in a handkerchief she bound,
   And laid them under the almond tree.
   Kywitt, kywitt, kywitt, I cry,
   Oh what a beautiful bird am I ! "

And when he had finished, he spread his wings, having ir
the right claw the chain, and in the left claw the shoes, and
round his neck the millstone, and he flew away to his father':
house.

In the parlour sat the father, the mother, and Marjory at
the table ; the father said,

" How light-hearted and cheerful I feel."

"Nay," said the mother, "I feel very low, just as if a great storm were coming."

But Marjory sat weeping; and the bird came flying, and perched on the roof.

"Oh," said the father, "I feel so joyful, and the sun is shining so bright; it is as if I were going to meet with an old friend."

"Nay," said the wife, "I am terrified, my teeth chatter, and there is fire in my veins," and she tore open her dress to get air; and Marjory sat in a corner and wept, with her plate before her, until it was quite full of tears. Then the bird perched on the almond tree, and sang,

> "It was my mother who murdered me;"

And the mother stopped her ears and hid her eyes, and would neither see nor hear; nevertheless, the noise of a fearful storm was in her ears, and in her eyes a quivering and burning as of lightning.

> "It was my father who ate of me;"

"O mother!" said the father, "there is a beautiful bird singing so finely, and the sun shines, and everything smells as sweet as cinnamon.

> "It was my sister Marjory"

Marjory hid her face in her lap and wept, and the father said,

"I must go out to see the bird."

"Oh do not go!" said the wife, "I feel as if the house were on fire."

But the man went out and looked at the bird.

> "Who all my bones in pieces found;
> Them in a handkerchief she bound,
> And laid them under the almond tree.
> Kywitt, kywitt, kywitt, I cry,
> Oh what a beautiful bird am I!"

With that the bird let fall the gold chain upon his father's neck, and it fitted him exactly. So he went indoors and said, "Look what a beautiful chain the bird has given me."

Then his wife was so terrified that she fell all along on th
floor, and her cap came off. Then the bird began again to sing

"It was my mother who murdered me;"

"Oh," groaned the mother, "that I were a thousand
fathoms under ground, so as not to be obliged to hear it."

"It was my father who ate of me;"

Then the woman lay as if she were dead.

"It was my sister Marjory"

"Oh," said Marjory, "I will go out, too, and see if the bird
will give me anything." And so she went.

"Who all my bones in pieces found;
Them in a handkerchief she bound,"

Then he threw the shoes down to her.

"And laid them under the almond tree.
Kywitt, kywitt, kywitt, I cry,
Oh what a beautiful bird am I!"

And poor Marjory all at once felt happy and joyful, and
put on her red shoes, and danced and jumped for joy.

"Oh dear," said she, "I felt so sad before I went outside,
and now my heart is so light! He is a charming bird to have
given me a pair of red shoes."

But the mother's hair stood on end, and looked like flame,
and she said,

"Even if the world is coming to an end, I must go out
for a little relief."

Just as she came outside the door, crash went the millstone on her head, and crushed her flat. The father and
daughter rushed out, and saw smoke and flames of fire rise
up; but when that had gone by, there stood the little brother;
and he took his father and Marjory by the hand, and they felt
very happy and content, and went indoors, and sat to the
table, and had their dinner.

⁕ OLD ⁕ SULTAN ⁕

THERE was once a peasant who owned a faithful dog called Sultan, now grown so old that he had lost all his teeth, and could lay hold of nothing. One day the man was standing at the door of his house with his wife, and he said,

"I shall kill old Sultan to-morrow; he is of no good any longer."

His wife felt sorry for the poor dog, and answered, "He has served us for so many years, and has kept with us so faithfully, he deserves food and shelter in his old age."

"Dear me, you do not seem to understand the matter," said the husband; "he has never a tooth, and no thief would mind him in the least, so I do not see why he should not be made away with. If he has served us well, we have given him plenty of good food."

The poor dog, who was lying stretched out in the sun not far off, heard all they said, and was very sad to think that the next day would be his last. He bethought him of his great friend the wolf, and slipped out in the evening to the wood to see him, and related to him the fate that was awaiting him.

"Listen to me, old fellow," said the wolf; "be of good courage, I will help you in your need. I have thought of a way. Early to-morrow morning your master is going hay-making with his wife, and they will take their child with them, so that no one will be left at home. They will be sure to lay the child in the shade behind the hedge while they are at work; you must lie by its side, just as if you were watching it. Then

I will come out of the wood and steal away the child; you must rush after me, as if to save it from me. Then I must let it fall, and you must bring it back again to its parents, who will think that you have saved it, and will be much too grateful to do you any harm; on the contrary, you will be received into full favour, and they will never let you want for anything again."

The dog was pleased with the plan, which was carried out accordingly. When the father saw the wolf running away with his child he cried out, and when old Sultan brought it back again, he was much pleased with him, and patted him, saying,

"Not a hair of him shall be touched; he shall have food and shelter as long as he lives." And he said to his wife,

"Go home directly and make some good stew for old Sultan, something that does not need biting; and get the pillow from my bed for him to lie on."

From that time old Sultan was made so comfortable that he had nothing left to wish for. Before long the wolf paid him a visit, to congratulate him that all had gone so well.

"But, old fellow," said he, "you must wink at my making off by chance with a fat sheep of your master's; perhaps one will escape some fine day."

"Don't reckon on that," answered the dog; "I cannot consent to it; I must remain true to my master."

But the wolf, not supposing it was said in earnest, came sneaking in the night to carry off the sheep. But the master, who had been warned by the faithful Sultan of the wolf's intention, was waiting for him, and gave him a fine hiding with the threshing-flail. So the wolf had to make his escape, calling out to the dog,

"You shall pay for this, you traitor!"

The next morning the wolf sent the wild boar to call out the dog; and to appoint a meeting in the wood to receive satisfaction from him. Old Sultan could find no second but a cat with three legs; and as they set off together, the poor thing went limping along, holding her tail up in the air. The wolf and his second were already on the spot; when they saw their antagonists coming, and caught sight of the elevated tail of the cat, they thought it was a sabre they were bringing with them. And as the poor thing came limping on three legs, they supposed it was lifting a big stone to throw at them. This frightened them very much; the wild boar crept among the leaves, and the wolf clambered up into a tree. And when the dog and cat came up, they were surprised not to see any one there. However, the wild boar was not perfectly hidden in the leaves, and the tips of his ears peeped out. And when the cat caught sight of one, she thought it was a mouse, and sprang upon it, seizing it with her teeth. Out leaped the wild boar with a dreadful cry, and ran away shouting,

"There is the culprit in the tree!"

And the dog and the cat looking up caught sight of the wolf, who came down, quite ashamed of his timidity, and made peace with the dog once more.

-THE·SIX-SWANS-

ONCE on a time a king was hunting in a great wood, and he pursued a wild animal so eagerly that none of his people could follow him. When evening came he stood still, and looking round him he found that he had lost his way; and seeking a path, he found none. Then all at once he saw an old woman with a nodding head coming up to him; and it was a witch.

"My good woman," said he, "can you show me the way out of the wood?"

"Oh yes, my lord king," answered she, "certainly I can; but I must make a condition, and if you do not fulfil it, you will never get out of the wood again, but die there of hunger."

"What is the condition?" asked the king.

"I have a daughter," said the old woman, "who is as fair as any in the world, and if you will take her for your bride, and make her queen, I will show you the way out of the wood."

The king consented, because of the difficulty he was in, and the old woman led him into her little house, and there her daughter was sitting by the fire.

She received the king just as if she had been expecting him, and though he saw that she was very beautiful, she did not please him, and he could not look at her without an inward shudder. Nevertheless, he took the maiden before him on his horse, and the old woman showed him the way, and

THE · SIX · SWANS

THE · SWANS · CAME · CLOSE · UP · TO
HER · WITH · RUSHING · WINGS; &
STOOPED · ROUND · HER; SO · THAT
SHE · COULD · THROW · THE · SHIRTS
OVER · THEM: "

SWAIN SC

soon he was in his royal castle again, where the wedding was held.

The king had been married before, and his first wife had left seven children, six boys and one girl, whom he loved better than all the world, and as he was afraid the step-mother might not behave well to them, and perhaps would do them some mischief, he took them to a lonely castle standing in the middle of a wood. There they remained hidden, for the road to it was so hard to find that the king himself could not have found it, had it not been for a clew of yarn, possessing wonderful properties, that a wise woman had given him; when he threw it down before him, it unrolled itself and showed him the way. And the king went so often to see his dear children, that the queen was displeased at his absence; and she became curious and wanted to know what he went out into the wood for so often alone. She bribed his servants with much money, and they showed her the secret, and told her of the clew of yarn, which alone could point out the way; then she gave herself no rest until she had found out where the king kept the clew, and then she made some little white silk shirts, and sewed a charm in each, as she had learned witchcraft of her mother. And once when the king had ridden to the hunt, she took the little shirts and went into the wood, and the clew of yarn showed her the way. The children seeing some one in the distance, thought it was their dear father coming to see them, and came jumping for joy to meet him. Then the wicked queen threw over each one of the little shirts, and as soon as the shirts touched their bodies, they were changed into swans, and flew away through the wood. So the queen went home very pleased to think she had got rid of her step-children; but the maiden had not run out with her brothers, and so the queen knew nothing about her. The next day the king went to see his children, but he found nobody but his daughter.

" Where are thy brothers? " asked the king.

" Ah, dear father," answered she, " they are gone away and have left me behind," and then she told him how she had seen from her window her brothers in the guise of swans fly away through the wood, and she showed him the feathers which they had let fall in the courtyard, and which she had picked up. The

king was grieved, but he never dreamt that it was the queen
who had done this wicked deed, and as he feared lest the
maiden also should be stolen away from him, he wished to
take her away with him. But she was afraid of the step-mother,
and begged the king to let her remain one more night in the
castle in the wood.

Then she said to herself,

"I must stay here no longer, but go and seek for my
brothers."

And when the night came, she fled away and went straight
into the wood. She went on all that night and the next day,
until she could go no longer for weariness. At last she saw a
rude hut, and she went in and found a room with six little
beds in it ; she did not dare to lie down in one, but she crept
under one and lay on the hard boards and wished for night.
When it was near the time of sun-setting she heard a rustling
sound, and saw six swans come flying in at the window. They
alighted on the ground, and blew at one another until they
had blown all their feathers off, and then they stripped off
their swan-skin as if it had been a shirt. And the maiden
looked at them and knew them for her brothers, and was very
glad, and crept from under the bed. The brothers were not less
glad when their sister appeared, but their joy did not last long.

"You must not stay here," said they to her; "this is a
robbers' haunt, and if they were to come and find you here,
they would kill you."

"And cannot you defend me?" asked the little sister.

"No," answered they, "for we can only get rid of our
swan-skins and keep our human shape every evening for a
quarter of an hour, but after that we must be changed again
into swans."

Their sister wept at hearing this, and said,

"Can nothing be done to set you free?"

"Oh no," answered they, "the work would be too hard for
you. For six whole years you would be obliged never to speak
or laugh, and make during that time six little shirts out of
aster-flowers. If you were to let fall a single word before the
work was ended, all would be of no good."

And just as the brothers had finished telling her this, the

quarter of an hour came to an end, and they changed into swans and flew out of the window.

But the maiden made up her mind to set her brothers free, even though it should cost her her life. She left the hut, and going into the middle of the wood, she climbed a tree, and there passed the night. The next morning she set to work and gathered asters and began sewing them together: as for speaking, there was no one to speak to, and as for laughing, she had no mind to it; so she sat on and looked at nothing but her work. When she had been going on like this for a long time, it happened that the king of that country went a-hunting in the wood, and some of his huntsmen came up to the tree in which the maiden sat. They called out to her, saying, "Who art thou?" But she gave no answer. "Come down," cried they; "we will do thee no harm." But she only shook her head. And when they tormented her further with questions she threw down to them her gold necklace, hoping they would be content with that. But they would not leave off, so she threw down to them her girdle, and when that was no good, her garters, and one after another everything she had on and could possibly spare, until she had nothing left but her smock. But all was no good, the huntsmen would not be put off any longer, and they climbed the tree, carried the maiden off, and brought her to the king. The king asked, "Who art thou? What wert thou doing in the tree?" But she answered nothing. He spoke to her in all the languages he knew, but she remained dumb: but, being very beautiful, the king inclined to her, and he felt a great love rise up in his heart towards her; and casting his mantle round her, he put her before him on his horse and brought her to his castle. Then he caused rich clothing to be put upon her, and her beauty shone as bright as the morning, but no word would she utter. He seated her by his side at table, and her modesty and gentle mien so pleased him, that he said,

"This maiden I choose for wife, and no other in all the world," and accordingly after a few days they were married.

But the king had a wicked mother, who was displeased with the marriage, and spoke ill of the young queen.

"Who knows where the maid can have come from?" said

she, "and not able to speak a word! She is not worthy of a king!"

After a year had passed, and the queen brought her first child into the world, the old woman carried it away, and marked the queen's mouth with blood as she lay sleeping. Then she went to the king and declared that his wife was an eater of human flesh. The king would not believe such a thing, and ordered that no one should do her any harm. And the queen went on quietly sewing the shirts and caring for nothing else. The next time that a fine boy was born, the wicked step-mother used the same deceit, but the king would give no credence to her words, for he said,

"She is too tender and good to do any such thing, and if she were only not dumb, and could justify herself, then her innocence would be as clear as day."

When for the third time the old woman stole away the new-born child and accused the queen, who was unable to say a word in her defence, the king could do no other but give her up to justice, and she was sentenced to suffer death by fire.

The day on which her sentence was to be carried out was the very last one of the sixth year of the years during which she had neither spoken nor laughed, to free her dear brothers from the evil spell. The six shirts were ready, all except one which wanted the left sleeve. And when she was led to the pile of wood, she carried the six shirts on her arm, and when she mounted the pile and the fire was about to be kindled, all at once she cried out aloud, for there were six swans coming flying through the air; and she saw that her deliverance was near, and her heart beat for joy. The swans came close up to her with rushing wings, and stooped round her, so that she could throw the shirts over them; and when that had been done the swan-skins fell off them, and her brothers stood before her in their own bodies quite safe and sound; but as one shirt wanted the left sleeve, so the youngest brother had a swan's wing instead of a left arm. They embraced and kissed each other, and the queen went up to the king, who looked on full of astonishment, and began to speak to him and to say,

"Dearest husband, now I may dare to speak and tell you that I am innocent, and have been falsely accused," and she related to him the treachery of the step-mother, who had taken away the three children and hidden them. And she was reconciled to the king with great joy, and the wicked step-mother was bound to the stake on the pile of wood and burnt to ashes.

And the king and queen lived many years with their six brothers in peace and joy.

⊹THE⊹SLEEPING⊹BEAUTY⊹

N times past there lived a king and queen, who said to each other every day of their lives, "Would that we had a child!" and yet they had none. But it happened once that when the queen was bathing, there came a frog out of the water, and he squatted on the ground, and said to her,

"Thy wish shall be fulfilled; before a year has gone by, thou shalt bring a daughter into the world."

And as the frog foretold, so it happened; and the queen bore a daughter so beautiful that the king could not contain himself for joy, and he ordained a great feast. Not only did he bid to it his relations, friends, and acquaintances, but also the wise women, that they might be kind and favourable to the child. There were thirteen of them in his kingdom, but as he had only provided twelve golden plates for them to eat from, one of them had to be left out. However, the feast was celebrated with all splendour; and as it drew to an end, the wise women stood forward to present to the child their wonderful gifts: one bestowed virtue, one beauty, a third riches, and so on, whatever there is in the world to wish for. And when eleven of them had said their say, in came the uninvited thirteenth, burning to revenge herself, and without greeting or respect, she cried with a loud voice,

"In the fifteenth year of her age the princess shall prick herself with a spindle and shall fall down dead."

And without speaking one more word she turned away and

left the hall. Every one was terrified at her saying, when the twelfth came forward, for she had not yet bestowed her gift, and though she could not do away with the evil prophecy, yet she could soften it, so she said,

"The princess shall not die, but fall into a deep sleep for a hundred years."

Now the king, being desirous of saving his child even from this misfortune, gave commandment that all the spindles in his kingdom should be burnt up.

The maiden grew up, adorned with all the gifts of the wise women; and she was so lovely, modest, sweet, and kind and clever, that no one who saw her could help loving her.

It happened one day, she being already fifteen years old, that the king and queen rode abroad, and the maiden was left behind alone in the castle. She wandered about into all the nooks and corners, and into all the chambers and parlours, as the fancy took her, till at last she came to an old tower. She climbed the narrow winding stair which led to a little door, with a rusty key sticking out of the lock; she turned the key, and the door opened, and there in the little room sat an old woman with a spindle, diligently spinning her flax.

"Good day, mother," said the princess, "what are you doing?"

"I am spinning," answered the old woman, nodding her head.

"What thing is that that twists round so briskly?" asked the maiden, and taking the spindle into her hand she began to spin; but no sooner had she touched it than the evil prophecy was fulfilled, and she pricked her finger with it. In that very moment she fell back upon the bed that stood there, and lay in a deep sleep. And this sleep fell upon the whole castle; the king and queen, who had returned and were in the great hall, fell fast asleep, and with them the whole court. The horses in their stalls, the dogs in the yard, the pigeons on the roof, the flies on the wall, the very fire that flickered on the hearth, became still, and slept like the rest; and the meat on the spit ceased roasting, and the cook, who was going to pull the scullion's hair for some mistake he had made, let him go, and went to sleep. And the wind ceased, and not a leaf fell from the trees about the castle.

Then round about that place there grew a hedge of thorns thicker every year, until at last the whole castle was hidden from view, and nothing of it could be seen but the vane on the roof. And a rumour went abroad in all that country of the beautiful sleeping Rosamond, for so was the princess called; and from time to time many kings' sons came and tried to force their way through the hedge; but it was impossible for them to do so, for the thorns held fast together like strong hands, and the young men were caught by them, and not being able to get free, there died a lamentable death.

Many a long year afterwards there came a king's son into that country, and heard an old man tell how there should be a castle standing behind the hedge of thorns, and that there a beautiful enchanted princess named Rosamond had slept for a hundred years, and with her the king and queen, and the whole court. The old man had been told by his grandfather that many king's sons had sought to pass the thorn-hedge, but had been caught and pierced by the thorns, and had died a miserable death. Then said the young man, "Nevertheless, I do not fear to try; I shall win through and see the lovely Rosamond." The good old man tried to dissuade him, but he would not listen to his words.

For now the hundred years were at an end, and the day had come when Rosamond should be awakened. When the prince drew near the hedge of thorns, it was changed into a hedge of beautiful large flowers, which parted and bent aside to let him pass, and then closed behind him in a thick hedge. When he reached the castle-yard, he saw the horses and brindled hunting-dogs lying asleep, and on the roof the pigeons were sitting with their heads under their wings. And when he came indoors, the flies on the wall were asleep, the cook in the kitchen had his hand uplifted to strike the scullion, and the kitchen-maid had the black fowl on her lap ready to pluck. Then he mounted higher, and saw in the hall the whole court lying asleep, and above them, on their thrones, slept the king and the queen. And still he went farther, and all was so quiet that he could hear his own breathing; and at last he came to the tower, and went up the winding stair, and opened the door of the little room where Rosamond lay. And when he saw her looking so lovely in her sleep, he could not turn away his eyes; and presently he stooped and kissed her, and she awaked, and opened her eyes, and looked very kindly on him. And she rose, and they went forth together, and the king and the queen and whole court waked up, and gazed on each other with great eyes of wonderment. And the horses in the yard got up and shook themselves, the hounds sprang up and wagged their tails, the pigeons on the roof drew their heads from under their wings, looked round, and flew into the field, the flies on the wall crept on a little farther, the kitchen fire leapt up and blazed, and cooked the meat, the joint on the spit began to roast, the cook gave the scullion such a box on the ear that he roared out, and the maid went on plucking the fowl.

Then the wedding of the Prince and Rosamond was held with all splendour, and they lived very happily together until their lives' end.

⸱KING⸱THRUSHBEARD⸱

A KING had a daughter who was beautiful beyond measure, but so proud and overbearing that none of her suitors were good enough for her; she not only refused one after the other, but made a laughing-stock of them. Once the king appointed a great feast, and bade all the marriageable men to it from far and near. And they were all put in rows, according to their rank and station; first came the kings, then the princes, the dukes, the earls, the barons, and lastly the noblemen. The princess was led in front of the rows, but she had a mocking epithet for each. One was too fat, "What a tub!" said she. Another too tall, "Long and lean is ill to be seen," said she. A third too short, "Fat and short, not fit to court," said she. A fourth was too pale, "A regular death's-head;" a fifth too red-faced, "A game-cock," she called him. The sixth was not well-made enough, "Green wood ill dried!" cried she. So every one had something against him, and she made especially merry over a good king who was very tall, and whose chin had grown a little peaked.

"Only look," cried she, laughing, "he has a chin like a thrush's beak."

And from that time they called him King Thrushbeard. But the old king, when he saw that his daughter mocked every one, and scorned all the assembled suitors, swore in his anger that she should have the first beggar that came to the door for a husband.

A few days afterwards came a travelling ballad-singer, and sang under the window in hopes of a small alms. When the king heard of it, he said that he must come in. And so the ballad-singer entered in his dirty tattered garments, and sang before the king and his daughter; when he had done, he asked for a small reward. But the king said,

"Thy song has so well pleased me, that I will give thee my daughter to wife."

The princess was horrified; but the king said,

"I took an oath to give you to the first beggar that came, and so it must be done."

There was no remedy. The priest was fetched, and she had to be married to the ballad-singer out of hand. When all was done, the king said,

"Now, as you are a beggar-wife, you can stay no longer in my castle, so off with you and your husband."

The beggar-man led her away, and she was obliged to go forth with him on foot. On the way they came to a great wood, and she asked,

"Oh, whose is this forest, so thick and so fine?"

He answered,

"It is King Thrushbeard's, and might have been thine."

And she cried,

"Oh, I was a silly young thing, I'm afeared;
Would I had taken that good King Thrushbeard!"

Then they passed through a meadow, and she asked,

"Oh, whose is this meadow, so green and so fine?"

He answered,

"It is King Thrushbeard's, and might have been thine."

And she cried,

"I was a silly young thing, I'm afeared,
Would I had taken that good King Thrushbeard!"

Then they passed through a great town, and she asked,

"Whose is this city, so great and so fine?"

He answered,

> " Oh, it is King Thrushbeard's, and might have been thine."

And she cried,

> " I was a silly young thing, I'm afeared,
> Would I had taken that good King Thrushbeard ! "

Then said the beggar-man,
" It does not please me to hear you always wishing for another husband ; am I not good enough for you ? "
At last they came to a very small house, and she said,

> " Oh dear me ! what poor little house do I see ?
> And whose, I would know, may the wretched hole be ? "

The man answered,
" That is my house and thine, where we must live together."
She had to stoop before she could go in at the door.
" Where are the servants ? " asked the king's daughter.
" What servants ? " answered the beggar-man, " what you want to have done you must do yourself.   Make a fire quick, and put on water, and cook me some food ; I am very tired."
But the king's daughter understood nothing about fire-making and cooking, and the beggar-man had to lend a hand himself in order to manage it at all.   And when they had eaten their poor fare, they went to bed ; but the man called up his wife very early in the morning, in order to clean the house.   For a few days they lived in this indifferent manner, until they came to the end of their store.
" Wife," said the man, " this will not do, stopping here and earning nothing ; you must make baskets."
So he went out and cut willows, and brought them home ; and she began to weave them, but the hard twigs wounded her tender hands.
" I see this will not do," said the man, " you had better try spinning."
So she sat her down and tried to spin, but the harsh thread cut her soft fingers, so that the blood flowed.
" Look now ! " said the man, " you are no good at any sort of work ; I made a bad bargain when I took you.   I must see

what I can do to make a trade of pots and earthen vessels;
you can sit in the market and offer them for sale."

"Oh dear!" thought she, "suppose while I am selling in
the market people belonging to my father's kingdom should
see me, how they would mock at me!"

But there was no help for it; she had to submit, or else
die of hunger.

The first day all went well; the people bought her wares
eagerly, because she was so beautiful, and gave her whatever
she asked, and some of them gave her the money and left the
pots after all behind them. And they lived on these earnings
as long as they lasted; and then the man bought a number of
new pots. So she seated herself in a corner of the market,
and stood the wares before her for sale. All at once a drunken
horse-soldier came plunging by, and rode straight into the
midst of her pots, breaking them into a thousand pieces. She
could do nothing for weeping.

"Oh dear, what will become of me," cried she; "what will
my husband say?" and she hastened home and told him her
misfortune.

"Who ever heard of such a thing as sitting in the corner
of the market with earthenware pots!" said the man; "now
leave off crying; I see you are not fit for any regular work. I
have been asking at your father's castle if they want a kitchen-
maid, and they say they don't mind taking you; at any rate
you will get your victuals free."

And the king's daughter became a kitchen-maid, to be at
the cook's beck and call, and to do the hardest work. In each
of her pockets she fastened a little pot, and brought home in
them whatever was left, and upon that she and her husband were
fed. It happened one day, when the wedding of the eldest prince
was celebrated, the poor woman went upstairs, and stood by the
parlour door to see what was going on. And when the place
was lighted up, and the company arrived, each person hand-
somer than the one before, and all was brilliancy and splendour,
she thought on her own fate with a sad heart, and bewailed her
former pride and haughtiness which had brought her so low,
and plunged her in so great poverty. And as the rich and
delicate dishes smelling so good were carried to and fro every
now and then, the servants would throw her a few fragments,

which she put in her pockets, intending to take home. And then the prince himself passed in clothed in silk and velvet with a gold chain round his neck. And when he saw the beautiful woman standing in the doorway, he seized her hand and urged her to dance with him, but she refused, all trembling, for she saw it was King Thrushbeard, who had come to court her, whom she had turned away with mocking. It was of no use her resisting, he drew her into the room; and all at once the band to which her pockets were fastened broke, and the pots fell out, and the soup ran about, and the fragments were scattered all round. And when the people saw that, there was great laughter and mocking, and she felt so ashamed, that she wished herself a thousand fathoms underground. She rushed to the door to fly from the place, when a man caught her just on the steps, and when she looked at him, it was King Thrushbeard again. He said to her in a kind tone,

"Do not be afraid, I and the beggar-man with whom you lived in the wretched little hut are one. For love of you I disguised myself, and it was I who broke your pots in the guise of a horse-soldier. I did all that to bring down your proud heart, and to punish your haughtiness, which caused you to mock at me." Then she wept bitterly, and said,

"I have done great wrong, and am not worthy to be your wife."

But he said,

"Take courage, the evil days are gone over; now let us keep our wedding-day."

Then came the ladies-in-waiting and put on her splendid clothing; and her father came, and the whole court, and wished her joy on her marriage with King Thrushbeard; and then the merry-making began in good earnest. I cannot help wishing that you and I could have been there too.

SNOW·WHITE·

"QUEEN·THOU·ART·OF·BEAUTY·RARE·
BUT·SNOW-WHITE·LIVING·IN·THE
WITH·THE·SEVEN·LITTLE·MEN· GLEN,
IS·A·THOUSAND·TIMES·MORE·
FAIR·"

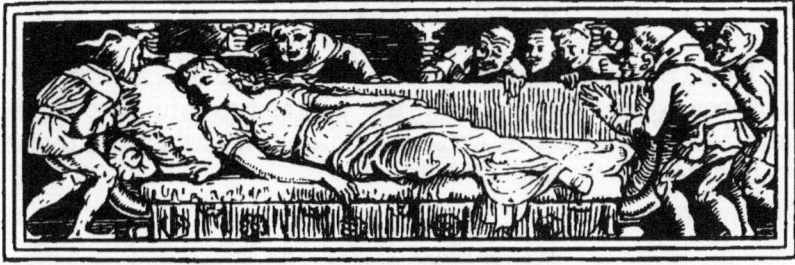

·SNOW-WHITE·

T was the middle of winter, and the snow-flakes were falling like feathers from the sky, and a queen sat at her window working, and her embroidery-frame was of ebony. And as she worked, gazing at times out on the snow, she pricked her finger, and there fell from it three drops of blood on the snow. And when she saw how bright and red it looked, she said to herself, "Oh that I had a child as white as snow, as red as blood, and as black as the wood of the embroidery frame!"

Not very long after she had a daughter, with a skin as white as snow, lips as red as blood, and hair as black as ebony, and she was named Snow-white. And when she was born the queen died.

After a year had gone by the king took another wife, a beautiful woman, but proud and overbearing, and she could not bear to be surpassed in beauty by any one. She had a magic looking-glass, and she used to stand before it, and look in it, and say,

> " Looking-glass upon the wall,
> Who is fairest of us all?"

And the looking-glass would answer,

> " You are fairest of them all."

And she was contented, for she knew that the looking-glass spoke the truth.

Now, Snow-white was growing prettier and prettier, and when she was seven years old she was as beautiful as day, far more so than the queen herself. So one day when the queen went to her mirror and said,

> " Looking-glass upon the wall,
> Who is fairest of us all ? "

It answered,

> " Queen, you are full fair, 'tis true,
> But Snow-white fairer is than you."

This gave the queen a great shock, and she became yellow and green with envy, and from that hour her heart turned against Snow-white, and she hated her. And envy and pride like ill weeds grew in her heart higher every day, until she had no peace day or night. At last she sent for a huntsman, and said,

"Take the child out into the woods, so that I may set eyes on her no more. You must put her to death, and bring me her heart for a token."

The huntsman consented, and led her away ; but when he drew his cutlass to pierce Snow-white's innocent heart, she began to weep, and to say,

"Oh, dear huntsman, do not take my life ; I will go away into the wild wood, and never come home again."

And as she was so lovely the huntsman had pity on her, and said,

"Away with you then, poor child ;" for he thought the wild animals would be sure to devour her, and it was as if a stone had been rolled away from his heart when he spared to put her to death. Just at that moment a young wild boar came running by, so he caught and killed it, and taking out its heart, he brought it to the queen for a token. And it was salted and cooked, and the wicked woman ate it up, thinking that there was an end of Snow-white.

Now, when the poor child found herself quite alone in the wild woods, she felt full of terror, even of the very leaves on the trees, and she did not know what to do for fright. Then she began to run over the sharp stones and through the thorn bushes, and the wild beasts after her, but they did her no harm.

She ran as long as her feet would carry her; and when the evening drew near she came to a little house, and she went inside to rest. Everything there was very small, but as pretty and clean as possible. There stood the little table ready laid, and covered with a white cloth, and seven little plates, and seven knives and forks, and drinking-cups. By the wall stood seven little beds, side by side, covered with clean white quilts. Snow-white, being very hungry and thirsty, ate from each plate a little porridge and bread, and drank out of each little cup a drop of wine, so as not to finish up one portion alone. After that she felt so tired that she lay down on one of the beds, but it did not seem to suit her; one was too long, another too short, but at last the seventh was quite right; and so she lay down upon it, committed herself to heaven, and fell asleep.

When it was quite dark, the masters of the house came home. They were seven dwarfs, whose occupation was to dig underground among the mountains. When they had lighted their seven candles, and it was quite light in the little house, they saw that some one must have been in, as everything was not in the same order in which they left it. The first said,

"Who has been sitting in my little chair?"

The second said,

"Who has been eating from my little plate?"

The third said,

"Who has been taking my little loaf?"

The fourth said,

"Who has been tasting my porridge?"

The fifth said,

"Who has been using my little fork?"

The sixth said,

"Who has been cutting with my little knife?"

The seventh said,

"Who has been drinking from my little cup?"

Then the first one, looking round, saw a hollow in his bed, and cried,

"Who has been lying on my bed?"

And the others came running, and cried,

"Some one has been on our beds too!"

But when the seventh looked at his bed, he saw little Snow-white lying there asleep. Then he told the others, who

came running up, crying out in their astonishment, and holding
up their seven little candles to throw a light upon Snow-white.

"O goodness! O gracious!" cried they, "what beautiful
child is this?" and were so full of joy to see her that they
did not wake her, but let her sleep on. And the seventh
dwarf slept with his comrades, an hour at a time with each,
until the night had passed.

When it was morning, and Snow-white awoke and saw the
seven dwarfs, she was very frightened; but they seemed quite
friendly, and asked her what her name was, and she told them;
and then they asked how she came to be in their house.
And she related to them how her step-mother had wished her
to be put to death, and how the huntsman had spared her life,
and how she had run the whole day long, until at last she had
found their little house. Then the dwarfs said,

"If you will keep our house for us, and cook, and wash,
and make the beds, and sew and knit, and keep everything tidy
and clean, you may stay with us, and you shall lack nothing."

"With all my heart," said Snow-white; and so she stayed,
and kept the house in good order. In the morning the dwarfs
went to the mountain to dig for gold; in the evening they
came home, and their supper had to be ready for them. All
the day long the maiden was left alone, and the good little
dwarfs warned her, saying,

"Beware of your step-mother, she will soon know you are
here. Let no one into the house."

Now the queen, having eaten Snow-white's heart, as she
supposed, felt quite sure that now she was the first and fairest,
and so she came to her mirror, and said,

> " Looking-glass upon the wall,
> Who is fairest of us all?"

And the glass answered,

> " Queen, thou art of beauty rare,
> But Snow-white living in the glen
> With the seven little men
> Is a thousand times more fair."

Then she was very angry, for the glass always spoke the
truth, and she knew that the huntsman must have deceived

her, and that Snow-white must still be living.   And she thought
and thought how she could manage to make an end of her,
for as long as she was not the fairest in the land, envy left her
no rest.   At last she thought of a plan ; she painted her face
and dressed herself like an old pedlar woman, so that no one
would have known her.   In this disguise she went across the
seven mountains, until she came to the house of the seven
little dwarfs, and she knocked at the door and cried,

"Fine wares to sell ! fine wares to sell !"

Snow-white peeped out of the window and cried,

"Good-day, good woman, what have you to sell ? "

"Good wares, fine wares," answered she, "laces of all
colours ;" and she held up a piece that was woven of variegated
silk.

"I need not be afraid of letting in this good woman,"
thought Snow-white, and she unbarred the door and bought
the pretty lace.

"What a figure you are, child !" said the old woman,
" come and let me lace you properly for once."

Snow-white, suspecting nothing, stood up before her, and
let her lace her with the new lace ; but the old woman laced
so quick and tight that it took Snow-white's breath away, and
she fell down as dead.

"Now you have done with being the fairest," said the old
woman as she hastened away.

Not long after that, towards evening, the seven dwarfs came
home, and were terrified to see their dear Snow-white lying
on the ground, without life or motion ; they raised her up,
and when they saw how tightly she was laced they cut the
lace in two ; then she began to draw breath, and little by little
she returned to life.   When the dwarfs heard what had
happened they said,

"The old pedlar woman was no other than the wicked
queen ; you must beware of letting any one in when we are
not here ! "

And when the wicked woman got home she went to her
glass and said,

> " Looking-glass against the wall,
> Who is fairest of us all ?"

And it answered as before,

> " Queen, thou art of beauty rare,
> But Snow-white living in the glen
> With the seven little men
> Is a thousand times more fair."

When she heard that she was so struck with surprise that all the blood left her heart, for she knew that Snow-white must still be living.

"But now," said she, "I will think of something that will be her ruin." And by witchcraft she made a poisoned comb. Then she dressed herself up to look like another different sort of old woman. So she went across the seven mountains and came to the house of the seven dwarfs, and knocked at the door and cried,

"Good wares to sell! good wares to sell!"

Snow-white looked out and said,

"Go away, I must not let anybody in."

"But you are not forbidden to look," said the old woman, taking out the poisoned comb and holding it up. It pleased the poor child so much that she was tempted to open the door; and when the bargain was made the old woman said,

"Now, for once your hair shall be properly combed."

Poor Snow-white, thinking no harm, let the old woman do as she would, but no sooner was the comb put in her hair than the poison began to work, and the poor girl fell down senseless.

"Now, you paragon of beauty," said the wicked woman, "this is the end of you," and went off. By good luck it was now near evening, and the seven little dwarfs came home. When they saw Snow-white lying on the ground as dead, they thought directly that it was the step-mother's doing, and looked about, found the poisoned comb, and no sooner had they drawn it out of her hair than Snow-white came to herself, and related all that had passed. Then they warned her once more to be on her guard, and never again to let any one in at the door.

And the queen went home and stood before the looking-glass and said,

> " Looking-glass against the wall,
> Who is fairest of us all?"

And the looking-glass answered as before,

> " Queen, thou art of beauty rare,
> But Snow-white living in the glen
> With the seven little men
> Is a thousand times more fair."

When she heard the looking-glass speak thus she trembled and shook with anger.

"Snow-white shall die," cried she, "though it should cost me my own life!" And then she went to a secret lonely chamber, where no one was likely to come, and there she made a poisonous apple. It was beautiful to look upon, being white with red cheeks, so that any one who should see it must long for it, but whoever ate even a little bit of it must die. When the apple was ready she painted her face and clothed herself like a peasant woman, and went across the seven mountains to where the seven dwarfs lived. And when she knocked at the door Snow-white put her head out of the window and said,

"I dare not let anybody in; the seven dwarfs told me not."

"All right," answered the woman; "I can easily get rid of my apples elsewhere. There, I will give you one."

"No," answered Snow-white, "I dare not take anything."

"Are you afraid of poison?" said the woman, "look here, I will cut the apple in two pieces; you shall have the red side, I will have the white one."

For the apple was so cunningly made, that all the poison was in the rosy half of it. Snow-white longed for the beautiful apple, and as she saw the peasant woman eating a piece of it she could no longer refrain, but stretched out her hand and took the poisoned half. But no sooner had she taken a morsel of it into her mouth than she fell to the earth as dead. And the queen, casting on her a terrible glance, laughed aloud and cried,

"As white as snow, as red as blood, as black as ebony! this time the dwarfs will not be able to bring you to life again."

And when she went home and asked the looking-glass,

> " Looking-glass against the wall,
> Who is fairest of us all?"

at last it answered,

"You are the fairest now of all."

Then her envious heart had peace, as much as an envious heart can have.

The dwarfs, when they came home in the evening, found Snow-white lying on the ground, and there came no breath out of her mouth, and she was dead. They lifted her up, sought if anything poisonous was to be found, cut her laces, combed her hair, washed her with water and wine, but all was of no avail, the poor child was dead, and remained dead. Then they laid her on a bier, and sat all seven of them round it, and wept and lamented three whole days. And then they would have buried her, but that she looked still as if she were living, with her beautiful blooming cheeks. So they said,

"We cannot hide her away in the black ground." And they had made a coffin of clear glass, so as to be looked into from all sides, and they laid her in it, and wrote in golden letters upon it her name, and that she was a king's daughter. Then they set the coffin out upon the mountain, and one of them always remained by it to watch. And the birds came too, and mourned for Snow-white, first an owl, then a raven, and lastly, a dove.

Now, for a long while Snow-white lay in the coffin and never changed, but looked as if she were asleep, for she was still as white as snow, as red as blood, and her hair was as black as ebony. It happened, however, that one day a king's son rode through the wood and up to the dwarfs' house, which was near it. He saw on the mountain the coffin, and beautiful Snow-white within it, and he read what was written in golden letters upon it. Then he said to the dwarfs,

"Let me have the coffin, and I will give you whatever you like to ask for it."

But the dwarfs told him that they could not part with it for all the gold in the world. But he said,

"I beseech you to give it me, for I cannot live without looking upon Snow-white; if you consent I will bring you to great honour, and care for you as if you were my brethren."

When he so spoke the good little dwarfs had pity upon him and gave him the coffin, and the king's son called his servants and bid them carry it away on their shoulders. Now it happened that as they were going along they stumbled over a bush, and with the shaking the bit of poisoned apple flew out of her throat. It was not long before she opened her eyes, threw up the cover of the coffin, and sat up, alive and well.

"Oh dear! where am I?" cried she. The king's son answered, full of joy, "You are near me," and, relating all that had happened, he said,

"I would rather have you than anything in the world; come with me to my father's castle and you shall be my bride."

And Snow-white was kind, and went with him, and their wedding was held with pomp and great splendour.

But Snow-white's wicked step-mother was also bidden to the feast, and when she had dressed herself in beautiful clothes she went to her looking-glass and said,

> " Looking-glass upon the wall,
> Who is fairest of us all?"

The looking-glass answered,

> " O Queen, although you are of beauty rare,
> The young bride is a thousand times more fair."

Then she railed and cursed, and was beside herself with disappointment and anger. First she thought she would not go to the wedding; but then she felt she should have no peace until she went and saw the bride. And when she saw her she knew her for Snow-white, and could not stir from the place for anger and terror. For they had ready red-hot iron shoes, in which she had to dance until she fell down dead.

The KNAPSACK, the HAT, and the HORN

NCE there were three brothers, and they grew poorer and poorer, until at last their need was so great that they had nothing left to bite or to break. Then they said, "This will not do; we had better go out into the world and seek our fortune."

So they set out, and went some distance through many green fields, but they met with no good fortune. One day they came to a great wood, in the midst of which was a hill, and when they came near to it, they saw that it was all of silver. Then said the eldest,

"Now here is good fortune enough for me, and I desire no better."

And he took of the silver as much as he could carry, turned round, and went back home. But the other two said,

"We must have something better than mere silver," and they would not touch it, but went on farther. After they had gone on a few days longer, they came to a hill that was all of gold. The second brother stood still and considered, and was uncertain.

"What shall I do?" said he; "shall I take of the gold enough to last me my life, or shall I go farther?"

At last, coming to a conclusion, he filled his pockets as full as they would hold, bid good-bye to his brother, and went home. But the third brother said to himself,

"Silver and gold do not tempt me; I will not gainsay fortune, who has better things in store for me."

So he went on, and when he had journeyed for three days, he came to a wood still greater than the former ones, so that there was no end to it; and in it he found nothing to eat or to drink, so that he was nearly starving. He got up into a high tree, so as to see how far the wood reached, but as far as his eyes could see, there was nothing but the tops of the trees. And as he got down from the tree, hunger pressed him sore, and he thought,

"Oh that for once I could have a good meal!"

And when he reached the ground he saw to his surprise a table beneath the tree richly spread with food, and that smoked before him.

"This time at least," said he, "I have my wish," and without stopping to ask who had brought the meal there, and who had cooked it, he came close to the table and ate with relish, until his hunger was appeased. When he had finished, he thought,

"It would be a pity to leave such a good table-cloth behind in the wood," so he folded it up neatly and pocketed it. Then he walked on, and in the evening, when hunger again seized him, he thought he would put the table-cloth to the proof, and he brought it out and said,

"Now I desire that thou shouldst be spread with a good meal," and no sooner were the words out of his mouth, than there stood on it as many dishes of delicious food as there was room for.

"Now that I see," said he, "what sort of a cook thou art, I hold thee dearer than the mountains of silver and of gold," for he perceived that it was a wishing-cloth. Still he was not satisfied to settle down at home with only a wishing-cloth, so he determined to wander farther through the world and seek his fortune. One evening, in a lonely wood, he came upon a begrimed charcoal-burner at his furnace, who had put some potatoes to roast for his supper.

"Good evening, my black fellow," said he, "how do you get on in this lonely spot?"

"One day is like another," answered the charcoal-burner;

"every evening I have potatoes; have you a mind to be my guest?"

"Many thanks," answered the traveller, "I will not deprive you; you did not expect a guest; but if you do not object, you shall be the one to be invited."

"How can that be managed?" said the charcoal-burner; "I see that you have nothing with you, and if you were to walk two hours in any direction, you would meet with no one to give you anything."

"For all that," answered he, "there shall be a feast so good, that you have never tasted the like."

Then he took out the table-cloth from his knapsack, and spreading it on the ground, said,

"Cloth, be covered," and immediately there appeared boiled and roast meat, quite hot, as if it had just come from the kitchen. The charcoal-burner stared, but did not stay to be asked twice, and fell to, filling his black mouth with ever bigger and bigger pieces. When they had finished eating, the charcoal-burner smiled, and said,

"Look here, I approve of your table-cloth; it would not be a bad thing for me to have here in the wood, where the cooking is not first-rate. I will strike a bargain with you. There hangs a soldier's knapsack in the corner, which looks old and unsightly, but it has wonderful qualities; as I have no further occasion for it, I will give it to you in exchange for the table-cloth."

"First, I must know what these wonderful qualities are," returned the other.

"I will tell you," answered the charcoal-burner; "if you strike it with your hand, there will appear a corporal and six men with swords and muskets, and whatever you wish to have done, that will they do."

"Well, for my part," said the other, "I am quite willing to make the exchange." And he gave the table-cloth to the charcoal-burner, took down the knapsack from its hook, slung it over his shoulder, and took his leave. Before he had gone far he began to want to make a trial of his wonderful knapsack, so he struck it a blow. At once seven soldiers appeared before him, and the corporal said,

"What does my lord and master please to want?"

"March in haste to the charcoal-burner and demand my wishing-cloth back," said the man.   They wheeled round to the left, and were not long before they had accomplished his desire, and taken away, without wasting many words, the wishing-cloth from the charcoal-burner.   Having dismissed them, he wandered on, expecting still more wonderful luck. About sunset he fell in with another charcoal-burner, who was getting his supper ready at the fire.

"Will you join me?" said this black fellow; "potatoes and salt, without butter; sit down to it with me."

"No," answered he, "this time you shall be my guest." And he spread out his table-cloth, and it was directly covered with the most delicious victuals.   So they ate and drank together and were merry.   After the meal was over the charcoal-burner said,

"Over there, on the bench, lies an old worn-out hat, which has wonderful properties: if you put it on and draw it well over your head it is as if a dozen field-pieces went off, one after the other, shooting everything down, so that no one can stand against them.   This hat is of no use to me, and I will give it to you in exchange for the table-cloth."

"All right," answered the other, taking the hat and carrying it off, and leaving the table-cloth behind him.   Before he had gone far he struck upon the knapsack, and summoned his soldiers to fetch back the table-cloth again.

"First one thing, and then another," thought he, "just as if my luck were never to end."   And so it seemed, for at the end of another day's journey he came up to another charcoal-burner, who was roasting his potatoes just like the others. He invited him to eat with him off his wishing-cloth, to which the charcoal-burner took such a fancy, that he gave him for it a horn, which had different properties still from the hat.   If a man blew on it down fell all walls and fortresses, and finally towns and villages in heaps.   So the man gave the table-cloth in exchange for it to the charcoal-burner, afterwards sending his men to fetch it back, so that at last he had in his possession knapsack, hat, and horn, all at one time.

"Now," said he, "I am a made man, and it is time to go home again and see how my brothers are faring."

When he reached home he found that his brothers had

built themselves a fine house with their silver and gold, and
lived in clover. He went to see them, but because he wore a
half-worn-out coat, a shabby hat, and the old knapsack on his
back, they would not recognise him as their brother. They
mocked him and said,

" It is of no use your giving yourself out to be our brother
he who scorned silver and gold, seeking for better fortune
will return in great splendour, as a mighty king, not as a
beggar-man." And they drove him from their door. Then
he flew into a great rage, and struck upon his knapsack until
a hundred and fifty men stood before him, rank and file. He
ordered them to surround his brothers' house, and that two of
them should take hazel-rods, and should beat the brothers
until they knew who he was. And there arose a terrible noise
the people ran together and wished to rescue the brothers in
their extremity, but they could do nothing against the soldiers
It happened at last that the king of the country heard of it
and he was indignant, and sent a captain with his troops to
drive the disturber of the peace out of the town : but the man
with his knapsack soon assembled a greater company, who
beat back the captain and his people, sending them off with
bleeding noses. Then the king said,

" This vagabond fellow must be put down," and he sent
the next day a larger company against him, but they could do
nothing : for he assembled more men than ever, and in order
to bring them more quickly, he pulled his hat twice lower
over his brows ; then the heavy guns came into play, and the
king's people were beaten and put to flight.

" Now," said he, " I shall not make peace until the king
gives me his daughter to wife, and lets me rule the whole
kingdom in his name."

This he caused to be told to the king, who said to his
daughter,

" This is a hard nut to crack ; there is no choice but for
me to do as he asks ; if I wish to have peace and keep the
crown on my head, I must give in to him."

So the wedding took place, but the king's daughter was
angry that the bridegroom should be a common man, who
wore a shabby hat, and carried an old knapsack. She wished
very much to get rid of him, and thought day and night how

to manage it.   Then it struck her that perhaps all his wonder-working power lay in the knapsack, and she pretended to be very fond of him, and when she had brought him into a good humour she said,—"Pray lay aside that ugly knapsack; it misbecomes you so much that I feel ashamed of you."

"My dear child," answered he, "this knapsack is my greatest treasure; so long as I keep it I need not fear anything in the whole world," and then he showed her with what wonderful qualities it was endowed.   Then she fell on his neck as if she would have kissed him, but, by a clever trick, she slipped the knapsack over his shoulder and ran away with it.   As soon as she was alone she struck upon it and summoned the soldiers, and bade them seize her husband and bring him to the king's palace.   They obeyed, and the false woman had many more to follow behind, so as to be ready to drive him out of the country.   He would have been quite done for if he had not still kept the hat.   As soon as he could get his hands free he pulled it twice forward on his head; and then the cannon began to thunder and beat all down, till at last the king's daughter had to come and to beg pardon. And as she so movingly prayed and promised to behave better, he raised her up and made peace with her.   Then she grew very kind to him, and seemed to love him very much, and he grew so deluded, that one day he confided to her that even if he were deprived of his knapsack nothing could be done against him as long as he should keep the old hat.   And when she knew the secret she waited until he had gone to sleep; then she carried off the hat, and had him driven out into the streets.   Still the horn remained to him, and in great wrath he blew a great blast upon it, and down came walls and fortresses, towns and villages, and buried the king and his daughter among their ruins.   If he had not set down the horn when he did, and if he had blown a little longer, all the houses would have tumbled down, and there would not have been left one stone upon another.   After this no one dared to withstand him, and he made himself king over the whole country.

⁕RUMPELSTILTSKIN⁕

HERE was once a miller who was poor, but he had one beautiful daughter. It happened one day that he came to speak with the king, and, to give himself consequence, he told him that he had a daughter who could spin gold out of straw. The king said to the miller,

"That is an art that pleases me well; if thy daughter is as clever as you say, bring her to my castle to-morrow, that I may put her to the proof."

When the girl was brought to him, he led her into a room that was quite full of straw, and gave her a wheel and spindle, and said,

"Now set to work, and if by the early morning thou hast not spun this straw to gold thou shalt die." And he shut the door himself, and left her there alone.

And so the poor miller's daughter was left there sitting, and could not think what to do for her life: she had no notion how to set to work to spin gold from straw, and her distress grew so great that she began to weep. Then all at once the door opened, and in came a little man, who said,

"Good evening, miller's daughter; why are you crying?"

"Oh!" answered the girl, "I have got to spin gold out of straw, and I don't understand the business."

Then the little man said,

"What will you give me if I spin it for you?"

"My necklace," said the girl.

The little man took the necklace, seated himself before

the wheel, and whirr, whirr, whirr! three times round and the bobbin was full; then he took up another, and whirr, whirr, whirr! three times round, and that was full; and so he went on till the morning, when all the straw had been spun, and all the bobbins were full of gold. At sunrise came the king, and when he saw the gold he was astonished and very much rejoiced, for he was very avaricious. He had the miller's daughter taken into another room filled with straw, much bigger than the last, and told her that as she valued her life she must spin it all in one night. The girl did not know what to do, so she began to cry, and then the door opened, and the little man appeared and said,

"What will you give me if I spin all this straw into gold?"

"The ring from my finger," answered the girl.

So the little man took the ring, and began again to send the wheel whirring round, and by the next morning all the straw was spun into glistening gold. The king was rejoiced beyond measure at the sight, but as he could never have enough of gold, he had the miller's daughter taken into a still larger room full of straw, and said,

"This, too, must be spun in one night, and if you accomplish it you shall be my wife." For he thought, "Although she is but a miller's daughter, I am not likely to find any one richer in the whole world."

As soon as the girl was left alone, the little man appeared for the third time and said,

"What will you give me if I spin the straw for you this time?"

"I have nothing left to give," answered the girl.

"Then you must promise me the first child you have after you are queen," said the little man.

"But who knows whether that will happen?" thought the girl; but as she did not know what else to do in her necessity, she promised the little man what he desired, upon which he began to spin, until all the straw was gold. And when in the morning the king came and found all done according to his wish, he caused the wedding to be held at once, and the miller's pretty daughter became a queen.

In a year's time she brought a fine child into the world,

and thought no more of the little man ; but one day he came
suddenly into her room, and said,

"Now give me what you promised me."

The queen was terrified greatly, and offered the little man
all the riches of the kingdom if he would only leave the child ;
but the little man said,

"No, I would rather have something living than all the
treasures of the world."

Then the queen began to lament and to weep, so that
the little man had pity upon her.

"I will give you three days," said he, "and if at the end
of that time you cannot tell my name, you must give up the
child to me."

Then the queen spent the whole night in thinking over all
the names that she had ever heard, and sent a messenger through
the land to ask far and wide for all the names that could be
found.   And when the little man came next day, (beginning
with Caspar, Melchior, Balthazar) she repeated all she knew,
and went through the whole list, but after each the little man
said,

"That is not my name."

The second day the queen sent to inquire of all the
neighbours what the servants were called, and told the little
man all the most unusual and singular names, saying,

"Perhaps you are called Roast-ribs, or Sheepshanks, or
Spindleshanks?"   But he answered nothing but

"That is not my name."

The third day the messenger came back again, and said,

"I have not been able to find one single new name ; but
as I passed through the woods I came to a high hill, and near
it was a little house, and before the house burned a fire, and
round the fire danced a comical little man, and he hopped on
one leg and cried,

> "To-day do I bake, to-morrow I brew,
>   The day after that the queen's child comes in ;
>   And oh ! I am glad that nobody knew
>   That the name I am called is Rumpelstiltskin !"

You cannot think how pleased the queen was to hear that
name, and soon afterwards, when the little man walked in and

said, " Now, Mrs. Queen, what is my name?" she said at first,

" Are you called Jack?"

" No," answered he.

" Are you called Harry?" she asked again.

" No," answered he. And then she said,

" Then perhaps your name is Rumpelstiltskin!"

" The devil told you that! the devil told you that!" cried the little man, and in his anger he stamped with his right foot so hard that it went into the ground above his knee; then he seized his left foot with both his hands in such a fury that he split in two, and there was an end of him.

✣ ROLAND ✣

HERE was once a woman who was a witch, and she had two daughters, one ugly and wicked, whom she loved the best, because she was her very own daughter, and one pretty and good, whom she hated because she was her step-daughter. One day the step-daughter put on a pretty apron, which the other daughter liked so much that she became envious, and said to her mother that she must and should have the apron.

"Be content, my child," said the old woman, "thou shalt have it. Thy step-sister has long deserved death, and to-night, while she is asleep, I shall come and cut off her head. Take care to lie at the farthest side of the bed, and push her to the outside."

And it would have been all over with the poor girl, if she had not been standing in a corner near and heard it all. She did not dare to go outside the door the whole day long, and when bed-time came the other one got into bed first, so as to lie on the farthest side; but when she had gone to sleep, the step-daughter pushed her towards the outside, and took the inside place next the wall. In the night the old woman came sneaking; in her right hand she held an axe, and with her left she felt for the one who was lying outside, and then she heaved up the axe with both hands, and hewed the head off her only daughter.

When she had gone away, the other girl got up and went

to her sweetheart's, who was called Roland, and knocked at his door.   When he came to her, she said,

"Listen, dear Roland, we must flee away in all haste ; my step-mother meant to put me to death, but she has killed her only child instead.   When the day breaks, and she sees what she has done, we are lost."

"But I advise you," said Roland, "to bring away her magic wand with you ; otherwise we cannot escape her when she comes after to overtake us."   So the maiden fetched the magic wand, and she took up the head of her step-sister and let drop three drops of blood on the ground,—one by the bed, one in the kitchen, and one on the steps.   Then she hastened back to her sweetheart.

When the old witch got up in the morning, she called out to her daughter, to give her the apron, but no daughter came. Then she cried out, "Where art thou?"

"Here, at the steps, sweeping!" answered one of the drops of blood.

The old woman went out, but she saw nobody at the steps, and cried again, "Where art thou?"

"Here in the kitchen warming myself," cried the second drop of blood.

So she went into the kitchen and found no one.   Then she cried again, "Where art thou?"

"Oh, here in bed fast asleep!" cried the third drop of blood.

Then the mother went into the room, and up to the bed, and there lay her only child, whose head she had cut off herself. The witch fell into a great fury, rushed to the window, for from it she could see far and wide, and she caught sight of her step-daughter, hastening away with her dear Roland.

"It will be no good to you," cried she, "if you get ever so far away, you cannot escape me."   Then she put on her boots, which took her an hour's walk at every stride, and it was not long before she had overtaken them.   But the maiden, when she saw the old woman striding up, changed, by means of the magic wand, her dear Roland into a lake, and herself into a duck swimming upon it.   The witch stood on the bank and threw in crumbs of bread, and took great pains to decoy the duck towards her, but the duck would not be de-

coyed, and the old woman was obliged to go back in the evening disappointed.   Then the maiden and her dear Roland
took again their natural shapes, and travelled on the whole
night through until daybreak.   Then the maiden changed
herself into a beautiful flower, standing in the middle of a
hedge of thorns, and her dear Roland into a fiddle-player.   It
was not long before the witch came striding up, and she said
to the musician,

"Dear musician, will you be so kind as to reach that
pretty flower for me?"

"Oh yes," said he, "I will strike up a tune to it."

Then as she crept quickly up to the hedge to break off the
flower, for she knew well who it was, he began to play, and
whether she liked it or not, she was obliged to dance, for there
was magic in the tune.   The faster he played the higher she
had to jump, and the thorns tore her clothes, and scratched
and wounded her, and he did not cease playing until she was
spent, and lay dead.

So now they were saved, and Roland said,

"I will go to my father and prepare for the wedding."

"And I will stay here," said the maiden, "and wait for
you, and so that no one should know me, I will change myself
into a red milestone."   So away went Roland, and the maiden
in the likeness of a stone waited in the field for her beloved.

But when Roland went home he fell into the snares of
another maiden, who wrought so, that he forgot his first love.

And the poor girl waited a long time, but at last, seeing
that he did not come, she was filled with despair, and changed
herself into a flower, thinking "Perhaps some one in passing
will put his foot upon me and crush me."

But it happened that a shepherd, tending his flock, saw
the flower, and as it was so beautiful, he gathered it, took it
home with him, and put it in his chest.   From that time
everything went wonderfully well in the shepherd's house.
When he got up in the morning, all the work was already
done; the room was swept, the tables and benches rubbed,
fire kindled on the hearth, and water ready drawn; and when
he came home in the middle of the day, the table was laid,
and a good meal spread upon it.   He could not understand
how it was done, for he never saw anybody in his house, and

it was too little for anybody to hide in. The good serving pleased him well; but in the end he became uneasy, and went to a wise woman to take counsel of her. The wise woman said,

"There is magic in it: get up early some morning, and if you hear something moving in the room, be it what it may, throw a white cloth over it, and the charm will be broken."

The shepherd did as she told him, and the next morning at daybreak he saw the chest open, and the flower come out. Then he jumped up quickly and threw a white cloth over it. So the spell was broken, and a lovely maiden stood before him; and she told him that she had been the flower, and had until now cared for his household matters. She told him all that had happened to her, and she pleased him so much that he asked her to marry him, but she answered "No," because she still remained true to her dear Roland, though he had forsaken her; but she promised not to leave the shepherd, but to go on taking care of his house.

Now the time came when Roland's wedding was to be held; and there was an old custom in that country that all the girls should be present, and should sing in honour of the bride and bridegroom. The faithful maiden, when she knew this, was so sorrowful that she felt as if her heart would break; and she would not go, until the others came and fetched her. And when her turn came to sing she slipped behind, so that she stood alone, and so began to sing: and as soon as her song reached Roland's ear he sprang up and cried,

"I know that voice! that is the right bride, and no other will I have." And everything that he had forgotten, and that had been swept out of his mind, came suddenly home to him in his heart. And the faithful maiden was married to her dear Roland; her sorrow came to an end and her joy began.

~ THE·GOLDEN·BIRD ~

IN times gone by there was a king who had at the back of his castle a beautiful pleasure-garden, in which stood a tree that bore golden apples. As the apples ripened they were counted, but one morning one was missing. Then the king was angry, and he ordered that watch should be kept about the tree every night. Now the king had three sons, and he sent the eldest to spend the whole night in the garden; so he watched till midnight, and then he could keep off sleep no longer, and in the morning another apple was missing. The second son had to watch the following night; but it fared no better, for when twelve o'clock had struck he went to sleep, and in the morning another apple was missing. Now came the turn of the third son to watch, and he was ready to do so; but the king had less trust in him, and believed he would acquit himself still worse than his brothers, but in the end he consented to let him try. So the young man lay down under the tree to watch, and resolved that sleep should not be master. When it struck twelve something came rushing through the air, and he saw in the moonlight a bird flying towards him, whose feathers glittered like gold. The bird perched upon the tree, and had already pecked off an apple, when the young man let fly an arrow at it. The bird flew away, but the arrow had struck its plumage, and one of its golden feathers fell to the ground: the young man picked it up, and taking it next morning to the king, told him what had happened in the night. The king

THE
GOLDEN-BIRD

"—THE FOX SAID,
NOW WHAT WILL YOU GIVE ME
FOR MY REWARD?"

called his council together, and all declared that such a feather was worth more than the whole kingdom.

"Since the feather is so valuable," said the king, "one is not enough for me ; I must and will have the whole bird."

So the eldest son set off, and relying on his own cleverness he thought he should soon find the golden bird. When he had gone some distance he saw a fox sitting at the edge of a wood, and he pointed his gun at him. The fox cried out,

"Do not shoot me, and I will give you good counsel. You are on your way to find the golden bird, and this evening you will come to a village, in which two taverns stand facing each other. One will be brightly lighted up, and there will be plenty of merriment going on inside ; do not mind about that, but go into the other one, although it will look to you very uninviting."

"How can a silly beast give one any rational advice?" thought the king's son, and let fly at the fox, but missed him, and he stretched out his tail and ran quick into the wood. Then the young man went on his way, and towards evening he came to the village, and there stood the two taverns ; in one singing and dancing was going on, the other looked quite dull and wretched. "I should be a fool," said he, "to go into that dismal place, while there is anything so good close by." So he went into the merry inn, and there lived in clover, quite forgetting the bird and his father, and all good counsel.

As time went on, and the eldest son never came home, the second son set out to seek the golden bird. He met with the fox, just as the eldest did, and received good advice from him without attending to it. And when he came to the two taverns, his brother was standing and calling to him at the window of one of them, out of which came sounds of merriment ; so he could not resist, but went in and revelled to his heart's content.

And then, as time went on, the youngest son wished to go forth, and to try his luck, but his father would not consent.

"It would be useless," said he ; "he is much less likely to find the bird than his brothers, and if any misfortune were to happen to him he would not know how to help himself ; his wits are none of the best."

But at last, as there was no peace to be had, he let him go. By the side of the wood sat the fox, begged him to spare his life, and gave him good counsel. The young man was kind, and said,

" Be easy, little fox, I will do you no harm."

"You shall not repent of it," answered the fox, "and that you may get there all the sooner, get up and sit on my tail."

And no sooner had he done so than the fox began to run, and off they went over stock and stone, so that the wind whistled in their hair. When they reached the village the young man got down, and, following the fox's advice, went into the mean-looking tavern, without hesitating, and there he passed a quiet night. The next morning, when he went out into the field, the fox, who was sitting there already, said,

" I will tell you further what you have to do. Go straight on until you come to a castle, before which a great band of soldiers lie, but do not trouble yourself about them, for they will be all asleep and snoring ; pass through them and forward into the castle, and go through all the rooms, until you come to one where there is a golden bird hanging in a wooden cage. Near at hand will stand empty a golden cage of state, but you must beware of taking the bird out of his ugly cage and putting him into the fine one ; if you do so you will come to harm."

After he had finished saying this the fox stretched out his tail again, and the king's son sat him down upon it ; then away they went over stock and stone, so that the wind whistled through their hair. And when the king's son reached the castle he found everything as the fox had said : and he at last entered the room where the golden bird was hanging in a wooden cage, while a golden one was standing by ; the three golden apples too were in the room. Then, thinking it foolish to let the beautiful bird stay in that mean and ugly cage, he opened the door of it, took hold of it, and put it in the golden one. In the same moment the bird uttered a piercing cry. The soldiers awaked, rushed in, seized the king's son and put him in prison. The next morning he was brought before a judge, and, as he confessed everything, condemned to death. But the king said he would spare his life on one condition, that he should bring him the golden horse whose paces were swifter than the wind, and that then he should also receive the golden bird as a reward.

So the king's son set off to find the golden horse, but he sighed, and was very sad, for how should it be accomplished? And then he saw his old friend the fox sitting by the roadside.

"Now, you see," said the fox, "all this has happened, because you would not listen to me. But be of good courage, I will bring you through, and will tell you how you are to get the golden horse. You must go straight on until you come to a castle, where the horse stands in his stable; before the stable-door the grooms will be lying, but they will all be asleep and snoring; and you can go and quietly lead out the horse. But one thing you must mind—take care to put upon him the plain saddle of wood and leather, and not the golden one, which will hang close by; otherwise it will go badly with you."

Then the fox stretched out his tail, and the king's son seated himself upon it, and away they went over stock and stone until the wind whistled through their hair. And everything happened just as the fox had said, and he came to the stall where the golden horse was : and as he was about to put on him the plain saddle, he thought to himself,

"Such a beautiful animal would be disgraced were I not to put on him the good saddle, which becomes him so well." However, no sooner did the horse feel the golden saddle touch him than he began to neigh. And the grooms all awoke, seized the king's son and threw him into prison. The next morning he was delivered up to justice and condemned to death, but the king promised him his life, and also to bestow upon him the golden horse, if he could convey thither the beautiful princess of the golden castle.

With a heavy heart the king's son set out, but by great good luck he soon met with the faithful fox.

"I ought now to leave you to your own ill-luck," said the fox, "but I am sorry for you, and will once more help you in your need. Your way lies straight up to the golden castle : you will arrive there in the evening, and at night, when all is quiet, the beautiful princess goes to the bath. And as she is entering the bathing-house, go up to her and give her a kiss, then she will follow you, and you can lead her away; but do not suffer her first to go and take leave of her parents, or it will go ill with you."

Then the fox stretched out his tail; the king's son seated himself upon it, and away they went over stock and stone, so that the wind whistled through their hair. And when he came to the golden castle all was as the fox had said. He waited until midnight, when all lay in deep sleep, and then as the beautiful princess went to the bathing-house he went up to her and gave her a kiss, and she willingly promised to go with him, but she begged him earnestly, and with tears, that he would let her first go and take leave of her parents. At first he denied her prayer, but as she wept so much the more, and fell at his feet, he gave in at last. And no sooner had the princess reached her father's bedside than he, and all who were in the castle, waked up, and the young man was seized and thrown into prison.

The next morning the king said to him,

"Thy life is forfeit, but thou shalt find grace if thou canst level that mountain that lies before my windows, and over which I am not able to see: and if this is done within eight days thou shalt have my daughter for a reward."

So the king's son set to work, and dug and shovelled away without ceasing, but when, on the seventh day, he saw how little he had accomplished, and that all his work was as nothing, he fell into great sadness, and gave up all hope. But on the evening of the seventh day the fox appeared, and said,

"You do not deserve that I should help you, but go now and lie down to sleep, and I will do the work for you."

The next morning when he awoke, and looked out of the window, the mountain had disappeared. The young man hastened full of joy to the king, and told him that his behest was fulfilled, and, whether the king liked it or not, he had to keep to his word, and let his daughter go.

So they both went away together, and it was not long before the faithful fox came up to them.

"Well, you have got the best first," said he; "but you must know the golden horse belongs to the princess of the golden castle."

"But how shall I get it?" asked the young man.

"I am going to tell you," answered the fox. "First, go

to the king who sent you to the golden castle, and take to him the beautiful princess. There will then be very great rejoicing; he will willingly give you the golden horse, and they will lead him out to you; then mount him without delay, and stretch out your hand to each of them to take leave, and last of all to the princess, and when you have her by the hand swing her up on the horse behind you, and off you go! nobody will be able to overtake you, for that horse goes swifter than the wind."

And so it was all happily done, and the king's son carried off the beautiful princess on the golden horse. The fox did not stay behind, and he said to the young man,

" Now, I will help you to get the golden bird. When you draw near the castle where the bird is, let the lady alight, and I will take her under my care ; then you must ride the golden horse into the castle-yard, and there will be great rejoicing to see it, and they will bring out to you the golden bird; as soon as you have the cage in your hand, you must start off back to us, and then you shall carry the lady away."

The plan was successfully carried out ; and when the young man returned with the treasure, the fox said,

" Now, what will you give me for my reward ? "

" What would you like? " asked the young man.

" When we are passing through the wood, I desire that you should slay me, and cut my head and feet off."

" That were a strange sign of gratitude," said the king's son, " and I could not possibly do such a thing."

Then said the fox,

" If you will not do it, I must leave you ; but before I go let me give you some good advice. Beware of two things : buy no gallows-meat, and sit at no brook-side." With that the fox ran off into the wood.

The young man thought to himself, " That is a wonderful animal, with most singular ideas. How should any one buy gallows-meat? and I am sure I have no particular fancy for sitting by a brook-side."

So he rode on with the beautiful princess, and their way led them through the village where his two brothers had stayed. There they heard great outcry and noise, and when he asked what it was all about, they told him that two people

were going to be hanged. And when he drew near he saw
that it was his two brothers, who had done all sorts of evil
tricks, and had wasted all their goods. He asked if there
were no means of setting them free.

"Oh yes! if you will buy them off," answered the people;
"but why should you spend your money in redeeming such
worthless men?"

But he persisted in doing so; and when they were let
go they all went on their journey together.

After a while they came to the wood where the fox had
met them first, and there it seemed so cool and sheltered from
the sun's burning rays that the two brothers said,

"Let us rest here for a little by the brook, and eat and
drink to refresh ourselves."

The young man consented, quite forgetting the fox's warning, and he seated himself by the brook-side, suspecting no
evil. But the two brothers thrust him backwards into the
brook, seized the princess, the horse, and the bird, and went
home to their father.

"Is not this the golden bird that we bring?" said they;
"and we have also the golden horse, and the princess of the
golden castle."

Then there was great rejoicing in the royal castle, but the
horse did not feed, the bird did not chirp, and the princess
sat still and wept.

The youngest brother, however, had not perished. The
brook was, by good fortune, dry, and he fell on soft moss
without receiving any hurt, but he could not get up again.
But in his need the faithful fox was not lacking; he came up
running, and reproached him for having forgotten his advice.

"But I cannot forsake you all the same," said he; "I
will help you back again into daylight." So he told the young
man to grasp his tail, and hold on to it fast, and so he drew
him up again.

"Still you are not quite out of all danger," said the fox;
"your brothers, not being certain of your death, have surrounded the wood with sentinels, who are to put you to death
if you let yourself be seen."

A poor beggar-man was sitting by the path, and the young
man changed clothes with him, and went clad in that wise

into the king's courtyard. Nobody knew him, but the bird began to chirp, and the horse began to feed, and the beautiful princess ceased weeping.

"What does this mean?" said the king, astonished.

The princess answered,

"I cannot tell, except that I was sad, and now I am joyful; it is to me as if my rightful bridegroom had returned."

Then she told him all that happened, although the two brothers had threatened to put her to death if she let out anything. The king then ordered every person who was in the castle to be brought before him, and with the rest came the young man like a beggar in his wretched garments; but the princess knew him, and greeted him well, falling on his neck and kissing him. The wicked brothers were seized and put to death, and the youngest brother was married to the princess, and succeeded to the inheritance of his father.

But what became of the poor fox? Long afterwards the king's son was going through the wood, and the fox met him and said,

"Now, you have everything that you can wish for, but my misfortunes never come to an end, and it lies in your power to free me from them." And once more he prayed the king's son earnestly to slay him, and cut off his head and feet. So, at last, he consented, and no sooner was it done than the fox was changed into a man, and was no other than the brother of the beautiful princess; and thus he was set free from a spell that had bound him for a long, long time.

And now, indeed, there lacked nothing to their happiness as long as they lived.

⁃The DOG and the SPARROW⁃

HERE was once a sheep-dog whose master behaved ill to him and did not give him enough to eat, and when for hunger he could bear it no longer, he left his service very sadly. In the street he was met by a sparrow, who said,

"Dog, my brother, why are you so sad?"

And the dog answered,

"I am hungry and have nothing to eat."

Then said the sparrow,

"Dear brother, come with me into the town; I will give you plenty."

Then they went together into the town, and soon they came to a butcher's stall, and the sparrow said to the dog,

"Stay here while I reach you down a piece of meat," and he perched on the stall, looked round to see that no one noticed him, and pecked, pulled, and dragged so long at a piece that lay near the edge of the board that at last it slid to the ground. The dog picked it up, ran with it into a corner, and ate it up. Then said the sparrow,

"Now come with me to another stall, and I will get you another piece, so that your hunger may be satisfied."

When the dog had devoured a second piece the sparrow asked,

"Dog, my brother, are you satisfied now?"

"Yes, as to meat I am," answered he, "but I have had no bread."

Then said the sparrow,

"That also shall you have; come with me." And he led him to a baker's stall and pecked at a few little rolls until they fell to the ground, and as the dog still wanted more, they went to another stall farther on and got more bread. When that was done the sparrow said,

"Dog, my brother, are you satisfied yet?"

"Yes," answered he, "and now we will walk a little outside the town."

And they went together along the high road. It was warm weather, and when they had gone a little way the dog said,

"I am tired, and would like to go to sleep."

"Well, do so," said the sparrow; "in the meanwhile I will sit near on a bough." The dog laid himself in the road and fell fast asleep, and as he lay there a waggoner came up with a waggon and three horses, laden with two casks of wine; the sparrow, seeing that he was not going to turn aside but kept in the beaten track, just where the dog lay, cried out,

"Waggoner, take care, or you shall suffer for it!"

But the waggoner, muttering, "What harm can you do to me?" cracked his whip and drove his waggon over the dog, and he was crushed to death by the wheels. Then the sparrow cried,

"Thou hast killed the dog my brother, and it shall cost thee horses and cart!"

"Oh! horses and cart!" said the waggoner, "what harm can you do me, I should like to know?" and drove on. The sparrow crept under the covering of the waggon and pecked at the bung-hole of one of the casks until the cork came out, and all the wine ran out without the waggoner noticing. After a while, looking round, he saw that something dripped from the waggon, and on examining the casks he found that one of them was empty, and he cried out,

"I am a ruined man!"

"Not ruined enough yet!" said the sparrow, and flying to one of the horses he perched on his head and pecked at his eyes. When the waggoner saw that he took out his axe to hit the sparrow, who at that moment flew aloft, and the waggoner missing him struck the horse on the head, so that he fell down dead.

"Oh, I am a ruined man!" cried he.

"Not ruined enough yet!" said the sparrow, and as the waggoner drove on with the two horses that were left the sparrow crept again under the waggon-covering and pecked the cork out of the second cask, so that all the wine leaked out. When the waggoner became aware of it, he cried out again,

"Oh! I am a ruined man!" But the sparrow answered, "Not ruined enough yet!" and perched on the second horse's head and began pecking at his eyes. Back ran the waggoner and raised his axe to strike, but the sparrow flying aloft, the stroke fell on the horse, so that he was killed.

"Oh! I am a ruined man!" cried the waggoner.

"Not ruined enough yet!" said the sparrow, and perching on the third horse began pecking at his eyes. The waggoner struck out in his anger at the sparrow without taking aim, and missing him, he laid his third horse dead.

"Oh! I am a ruined man!" he cried.

"Not ruined enough yet!" answered the sparrow, flying off; "I will see to that at home."

So the waggoner had to leave his waggon standing, and went home full of rage.

"Oh!" said he to his wife, "what ill-luck I have had! the wine is spilt, and the horses are all three dead."

"O husband!" answered she, "such a terrible bird has come to this house; he has brought with him all the birds of the air, and there they are in the midst of our wheat devouring it." And he looked and there were thousands upon thousands of birds sitting on the ground, having eaten up all the wheat, and the sparrow in the midst, and the waggoner cried,

"Oh! I am a ruined man!"

"Not ruined enough yet!" answered the sparrow; "Waggoner, it shall cost thee thy life!" and he flew away.

Now the waggoner, having lost everything he possessed, went in-doors and sat down angry and miserable behind the stove. The sparrow was perched outside on the window-sill, and cried, "Waggoner, it shall cost thee thy life!" Then the waggoner seized his axe and threw it at the sparrow, but it broke the window sash in two and did not touch the sparrow, who now hopped inside, perched on the stove, and cried.

"Waggoner it shall cost thee thy life!" and he, mad and blind with rage, beat in the stove, and as the sparrow flew from one spot to another, hacked everything in pieces, furniture, looking-glasses, benches, table, and the very walls of his house, and yet did not touch the sparrow.

At last he caught and held him in his hand.

"Now," said his wife, "shall I not kill him?"

"No!" cried he, "that were too easy a death; I will swallow him," and as the bird was fluttering in the man's mouth, it stretched out its head, saying,

"Waggoner, it shall cost thee thy life!"

Then the waggoner reached the axe to his wife saying,

"Wife, strike me this bird dead."

The wife struck, but missed her aim, and the blow fell on the waggoner's head, and he dropped down dead.

But the sparrow flew over the hills and away.

⚡FRED and KATE⚡

THERE were once a young husband and wife, and their names were Fred and Kate. One day said Fred,

"I must go now to my work in the fields, Kate, and when I come back you must have on the table some roast meat to satisfy my hunger, and some cool drink to quench my thirst."

"All right, Fred," answered Kate; "be off with you, I will see to it."

When dinner-time began to draw near, she took down a sausage from the chimney, put it in a frying-pan with some butter, and stood it over the fire. The sausage began to frizzle and fry, and Kate stood holding the handle of the pan, and fell into deep thought; at last she said to herself,

"While the sausage is cooking I might as well be drawing the beer in the cellar."

So she saw that the frying-pan was standing firmly, and then took a can and went down into the cellar to draw the beer. Now, while Kate was watching the beer run into the can, a sudden thought came into her mind.

"Holloa! the dog is not fastened up; he may perhaps get at the sausage," and in a trice she was up the cellar steps: but already the dog had it in his mouth, and was making off with it. Then Kate, with all haste, followed after him and chased him a good way into the fields, but the dog was quicker than Kate, and, never letting slip the sausage, was soon at a great distance.

"Well, it can't be helped!" said Kate turning back, and

as she had tired herself with running, she took her time about going home, and walked slowly to cool herself. All this time the beer was running out of the cask, for Kate had not turned off the tap, and as the can was soon full, it began to run over on the cellar floor, and ran, and ran, until the cask was empty. Kate stood on the steps and saw the misfortune.

"Dear me!" cried she, "what am I to do to prevent Fred from noticing it!"

She considered for a while, and then remembered that there was remaining in the loft from the last fair time a sack of fine wheat-flour; she determined to bring it down, and strew it over the beer.

"To be sure," said she, "those who know how to save have somewhat in time of necessity."

And going up to the loft, she dragged the sack down and threw it right upon the can full of beer, so that Fred's drink ran about the cellar with the rest.

"It is all right," said Kate; "where some goes the rest must follow," and she strewed the meal all over the cellar. When all was done, she was highly pleased, and thought how clean and neat it looked.

At dinner-time home came Fred.

"Now, wife, what have you got for me?" said he.

"O Fred," answered she, "I was going to cook a sausage for you, but while I was drawing the beer the dog got it out of the pan, and while I was running after the dog the beer all ran away, and as I was going to stop up the beer with the wheat-meal I knocked over the can: but it is all right now; the cellar is quite dry again." But said Fred,

"O Kate, Kate! what have you been about, letting the sausage be carried off, and the beer run out of the cask, and then to waste all our good meal into the bargain?"

"Well, Fred, I did not know; you should have told me," said Kate. So the husband thought to himself,

"If my wife is like this, I must look after things a little better."

Now he had saved a very pretty sum of money, and he changed it all to gold, and said to Kate,

"Do you see these yellow counters? I am going to make a hole in the stable underneath the cows' manger and bury them; see that you do not meddle with them, or it will be the worse for you."

And she said, " Oh no, Fred, certainly I won't."

Now, one day when Fred was away, there came some pedlars to the village, with earthen pots and basins to sell, and they asked the young wife if she had nothing to give in exchange for them.

" O my good men," said Kate, " I have no money to buy anything with, but if you had any use for yellow counters, I might do some business with you."

" Yellow counters I why not? we might as well see them," said they.

"Then go into the stable and dig under the cows' manger, and you will find them; but I dare not go near the place."

So those rogues went and dug, and found the gold accordingly.   And they seized it quickly, and ran off with it, leaving the pots and pans behind them in the house.   Kate thought she must make some use of her new possessions, so, as she had no need of them in the kitchen, she spread them out on the ground, and then stuck them, one after another, for ornament, on the fence which ran round the house.   When Fred came home and saw the new decorations, he said, "Kate, what have you been doing?"

" I bought them every one, Fred, with those yellow counters that were buried under the manger, and I did not go there myself; the pedlars had to dig them up for themselves."

" O wife !" cried Fred, " what have you done? they were not counters, but pure gold, and all our capital; you should not have done so."

" Well, Fred, I did not know; you should have told me that before," answered Kate.

Then Kate stood still a little while to consider, and at last she said, " Listen, Fred, we may be able to get the gold back again.   Let us run after the thieves."

" Very well," said Fred, " we will try; only let us take some bread and cheese with us, that we may have something to eat on the way."

" All right," she answered.   So they set out, and as Fred was a better walker than Kate, she was soon left behind.

"All the better for me," said she, "for when we turn back I shall have so much the less distance to go."

And they came to a mountain, where, on both sides of the road, there were deep cart-ruts. And Kate said to herself,

"How sad to see the poor earth torn, and vexed, and oppressed in this way! it will never be healed again in all its life."

And with a compassionate heart, she took out her butter and smeared the cart-ruts right and left, so that they might not be so cut by the wheels; and as she was stooping to perform this merciful act a cheese fell out of her pocket and rolled down the mountain. And Kate said,

"I have walked over the ground once, and I am not going to do it again, but another shall run after that cheese, and bring it back." So saying, she took another cheese, and rolled it after the first one: and as it did not seem to be coming back again, she sent a third racing after them, thinking, "Perhaps they are waiting for company, and are not used to travelling alone." But when they all three delayed coming, she said,

"I can't think what this means! perhaps it is that the third one has lost his way, so I will send a fourth that he may call out to him as he goes by." But it went no better with the fourth than with the third. And Kate lost all patience and threw down the fifth and sixth, and that was all. A long while she stood and waited for them to come up, but as still they did not come, she said,

"Oh, it's like sending good money after bad; there is no getting you back again. If you suppose I am going to wait for you any longer, you are very much mistaken: I shall go on my way and you may overtake me; your legs are younger than mine." Kate then went on until she overtook Fred, who was standing still and waiting, as he wanted something to eat.

"Now, be quick," he said, "and hand over what you have brought." And she handed him the dry bread.

"Now for the butter and the cheese," said the man.

"O Fred," said Kate, "I anointed the cart-ruts with the butter, and the cheeses will soon be here, they are upon the road; one of them ran away, and I sent the others to fetch it back."

Then said Fred,

"It was very wrong of you, Kate, to waste the butter, and roll the cheeses down the hill."

And Kate answered, "Well then, you should have told me so."

As they were eating the dry bread together, Fred said,

"Kate, did you lock up the house before leaving?"

"No, Fred; you ought to have told me that before."

And her husband answered,

"Well, you must go home at once and lock up the house before we go any farther, and you might as well bring something more to eat with you, and I will wait for you here."

So Kate went, and she thought to herself.

"As Fred wants something more to eat, and he does not care much about butter and cheese, I will bring some dried apples and a jug of vinegar back with me."

Then she bolted the front door, but the back door she took off its hinges, and lifted it on her shoulders, thinking that if she had the door all safe no harm could come to the house. And she took her time on the way back, and thought to herself, "Fred will have so much the longer to rest." So when she got back to him, she called out,

"Fred, if the house-door is safe, no harm can come to the house!"

"Oh dear!" cried he, "what a prudent wife have I! to carry away the back-door, so that any one may get in, and to bolt the front door! It is too late now to go home, but as you have brought the door so far, you may carry it on farther."

"All right, I will carry the door, Fred," said she, "but the dried apples and the vinegar will be too heavy for me; I will hang them on the door and make it carry them."

Now they went into the wood to look for the thieves, but they could not find them. When it grew dark they got up into a tree to pass the night there. No sooner had they settled down when up came the pedlars, some of those fellows who carry away what should not go with them, and who find things before they are lost. They laid themselves down directly under the tree where Fred and Kate were, and they made a fire, and began to divide their spoil. Then Fred got down on the farther side of the tree and gathered together some stones, and then got up again, intending to stone the robbers to death with them. The stones, however, did not hit them, and they said,

"It will soon be morning; the wind is rising and shaking down the fir-cones."

Now all the time Kate had the door on her shoulder, and as it weighed upon her heavily, she thought it must be the the dried apples, and she said,

"Fred, I must throw down the dried apples."

"No, Kate, not now," answered he; "we might be discovered."

"Oh dear, Fred, but I must! they weigh me down so!" said she.

"Well then, do it, if you must, in the name of all that's tormenting!" cried he; and down rolled the apples between the boughs, and the robbers cried,

"There are birds in this tree!"

After a while, as the door still weighed her down heavily, Kate said, "O Fred, I must pour away the vinegar;" and he answered,

"No, Kate, you must not do that; we might be discovered."

"Oh dear me, Fred, but I must! it weighs me down so!"

"Then do it, if you must, in the name of all that's tormenting!"

And she poured out the vinegar, so that the men were all besprinkled.

And they said one to another,

"The morning dew is beginning to fall already."

At last Kate began to think that it must really be the door that weighed so heavy, and she said,

"Fred, I must throw down the door!" and he answered,

"No, Kate, not now; we might be discovered."

"Oh dear me, Fred, but I must! it weighs me down so."

"No, Kate, you must hold it fast."

"O Fred, it's slipping, it's falling!"

"Well then, let it fall in the name of torment!" cried Fred in a passion. And so it fell with a great crash, and the thieves below cried,

"There is something wrong about this tree!" and they got up in a great hurry and ran off, leaving their spoil behind them.

And early in the morning when Fred and Kate came down from the tree they got all their gold again and carried it home.

And when they reached their house again Fred said,

"Now, Kate, you must fall to and be very industrious and work hard."

"All right, Fred, I will go into the field and cut corn," said she.

And when she came into the field she said to herself,

"Shall I eat before I cut, or shall I sleep before I cut? well, I will eat first." And so she ate, and after that she felt sleepy, but she began to cut and went on half asleep cutting her own clothes, skirts, gown, and all, and when she at last woke up and found herself in rags, she said to herself,

"Is this really I or not? oh dear, it is not I!"

After a while night came on, and Kate ran into the village and knocked at her husband's door calling out, "Fred!"

"What is it?" said he.

"I want to know if Kate is at home," said she.

"Oh yes," he answered, "she is lying here fast asleep."

So she said to herself, "All right then, I am certainly at home," and she ran on farther.

Soon she came upon some thieves who were looking about for something to steal, and she went up to them and offered to help them, and the thieves thought she knew of a good place and opportunity, and were glad of her offer. But Kate walked in front of the houses calling out,

"Good people, what have you for us to steal?"

So the thieves thought to themselves, "This will never do," and wished themselves quit of her. At last they said to her,

"Just at the end of the village there are some turnips in the parson's field; go and fetch us some."

So Kate went into the field and began to pull some up, but very lazily, and never raised herself. Presently came by a man who saw her, and thought she was some evil thing grubbing for the turnips. So he ran quickly into the village and said to the parson,

"O parson, some evil creature is grubbing in your turnip-field!"

"Oh dear!" answered the parson, "I have a lame foot, I cannot go to drive it away."

And the man at once offered to take him on his back, and he did so.

Just as they reached the field Kate got up and stood upright.

"Oh, the devil!" cried the parson, and both took to their heels, and the parson was able, out of his great fear, to run faster with his lame foot than the man who had carried him on his back with both legs sound.

·THE·LITTLE·FARMER·.

HERE was a certain village where lived many rich farmers and only one poor one, whom they called the Little Farmer. He had not even a cow, and still less had he money to buy one; and he and his wife greatly wished for such a thing. One day he said to her,

"Listen, I have a good idea; it is that your godfather the joiner shall make us a calf of wood and paint it brown, so as to look just like any other; and then in time perhaps it will grow big and become a cow."

This notion pleased the wife, and godfather joiner set to work to saw and plane, and soon turned out a calf complete, with its head down and neck stretched out as if it were grazing.

The next morning, as the cows were driven to pasture, the Little Farmer called out to the drover,

"Look here, I have got a little calf to go, but it is still young and must be carried."

"All right!" said the drover, and tucked it under his arm, carried it into the meadows, and stood it in the grass. So the calf stayed where it was put, and seemed to be eating all the time, and the drover thought to himself,

"It will soon be able to run alone, if it grazes at that rate!"

In the evening, when the herds had to be driven home, he said to the calf, "If you can stand there eating like that, you can just walk off on your own four legs; I am not going to lug you under my arm again!"

But the Little Farmer was standing by his house-door, and

waiting for his calf; and when he saw the cow-herd coming through the village without it, he asked what it meant. The cow-herd answered, "It is still out there eating away, and never attended to the call, and would not come with the rest."

Then the Little Farmer said,

"I will tell you what, I must have my beast brought home."

And they went together through the fields in quest of it, but some one had stolen it, and it was gone. And the drover said,

"Most likely it has run away."

But the Little Farmer said "Not it!" and brought the cow-herd before the bailiff, who ordered him for his carelessness to give the Little Farmer a cow for the missing calf.

So now the Little Farmer and his wife possessed their long-wished-for cow; they rejoiced with all their hearts, but unfortunately they had no fodder for it, and could give it nothing to eat, so that before long they had to kill it. Its flesh they salted down, and the Little Farmer went to the town to sell the skin and buy a new calf with what he got for it. On the way he came to a mill, where a raven was sitting with broken wings, and he took it up out of pity and wrapped it in the skin. The weather was very stormy, and it blew and rained, so he turned into the mill and asked for shelter. The miller's wife was alone in the house, and she said to the Little Farmer,

"Well, come in and lay thee down in the straw," and she gave him a piece of bread and cheese. So the Little Farmer ate, and then lay down with his skin near him, and the miller's wife thought he was sleeping with fatigue. After a while in came another man, and the miller's wife received him very well, saying,

"My husband is out; we will make good cheer."

The Little Farmer listened to what they said, and when he heard good cheer spoken of, he grew angry to think he had been put off with bread and cheese. For the miller's wife presently brought out roast meat, salad, cakes, and wine.

Now as the pair were sitting down to their feast, there came a knock at the door.

"Oh dear," cried the woman, "it is my husband!" In a twinkling she popped the roast meat into the oven, the wine under the pillow, the salad in the bed, the cakes under the bed, and the man in the linen-closet. Then she opened the door to her husband, saying,

"Thank goodness, you are here! what weather it is, as if the world were coming to an end!"

When the miller saw the Little Farmer lying in the straw, he said,

"What fellow have you got there?"

"Oh!" said the wife, "the poor chap came in the midst of the wind and rain and asked for shelter, and I gave him some bread and cheese and spread some straw for him."

The husband answered, "Oh well, I have no objection, only get me something to eat at once."

But the wife said, "There is nothing but bread and cheese."

"Anything will do for me," answered the miller, "bread and cheese for ever!" and catching sight of the Little Farmer, he cried,

"Come along, and keep me company!" The Little Farmer did not wait to be asked twice, but sat down and ate. After a while the miller noticed the skin lying on the ground with the raven wrapped up in it, and he said, "What have you got there?"

The Little Farmer answered, "A fortune-teller."

And the miller asked "Can he tell my fortune?"

"Why not?" answered the Little Farmer. "He will tell four things, and the fifth he keeps to himself." Now the miller became very curious, and said, "Ask him to say something."

And the Little Farmer pinched the raven, so that it croaked, "Crr, crr." "What does he say?" asked the miller. And the Little Farmer answered,

"First he says that there is wine under the pillow."

"That would be jolly!" cried the miller, and he went to look, and found the wine, and then asked, "What next?"

So the Little Farmer made the raven croak again, and then said,

"He says, secondly, that there is roast meat in the oven."

"That would be jolly!" cried the miller, and he went and looked, and found the roast meat. The Little Farmer made the fortune-teller speak again, and then said,

"He says, thirdly, that there is salad in the bed."

"That would be jolly!" cried the miller, and went and looked, and found the salad. Once more the Little Farmer pinched the raven, so that he croaked, and said,

"He says, fourthly and lastly, that there are cakes under the bed."

"That would be jolly!" cried the miller, and he went and looked, and found the cakes.

And now the two sat down to table, and the miller's wife felt very uncomfortable, and she went to bed and took all the keys with her. The miller was eager to know what the fifth thing could be, but the Little Farmer said,

"Suppose we eat the four things in peace first, for the fifth thing is a great deal worse."

So they sat and ate, and while they ate, they bargained together as to how much the miller would give for knowing the fifth thing; and at last they agreed upon three hundred dollars. Then the Little Farmer pinched the raven, so that he croaked aloud. And the miller asked what he said, and the Little Farmer answered,

"He says that there is a demon in the linen-closet."

"Then," said the miller, "that demon must out of the linen-closet," and he unbarred the house-door, while the Little Farmer got the key of the linen-closet from the miller's wife, and opened it. Then the man rushed forth, and out of the house, and the miller said,

"I saw the black rogue with my own eyes; so that is a good riddance."

And the Little Farmer took himself off by daybreak next morning with the three hundred dollars.

And after this the Little Farmer by degrees got on in the world, and built himself a good house, and the other farmers said,

"Surely the Little Farmer has been where it rains gold pieces, and has brought home money by the bushel."

And he was summoned before the bailiff to say whence his riches came. And all he said was,

"I sold my calf's skin for three hundred dollars."

When the other farmers heard this they wished to share such good luck, and ran home, killed all their cows, skinned them in order to sell them also for the same high price as the

Little .Farmer. And the bailiff said, " I must be beforehand with them." So he sent his servant into the town to the skin-buyer, and he only gave her three dollars for the skin, and that was faring better than the others, for when they came, they did not get as much as that, for the skin-buyer said,

" What am I to do with all these skins ? "

Now the other farmers were very angry with the Little Farmer for misleading them, and they vowed vengeance against him, and went to complain of his deceit to the bailiff. The poor Little Farmer was with one voice sentenced to death, and to be put into a cask with holes in it, and rolled into the water. So he was led to execution, and a priest was fetched to say a mass for him, and the rest of the people had to stand at a distance. As soon as the Little Farmer caught sight of the priest he knew him for the man who was hid in the linen-closet at the miller's. And he said to him,

" As I let you out of the cupboard, you must let me out of the cask."

At that moment a shepherd passed with a flock of sheep, and the Little Farmer knowing him to have a great wish to become bailiff himself, called out with all his might,

" No, I will not, and if all the world asked me, I would not ! "

The shepherd, hearing him, came up and asked what it was he would not do. The Little Farmer answered,

" They want to make me bailiff, if I sit in this cask, but I will not do it ! "

The shepherd said,

" If that is all there is to do in order to become bailiff I will sit in the cask and welcome." And the Little Farmer answered,

" Yes, that is all, just you get into the cask, and you will become bailiff." So the shepherd agreed, and got in, and the Little Farmer fastened on the top ; then he collected the herd of sheep and drove them away. The priest went back to the parish-assembly, and told them the mass had been said. Then they came and began to roll the cask into the water, and as it went the shepherd inside called out, " I consent to be bailiff ! "

They thought that it was the Little Farmer who spoke, and they answered,

"All right; but first you must go down below and look about you a little," and they rolled the cask into the water.

Upon that the farmers went home, and when they reached the village, there they met the Little Farmer driving a flock of sheep, and looking quite calm and contented. The farmers were astonished and cried,

"Little Farmer, whence come you? how did you get out of the water?"

"Oh, easily," answered he, "I sank and sank until I came to the bottom; then I broke through the cask and came out of it, and there were beautiful meadows and plenty of sheep feeding, so I brought away this flock with me."

Then said the farmers, "Are there any left?"

"Oh yes," answered the Little Farmer, "more than you can possibly need."

Then the farmers agreed that they would go and fetch some sheep also, each man a flock for himself; and the bailiff said, "Me first." And they all went together, and in the blue sky there were little fleecy clouds like lambkins, and they were reflected in the water; and the farmers cried out,

"There are the sheep down there at the bottom."

When the bailiff heard that he pressed forward and said,

"I will go first and look about me, and if things look well, I will call to you."

And he jumped plump into the water, and they all thought that the noise he made meant "Come," so the whole company jumped in one after the other. So perished all the proprietors of the village, and the Little Farmer, as sole heir, became a rich man.

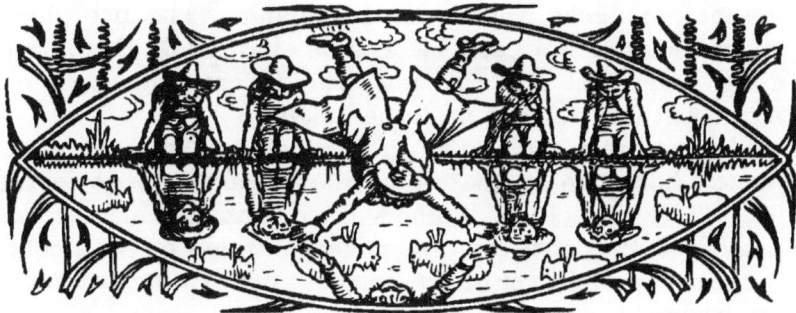

·THE·QUEEN·BEE·

WO king's sons once started to seek adventures, and fell into a wild, reckless way of living, and gave up all thoughts of going home again. Their third and youngest brother, who was called Witling, and had remained behind, started off to seek them; and when at last he found them, they jeered at his simplicity in thinking that he could make his way in the world, while they who were so much cleverer were unsuccessful. But they all three went on together until they came to an ant-hill, which the two eldest brothers wished to stir up, that they might see the little ants hurry about in their fright and carrying off their eggs, but Witling said,

"Leave the little creatures alone, I will not suffer them to be disturbed."

And they went on farther until they came to a lake, where a number of ducks were swimming about. The two eldest brothers wanted to catch a couple and cook them, but Witling would not allow it, and said, "Leave the creatures alone, I will not suffer them to be killed."

And then they came to a bee's-nest in a tree, and there was so much honey in it that it overflowed and ran down the trunk. The two eldest brothers then wanted to make a fire beneath the tree, that the bees might be stifled by the smoke, and then they could get at the honey. But Witling prevented them, saying,

" Leave the little creatures alone, I will not suffer them to be stifled."

At last the three brothers came to a castle where there were in the stables many horses standing, all of stone, and the brothers went through all the rooms until they came to a door at the end secured with three locks, and in the middle of the door a small opening through which they could look into the room. And they saw a little grey-haired man sitting at a table. They called out to him once, twice, and he did not hear, but at the third time he got up, undid the locks, and came out. Without speaking a word he led them to a table loaded with all sorts of good things, and when they had eaten and drunk he showed to each his bed-chamber. The next morning the little grey man came to the eldest brother, and beckoning him, brought him to a table of stone, on which were written three things directing by what means the castle could be delivered from its enchantment. The first thing was, that in the wood under the moss lay the pearls belonging to the princess—a thousand in number—and they were to be sought for and collected, and if he who should undertake the task had not finished it by sunset,—if but one pearl were missing,—he must be turned to stone. So the eldest brother went out, and searched all day, but at the end of it he had only found one hundred; just as was said on the table of stone came to pass and he was turned into stone. The second brother undertook the adventure next day, but it fared with him no better than with the first; he found two hundred pearls, and was turned into stone.

And so at last it was Witling's turn, and he began to search in the moss; but it was a very tedious business to find the pearls, and he grew so out of heart that he sat down on a stone and began to weep. As he was sitting thus, up came the ant-king with five thousand ants, whose lives had been saved through Witling's pity, and it was not very long before the little insects had collected all the pearls and put them in a heap.

Now the second thing ordered by the table of stone was to get the key of the princess's sleeping-chamber out of the lake.

And when Witling came to the lake, the ducks whose lives he had saved came swimming, and dived below, and brought up the key from the bottom. The third thing that had to be done was the most difficult, and that was to choose out the youngest and loveliest of the three princesses, as they lay sleeping. All bore a perfect resemblance each to the other, and only differed in this, that before they went to sleep each one had eaten a different sweetmeat,—the eldest a piece of sugar, the second a little syrup, and the third a spoonful of honey. Now the Queen-bee of those bees that Witling had protected from the fire came at this moment, and trying the lips of all three, settled on those of the one that had eaten honey, and so it was that the king's son knew which to choose. Then the spell was broken; every one awoke from stony sleep, and took their right form again.

And Witling married the youngest and loveliest princess, and became king after her father's death. But his two brothers had to put up with the two other sisters.

·THE·GOLDEN·GOOSE·

HERE was a man who had three sons, the youngest of whom was called the Simpleton, and was despised, laughed at, and neglected, on every occasion. It happened one day that the eldest son wished to go into the forest to cut wood, and before he went his mother gave him a delicious pancake and a flask of wine, that he might not suffer from hunger or thirst. When he came into the forest a little old grey man met him, who wished him good day, and said,

"Give me a bit of cake out of your pocket, and let me have a drink of your wine; I am so hungry and thirsty."

But the prudent youth answered,

"Give you my cake and my wine? I haven't got any; be off with you."

And leaving the little man standing there, he went off. Then he began to fell a tree, but he had not been at it long before he made a wrong stroke, and the hatchet hit him in the arm, so that he was obliged to go home and get it bound up. That was what came of the little grey man.

Afterwards the second son went into the wood, and the mother gave to him, as to the eldest, a pancake and a flask of wine. The little old grey man met him also, and begged for a little bit of cake and a drink of wine. But the second son spoke out plainly, saying,

"What I give you I lose myself, so be off with you."

And leaving the little man standing there, he went off.

The punishment followed; as he was chopping away at the tree, he hit himself in the leg so severely that he had to be carried home.

Then said the Simpleton,

"Father, let me go for once into the forest to cut wood; and the father answered, "Your brothers have hurt themselves by so doing; give it up, you understand nothing about it."

But the Simpleton went on begging so long, that the father said at last,

"Well, be off with you; you will only learn by experience."

The mother gave him a cake (it was only made with water, and baked in the ashes), and with it a flask of sour beer. When he came into the forest the little old grey man met him, and greeted him, saying,

"Give me a bit of your cake, and a drink from your flask; I am so hungry and thirsty."

And the Simpleton answered, "I have only a flour and water cake and sour beer; but if that is good enough for you, let us sit down together and eat." Then they sat down, and as the Simpleton took out his flour and water cake it became a rich pancake, and his sour beer became good wine; then they ate and drank, and afterwards the little man said,

"As you have such a kind heart, and share what you have so willingly, I will bestow good luck upon you. Yonder stands an old tree; cut it down, and at its roots you will find something," and thereupon the little man took his departure.

The Simpleton went there, and hewed away at the tree, and when it fell he saw, sitting among the roots, a goose with feathers of pure gold. He lifted it out and took it with him to an inn where he intended to stay the night. The landlord had three daughters who, when they saw the goose, were curious to know what wonderful kind of bird it was, and ended by longing for one of its golden feathers. The eldest thought, "I will wait for a good opportunity, and then I will pull out one of its feathers for myself;" and so, when the Simpleton was gone out, she seized the goose by its wing—but there her finger and hand had to stay, held fast. Soon after came the second sister with the same idea of plucking out one of the golden feathers for herself; but scarcely had she touched her sister, than she also was obliged to stay, held fast. Lastly came the third with the same intentions; but the others screamed out,

"Stay away! for heaven's sake stay away!"

But she did not see why she should stay away, and thought, "If they do so, why should not I?" and went towards them. But when she reached her sisters there she stopped, hanging on with them. And so they had to stay, all night. The next morning the Simpleton took the goose under his arm and went away, unmindful of the three girls that hung on to it. The three had always to run after him, left and right, wherever his legs carried him. In the midst of the fields they met the parson, who, when he saw the procession, said,

"Shame on you, girls, running after a young fellow through the fields like this," and forthwith he seized hold of the youngest by the hand to drag her away, but hardly had he touched her when he too was obliged to run after them himself. Not long after the sexton came that way, and seeing the respected parson following at the heels of the three girls, he called out,

"Ho, your reverence, whither away so quickly? You forget that we have another christening to-day;" and he seized hold of him by his gown; but no sooner had he touched him than he was obliged to follow on too. As the five tramped on, one after another, two peasants with their hoes came up from the fields, and the parson cried out to them, and begged them to come and set him and the sexton free, but no sooner had they touched the sexton than they had to follow on too; and now there were seven following the Simpleton and the goose.

By and by they came to a town where a king reigned, who had an only daughter who was so serious that no one could make her laugh; therefore the king had given out that whoever should make her laugh should have her in marriage. The Simpleton, when he heard this, went with his goose and his hangers-on into the presence of the king's daughter, and as soon as she saw the seven people following always one after the other, she burst out laughing, and seemed as if she could never stop. And so the Simpleton earned a right to her as his bride; but the king did not like him for a son-in-law and made all kinds of objections, and said he must first bring a man who could drink up a whole cellar of wine. The Simpleton thought that the little grey man would be able to help him, and went out into the forest, and there, on the very spot where he felled the tree, he saw a man sitting with a very sad countenance. The Simpleton asked him what was the matter, and he answered,

"I have a great thirst, which I cannot quench: cold water does not agree with me; I have indeed drunk up a whole cask of wine, but what good is a drop like that?"

Then said the Simpleton,

"I can help you; only come with me, and you shall have enough."

He took him straight to the king's cellar, and the man sat himself down before the big vats, and drank, and drank, and before a day was over he had drunk up the whole cellar-full. The Simpleton again asked for his bride, but the king was annoyed that a wretched fellow, called the Simpleton by everybody, should carry off his daughter, and so he made new conditions. He was to produce a man who could eat up a mountain of bread. The Simpleton did not hesitate long, but ran quickly off to the forest, and there in the same place sat a man who had fastened a strap round his body, making a very piteous face, and saying,

"I have eaten a whole bakehouse full of rolls, but what is the use of that when one is so hungry as I am? My stomach feels quite empty, and I am obliged to strap myself together, that I may not die of hunger."

The Simpleton was quite glad of this, and said,

"Get up quickly, and come along with me, and you shall have enough to eat."

He led him straight to the king's courtyard, where all the meal in the kingdom had been collected and baked into a mountain of bread. The man out of the forest settled himself down before it and hastened to eat, and in one day the whole mountain had disappeared.

Then the Simpleton asked for his bride the third time. The king, however, found one more excuse, and said he must have a ship that should be able to sail on land or on water.

"So soon," said he, "as you come sailing along with it, you shall have my daughter for your wife."

The Simpleton went straight to the forest, and there sat the

little old grey man with whom he had shared his cake, and he
said,

"I have eaten for you, and I have drunk for you, I will
also give you the ship; and all because you were kind to me
at the first."

Then he gave him the ship that could sail on land and on
water, and when the king saw it he knew he could no longer
withhold his daughter. The marriage took place immediately,
and at the death of the king the Simpleton possessed the
kingdom, and lived long and happily with his wife.